In Place of Inter-State Retaliation

In Place of Inter-State Retaliation

The European Union's Rejection of WTO-style Trade Sanctions and Trade Remedies

William Phelan

OXFORD
UNIVERSITY PRESS

OXFORD
UNIVERSITY PRESS

Great Clarendon Street, Oxford, OX2 6DP,
United Kingdom

Oxford University Press is a department of the University of Oxford.
It furthers the University's objective of excellence in research, scholarship,
and education by publishing worldwide. Oxford is a registered trade mark of
Oxford University Press in the UK and in certain other countries

First Edition published in 2015

Published in the United States of America by Oxford University Press
198 Madison Avenue, New York, NY 10016, United States of America

British Library Cataloguing in Publication Data
Data available

Library of Congress Control Number: 2014940451

ISBN 978–0–19–871279–4

Acknowledgments

I was fortunate to begin my dissertation research at a time when political science and legal scholarship on European integration was in full bloom at Harvard. I start therefore by acknowledging my dissertation committee. Andrew Moravcsik, most of all, helped me toward a particular way of thinking about international relations, and the European Union, ever since I took his seminar on international relations in Europe as a Kennedy School student. Andy also provided acute comments on a long paper version of this book's argument at a workshop in Princeton in April 2012. Peter Hall supported the project from start to finish with unwavering charm and detailed, tobacco-scented annotations. Michael Hiscox was always ready to talk about trade politics at the Grafton Street bar. I thank them all for their advice over the years. At Harvard Law School, Joseph Weiler allowed me the great opportunity of participating in his class on European law. Among the many other helpful professors and visitors, I am especially grateful to Jeff Frieden for his constant encouragement.

Since leaving Harvard, I have been fortunate to teach at Middlebury College, Vermont, and then at Trinity College, Dublin. At both institutions, my staff colleagues and the wonderful students have been a great support and stimulation. I thank them all, and in particular Erik Bleich, Matt Dickinson, Murray Dry, Ashley Esarey, and Quinn Mecham at Middlebury, and Ken Benoit, Michael Gallagher, Tim Hicks, René Lindstädt, Gail McElroy, Michael Marsh, Jon Slapin, and Robert Thomson at Trinity College, Dublin.

The scholarly study of European integration may have largely moved on from Harvard these days, but the Center for European Studies on Kirkland Street still provides a superb place to visit and study. That is where I finished the book manuscript in the spring and summer of 2012. I would like to thank my fellow visiting scholars at Harvard—Ulrich Krotz, Cornelia Woll, and especially Mareike Kleine—as well as Jonathan Laurence over at Boston College for making the experience so valuable.

A number of friends and colleagues read parts or more of this book in draft form. I thank Mark Copelovitch, Bill Davies, Carolin Huebner, Mareike Kleine, and Peter Lindseth for reading and criticizing more or less the complete manuscript at various stages of its progress. I would also like to thank those who were so kind as to read draft chapters, including Todd Allee, Andrew Glencross, Tim Hicks, Stephanie Rickard, Thomas Sattler, and Cornelia Woll. Among those who offered wise counsel over the years on many matters of trade politics, European politics, European law, and European integration are Hans Arnum, Francesca Bignami, Marius Brülhart, Gerard Conway, Christina Davis, Catherine Donnelly, John Gillingham, Andrew Glencross, Dieter Grimm, Trevor Hartley, Gerard Hogan, Ulrich Krotz, Andy Martin, Dermot McAleese, Gail McElroy, Imelda Maher, Franz Mayer, Christoph Moellers, Fernanda Nicola, Craig Parsons, Diarmuid Rossa Phelan, Thomas Raphael, Des Ryan, Philippe Schmitter, Jon Slapin, Holger Spamann, Francesca Strumia, Scott Siegel, Patrick Theiner, Robert Thomson, Christian Tomuschat, Helen Wallace, William Wallace, Daniel Ziblatt, and Michael Zürn. Responsibility for all faults remaining is, of course, my own.

I am particularly obliged to Wayne Vroman of the Urban Institute for generously making available his data on unemployment compensation systems around the world.

This book draws on material that has appeared in *European Law Journal, International Studies Review, Journal of European Public Policy,* and *International Theory.* I thank both editors and reviewers for all their feedback and criticism.

For financial assistance at various stages of this project, I would like to thank the Department of Political Science, the Arts and Social Sciences Benefactions Fund, and the Institute for International Integration Studies at Trinity College, the Department of Political Science at Middlebury College, the Center for European Studies at Harvard, and the BUNAC Educational Scholarship Trust. The Hertie School of Governance and the Deutsche Gesellschaft für Auswärtige Politik both kindly provided much-needed office space in Berlin. Small Project Grant G31090 from the Irish Research Council for the Humanities and Social Sciences (now the Irish Research Council) provided generous support for the years 2008–2010.

During a project of this length, one receives a great deal of unsolicited advice. Back in 2002, when informed that my dissertation project involved studying the constitutions of four European states to make an argument about the legal system of the European Union, the interviewing Immigration Officer at Logan Airport in Boston responded, "How will you ever finish?" Over many years, but particularly during the writing of the dissertation, many friends gave the support, intellectual and otherwise, that helped get the job done. Here, I would like to thank Fiona Barker, Laura Beers, Mark and Beth Copelovitch, Casey Klofstad, Jonathan Laurence, Thomas Raphael, Hillel Soifer, and Annie Stilz.

My greatest debt is to my parents, Cel and Bill, who encouraged me to pursue my education, wherever it led around the world.

Above all, my love to Haiyan and Hubert, who make every day worthwhile. I dedicate this book to them.

Contents

List of Tables and Figures

Tables

Figure

List of Abbreviations

ATJ	Andean Tribunal of Justice
CAP	Common Agricultural Policy
DSB	Dispute Settlement Body
DSU	Dispute Settlement Understanding
ECJ	European Court of Justice
EEC	European Economic Community
EU	European Union
GATT	General Agreement on Tariffs and Trade
ICJ	International Court of Justice
NAFTA	North American Free Trade Agreement
WDI	World Development Indicators
WTO	World Trade Organization

Nothing is more alien to Community law than the idea of a measure of retaliation or *reciprocity* proper to classical public international law.

Philippe Léger, Advocate General of the European Court of Justice,

Case C-5/94, *Hedley Lomas* (emphasis in the original)

Introduction

This book offers a new explanation of the European Union as a distinctive form of international organization. It does so by focusing on perhaps the most remarkable feature of that treaty regime—the European Union's rejection of inter-state retaliation as a mechanism to enforce its obligations. In many international trade organizations, perhaps most prominently in the World Trade Organization (WTO), states that defect from their obligations may be punished by trade sanctions—that is, by other member states suspending or withdrawing equivalent trading opportunities. The European Union (EU), however, forbids any use of such inter-state retaliation mechanisms and requires its member states to fulfill their EU obligations regardless of other member states' failures to do so. As the European Court of Justice stated in 1964, "international law allows a party, injured by the failure of another party to perform its obligations, to withhold performance of its own... However, this relationship between the obligations of parties cannot be recognized under [European] Community law.... Therefore the fact that the [other party] failed to carry out its obligations cannot relieve the defendants from carrying out theirs."[1] This rejection of inter-state countermeasures is intimately connected to the EU's equally unusual rejection of trade remedies—such as anti-dumping, countervailing duties, and industry safeguards—in the trade between its member states. Voon, in a review of more than 150 regional trade agreements, concluded that only the EU treaty had abolished all three of these trade remedies (Voon 2010: 647). Indeed, the EU as a whole makes full use of threats of retaliatory trade sanctions, and of unilateral "escape" mechanisms, such as anti-dumping, in its trading relationships with states *outside* the EU, but it forbids any use of such mechanisms between states *within* the EU.

[1] Cases 90 and 91/63 *Commission v. Luxembourg and Belgium* [1964] ECR 625.

Why does the EU not use the inter-state retaliation systems and legal escape mechanisms that seem to be so central to many other international agreements operating in issue-areas that require demanding adjustments? International legal scholars call an international regime that rejects the use of inter-state retaliatory measures a *self-contained regime*. Explaining the EU's break with inter-state retaliatory measures—explaining the EU as a self-contained regime—is the objective of this book.

This book, therefore, like others before it, offers an explanation for the development of, and effectiveness of, the EU's distinctive dispute settlement system. Given the widely acknowledged weaknesses of many international treaty systems, the European legal order, often referred to as "constitutional" or "federal," is one of the great novelties of contemporary world politics. Its development has often been explained by arguments that emphasize the politics of courts, particularly the relationship between the European Court of Justice (ECJ) and the national courts, that allows European law to benefit from enforcement by domestic courts within the member states.[2]

Current accounts of the development of the European legal order, however, rarely focus on why the EU does not use the inter-state retaliatory measures and trade remedy instruments that are so important to many other international trade regimes, including, prominently, the WTO. In fact, many distinguished explanations of the development of the European legal order do not so much as mention, let alone advance an explanation for, the EU's rejection of inter-state retaliation and trade remedy mechanisms. This oversight meets its counterpart in the scholarship on international trade politics that only rarely appears to be aware of the existence of an important international trade regime that does not use inter-state trade sanctions and trade remedies. Here, however, this remarkable aspect of the EU will be our central focus.

There is one great advantage to offering an explanation of the EU as an international organization that rejects the use of inter-state trade sanctions and trade remedies: such an approach directly connects the puzzle of the EU to mainstream topics of research in international relations. Unfortunately, the study of the EU is increasingly segregated from the wider study of international organizations. The reasons for this are many, to be sure. Nonetheless, the special obscurity of some EU-related discussions no

[2] When the Lisbon Treaty entered into force in 2009, the institution encompassing the several courts of the European Union was renamed the "Court of Justice of the European Union," or "CJEU," with the European Court of Justice itself being renamed simply the "Court of Justice." Since the Court was known as the ECJ for the vast majority of the time period we will be considering here, and is referred to as the ECJ throughout the relevant literature, we will continue with that terminology here. Note that the "constitutional" nature of the EU's legal regime should not be confused with the "constitutional treaty" agreed by the EU member states in 2004 and rejected in referenda in 2005. The EU's legal regime had been characterized as "constitutional" long before then, indeed since the 1960s.

doubt plays a significant role. Frankly put, generalist students and scholars often simply do not understand how the EU fits into wider debates. However, almost every student and scholar of international relations spends at least some time studying the WTO and its retaliation-based dispute settlement system. So, by addressing the EU not as a "quasi-federation," or as a "constitutional" international organization, but as an international organization that imposes demanding trade policy adjustments on its member states but rejects the use of inter-state retaliation measures, as well as common forms of trade remedies, the essential puzzle of the EU is made transparent, and important, to the widest possible audience.

Because this book is concerned with both the EU and the use of trade sanctions and trade remedies in international trade regimes, it discusses *two* well-developed, but largely separate literatures—on the European legal order, and on enforcement and escape in international trade politics. It demonstrates that neither offers a satisfactory explanation for the EU's ability to reject the use of inter-state countermeasures or trade remedies. The EU-specialist scholarship on the European legal order, focused on how the ECJ lured the national courts into cooperation through its human rights doctrines, legal seminars, and champagne lunches, does not address the EU as a trade regime that rejects the use of inter-state countermeasures and trade remedies (Weiler 1991: 2417–2418; Burley [Slaughter] and Mattli 1993: 62; Alter 2001: ix). The generalist international relations scholarship on enforcement and escape in international trade politics, on the other hand, tends to assume that a demanding international trade regime that rejects inter-state countermeasures and trade remedies is all but impossible (Downs and Rocke 1995; Rosendorff and Milner 2001). These literatures explain, respectively, variations in outcomes *within* the EU, which rejects the use of countermeasures and trade remedies, and *within* the WTO, where states make extensive use of countermeasures and trade remedies. Neither of these literatures has attempted to explain *cross-regime* variation in the role, or non-role, of inter-state countermeasures and trade remedies in international trade organizations.

This book therefore develops a new explanation for the EU's rejection of inter-state retaliation mechanisms and trade remedies, inspired by the literature on the role of domestic interests and institutions in trade politics. International regimes such as the EU provide rules, decision-making arrangements, and monitoring systems that allow states to improve on unilateral policy-making and manage international externalities (Keohane 1982; Krasner 1982). However, in issue-areas such as trade, the obligations required by international regimes change relative prices and thus create adjustment costs for politically influential narrow organized interests (Olson 1965; Olson 1982). These narrow interests then press policy-makers to unilaterally reject the costly adjustments required by treaty obligations through a variety of "escape" mechanisms (Rosendorff and Milner 2001). It is therefore the responsiveness of policy-makers to irresistible narrow interest group pressures demanding defection that leads international trade regimes to employ WTO-style trade remedies or trade retaliation mechanisms (Downs and Rocke 1995; Downs et al. 1996). So, for example, the responsiveness of US policy-makers to workers and owners in the American trucking industry who fiercely opposed NAFTA obligations eventually led to Mexico imposing retaliatory tariffs on a wide range of US exports (MacDonald 2009).

If the political power of narrow interest groups is the essential cause of the use of WTO-style retaliation mechanisms, and legal "escape" instruments, in international trade regimes, this suggests that as the politics of managing income loss by organized groups becomes less difficult, there is less need for the obligations of an international trade regime to be enforced by inter-state retaliation systems. Where economic exchange imposes fewer adjustment costs, as is the case where nations both import and export similar products ("intra-industry trade"), such escape mechanisms may be less necessary (Balassa 1966). Where democratic political institutions are both inclusive and authoritative, policy-makers are better able to manage the demands of narrow interests with incentives to impose costs on the rest of society regardless of the domestic or international consequences (Gerring and Thacker 2008). Where domestic social insurance systems reduce the income loss associated with trade liberalization, the intensity of narrow interest opposition to trade liberalization is diminished, again permitting policy-makers to better accept the constraints of binding reciprocal trade liberalization even if narrow interests face adjustments (Cameron 1978; Ruggie 1982). Thus, in a region, such as Europe, where policy-makers are chosen by relatively inclusive and centralized democratic institutions (such as parliamentary legislatures and proportional electoral systems), tax revenues are high, social welfare schemes are generously funded, and inter-state trade has distinctively been intra-industry trade, an international trade regime can impose a stream of demanding policy requirements on narrow organized interests in its member states without the use of WTO-style inter-state retaliation systems, or trade remedies such as anti-dumping and countervailing duties. The European Union should therefore be understood as a community of intra-industry trade, a community of parliamentary democracies, and, not least, a community of welfare states, because—in combination, of course, with high levels of economic interdependence—those are the characteristics of intra-European economic exchange and institutions in the member states that have facilitated the development of the EU's remarkable "community of law."

The approach of this book is therefore, as far as possible, to both describe and explain the distinctive features of the European legal order in ways that engage with broad themes in contemporary research on international relations. In many cases, that will involve the discussion of explanations for the behavior of states and non-state actors that are seldom connected to the development of the European legal order, although they are in widespread use in research on many other topics in international organization. Where special features of the EU's legal institutions are genuinely unusual in contemporary world politics, the importance of such innovations is clarified through a detailed comparison with more common forms of enforcement and escape in highly legalized international trade regimes. Such an approach will, we hope, better reveal how treaty-based dispute settlement mechanisms are transformed by the direct participation of domestic courts and private litigants, and how elements of the wider economic and political environment can contribute to making such a transformation possible. The European legal order can therefore be used to illustrate a distinctive, and generalizable, form of inter-state cooperation in international anarchy.

Plan of the Book

The first chapter sets out the empirical puzzle that the book will address. It first considers scholarly debates on the EU as a *sui generis*, hybrid institution, or "unidentified political object." It then builds on debates in international legal theory to show that the best, and most specific, understanding of the EU as a distinctive form of international organization is as a so-called *"self-contained regime."* A self-contained regime is an international treaty that imposes a stream of demanding policy adjustments on its participating states, but rejects the use of inter-state countermeasures and "reciprocal measures" as enforcement mechanisms. It also demonstrates that the EU, most unusually among contemporary trade agreements, rejects the use of trade remedy instruments such as anti-dumping and countervailing duties. This approach removes the EU from the opacity of "unidentified political object" debates to reveal a readily recognizable political economy puzzle. The rest of the book considers possible explanations for this remarkable outcome.

The second chapter starts the investigation by discussing political science scholarship on the development and operation of dispute settlement in the EU. Much of this scholarship explains the development of the European legal order by emphasizing the impact of the individual rights declared by the ECJ, the importance of legal networks, and the empowerment of national judges vis-à-vis their national governments. This chapter argues that while past scholarship has contributed a great deal to our understanding of the European legal order, it has not attempted to explain the EU's rejection of WTO-style trade sanctions and trade remedies. Furthermore, because this literature offers only a limited discussion of incentives for state policy-makers and interest groups to accept the EU's dispute settlement system, the material it discusses cannot easily be used to generate an explanation for the EU as a self-contained regime. By contrast, the literature rarely discusses the wider variables emphasized in the trade politics literature (such as the role of intra-industry trade, domestic constitutional structures, and social insurance systems) and its causal arguments may therefore be affected by omitted variable bias.

The third chapter, on the other hand, demonstrates that the generalist international relations scholarship on enforcement and escape in international trade politics does not expect that a demanding trade regime will be able to reject the use of inter-state retaliation mechanisms and trade remedies. Empirical scholarship in this area is heavily focused on the study of the WTO, where it is widely accepted that the logic of bilateral trade retaliation through "suspension of equivalent concessions" enforcement mechanisms is inescapable (e.g. Lawrence 2003; Bown 2009). Theoretical scholarship tends to assume that WTO-style retaliation and escape systems in international trade organizations are universal necessities, despite the trade disruption they generate, because they are needed to allow nation policy-makers to manage scenarios where domestic organized interests insist on rejecting international obligations (Downs and Rocke 1995; Downs et al. 1996; Rosendorff and Milner 2001; Kucik and Reinhardt 2008).

Against that background, the fourth chapter puts forward a new, more multicausal, argument for the ability of the EU to reject the role of inter-state countermeasures and trade remedies. It starts by demonstrating that the national application of treaty obligations as law by national courts is a potential substitute for the use of inter-state countermeasures as a mechanism to enforce treaty obligations. National court enforcement of treaty obligations is therefore not merely a mechanism for the protection of individual rights, or the empowerment of national judges, as current accounts of European legal integration tend to stress. It can also be an essential component in an inter-state bargain where states give up their right to use trade sanctions or similar inter-state countermeasures as instruments to enforce trade obligations because their partner states have allowed trade obligations to be applied as law by their national courts. In short, the EU member states use domestic court enforcement of European treaty obligations in place of inter-state retaliation mechanisms.

It then argues that the distinctive *state behavior* involved in a move from a "WTO-style" to an "EU-style" trade regime is, in comparative terms, the acceptance of a stream of more frequent, more intrusive, less predictable, and more binding trade-related policy adjustments on organized interests within the participating states. An EU-style trade regime is therefore possible between a group of highly interdependent states whose policy-makers are capable of sufficiently consistently accepting a stream of such trade policy adjustments on narrow interests in the interest of the management of their international interdependence. Such a regime might entirely eliminate the use of WTO-style "suspension of equivalent concessions" enforcement mechanisms in favor of a mutual commitment to automatic application of the regime's obligations as law by domestic courts. Because this regime would be accepted on a *reciprocal* basis, the outcome would rest in part on retaliation incentives, to avoid triggering trading partners' reversion to WTO-style retaliatory behaviors. At the same time, this outcome would also require forms of international economic exchange and domestic political institutions that incentivize policy-makers to behave in ways compatible with such a demanding international bargain. The last section of this chapter tests this argument empirically by showing that, in comparative terms, intra-European trade is intra-industry trade, that the political institutions of the EU member states tend to be both inclusive and authoritative, and that the EU member states possess generous social insurance systems, each of which reduces the difficulty for policy-makers in accepting more binding and intrusive trade policy commitments (Balassa 1966; Cameron 1978; Ruggie 1982; Rodrik 1998; Gerring and Thacker 2008; Vroman and Brusentsev 2005, 2009).

The fifth chapter builds on this explanation to put forward a new narrative of the development of the European legal order, with less emphasis on the individual rights declared by the ECJ, the networking of legal elites, and the way that the European legal order changes the relationship between national courts and the governments of their own states, and more emphasis on intra-industry trade, parliamentary forms of government, substantial welfare states, and the way that domestic court enforcement of trade treaty obligations changes the international relationship between states.

The final chapter evaluates the book's approach to explaining the EU as a self-contained regime, and discusses the implications of the book's argument for scholarship on EU politics, on enforcement and escape in international trade politics, and for broader topics in international relations scholarship.

Two final words before we start: first, readers specialized in EU studies may perhaps be initially uncomfortable with this book's description of the EU an international organization, solving international problems. The EU, so some say, is "European," not "international." But the word "international" is used here in an analytical sense, to mean relating to politics "above" and "between" nation states. The EU itself is not a state, possessing no "monopoly of legitimate violence" vis-à-vis its participating jurisdictions. From this analytical perspective, the EU is just as much an international organization, and is just as dependent on the cooperative behavior of its member states, as the WTO or the Universal Postal Union. To be sure, as is often correctly emphasized, the EU is very different from many other international organizations. Explaining perhaps the most profound of those differences is, indeed, the focus of this book.

Second, and more importantly, for different reasons for readers from different backgrounds, this book may present a challenge. Its central contribution involves the integration of already dense and well-developed, but as yet poorly integrated, scholarly literatures. The generalist student of international relations will therefore be introduced to the specialist vocabulary and debates of the European legal order—among others, the doctrine of direct effect, the "preliminary reference" procedure, the problem of "later-in-time" national legislation—as well as some of the ECJ's most important decisions, including *Van Gend en Loos* and *Commission v. Luxembourg and Belgium*. They will learn about both the all-embracing supremacy doctrine of European law as elaborated by the ECJ, and the more modest and limited "supremacy" acknowledged by the courts of the member states. The specialist in EU studies is likely to be well aware of such EU terminology and debates, but may perhaps be unfamiliar with important trade politics concepts such as "trigger strategies," "escape mechanisms," and "embedded liberalism." To help unfamiliar readers of different backgrounds, a simple glossary of such key terms is included at the end of this book, but integrating these different perspectives may nevertheless remain challenging. Furthermore, this book discusses the EU's distinctive features in a relatively unusual comparative context, and focuses on topics that are at least partially "taboo" among some EU specialists.[3] There is a reward for the effort, however, because this approach promises a better understanding of what is most distinctive about the EU as an international organization, and its significance for the study of international politics.

With that introduction, we invite the reader to begin by identifying the central puzzle that the EU poses to international relations scholarship.

[3] There have been several full-scale attempts by political scientists to explain the development of the European legal order using comparisons with the early United States (e.g. Goldstein et al. 2001; Glencross 2009), for example, but none to our knowledge that focus on the EU's outcome in comparison with the organizing principles of other contemporary trade regimes. For an attempt to explain variation in the *initial design* of international dispute settlement systems, incorporating both the EU and other trade regimes, see McCall Smith 2000. For the argument that explanations of the EU's dispute settlement system should focus on a comparison with contemporary international organizations employing bilateral reciprocity enforcement mechanisms, see Phelan 2011b. For the reluctance of EU legal scholars to discuss a possible reversion to general international law's enforcement mechanisms between the EU member states, see Simma 1985: 123–129, 127.

1

The Puzzle

The basic details of the European Union's institutional arrangements can be described very simply.[1] The European Economic Community (EEC), which came into being in 1958, was originally a trade liberalization and integration agreement providing for a common market between six member states (France, the Federal Republic of Germany, Italy, Luxembourg, Belgium, and the Netherlands). The founding agreement, the Treaty of Rome, established a well-developed set of treaty institutions, including an international secretariat (the "European Commission," or "Commission," with rights to make policy proposals and take legal action against the member states), an international tribunal enjoying compulsory and exclusive competence in relation to the treaty ("the European Court of Justice"), and a body composed of the political representatives of the member states (the "Council of Ministers," or "Council"), which could agree new rules and policies to complete the objectives of the treaty.[2]

Several features of the original treaty arrangements are worth noting: first, the member states' representatives in the Council could make rules that were to be automatically applied as law in the member states' own legal systems, without any requirement for a national ratifying or implementing act;[3] second, the Council could, in certain circumstances (and these were expanded over time), agree new rules by a majority of its member states, rather than requiring unanimous agreement; third, the treaty provided for an international parliamentary assembly, nowadays called the European Parliament; fourth, the range of issues which could potentially be addressed by the

[1] This chapter draws on an earlier publication by this author in *International Studies Review* (Phelan 2012).

[2] The European Economic Community built on, and modified, the institutions and procedures established by the European Coal and Steel Community, established by the Treaty of Paris, signed by the same six states in 1951.

[3] Art. 189 of the Treaty of Rome: "Regulations shall have a general application. They shall be binding in every respect and directly applicable in each Member State."

European institutions was initially broad, and extended much further over time; and, finally, the treaty declared itself open to the membership of other European states, and over the decades since 1958, the number of member states grew to reach twenty-seven in 2007.[4]

Even if we restrict our attention to trade-related aspects, the obligations that the EU imposes on its member states are ambitious and demanding. After all, the member states are required by EU rules to end all tariffs and quotas in their trade with other EU states; to adopt a common external tariff; to submit to extensive and ambitious controls of non-tariff barriers (Gormley 1985; Maduro 1998); to accept controls on state subsidies and on anti-competitive practices by firms ("competition policy"); to submit to compulsory and exclusive dispute resolution arrangements that are open to non-state complainants; and to accept a stream of demanding policy adjustments derived from a rule-making system which can impose new obligations without the unanimous agreement of the member states. These elements distinguish the EU even from other well-developed international trade regimes.

This book does not offer a comprehensive survey of the many and diverse economic obligations that the EU imposes on the member states (Gormley 1985; Maduro 1998). Instead, we will proceed on the basis that many EU obligations involve policy adjustments that affect organized interests within the member states. Scholarship on international organization has long recognized that some important inter-state interactions should be understood as "coordination games," where states may have difficulty in agreeing to a common policy, but afterwards have no incentives to defect (Stein 1982; Martin 1992b). Some of the EU's obligations can, no doubt, be characterized in this manner, but the EU's many and diverse trade-related obligations expand international markets in ways that are commonly understood to create interest-group pressure on policy-makers to defect on previous agreements. Indeed, the EU's trade-related obligations are, by common consent, considerably more ambitious than those of many other trade agreements.[5] Furthermore, the EU member states are highly interdependent, with the level of intra-regional trade as a proportion of member-state GDP at over 20 percent by 1970 for the original six members, rising further as the EU enlarged over time.[6] The EU also regulates a considerable proportion of the total trade activities of its member states: 61 percent of the EU member states' imports

[4] The initial manuscript of this book was completed in September 2012, so its analysis refers to the twenty-seven members of the European Union at that date. Croatia became the twenty-eighth member of the EU in July 2013.

[5] For comparisons between restrictions on barriers to trade in the EU and WTO, see e.g. Gaines et al. 2012, Sorensen 2012, and especially Cottier and Oesch 2012. For a comparison of "internal market rules" within the EU and the USA, see Hoffmann 2011.

[6] For trends in trade integration over time between the EU member states, see Mongelli et al. 2005: especially p. 12.

in 2005 derived from intra-EU trade.[7] The EU's obligations are demanding and affect a large proportion of the member states' economies and trading relationships, and any explanation of the EU as a distinctive international organization therefore involves an explanation of an institution whose obligations produce a significant stream of ambitious trade-related policy adjustments on organized interests in highly interdependent member states.

This concise introduction to the EU's institutions and obligations is unlikely to sufficiently prepare the reader for the almost universal intellectual bafflement that the EU so often generates.[8] It is hard to think of any other area of social science research where scholars so freely admit to ignorance as they do when discussing the EU as a macro-institution. A few examples will suffice. First, leading international relations scholars Stephen Krasner:

> There is no commonly accepted term for the European Union. Is it a state, a commonwealth, a dominion, a confederation of states, a federation of states? Nevertheless it exists.
>
> (Krasner 1999: 235)

And Thomas Risse-Kappen:

> The EU is certainly an institution *sui generis* in the sense that no other international organization has reached a similar degree of integration and regional co-operation.
>
> (Risse-Kappen 1996: 56)

And Donald Puchala:

> Contemporary international integration is not federalism—at least it is not classical federalism...international integration could very well be something new that we have never before witnessed in international relations.
>
> (Puchala 1972: 269–270, 277)

Political theorist Glyn Morgan:

> The Treaty of Rome (1957) proclaimed that the aim of this process of integration was to create "an ever closer union...among the peoples of Europe." Now almost fifty years later—following the Single European Act (1986), the Treaty

[7] By contrast, the 1997 free-trade agreement between Canada and Chile, which—unusually—prohibited the use of anti-dumping duties in trade between these two states, covered only 1.4 percent of these states' imports in 2005 (Teh et al. 2007: 81; Voon 2010: 667). Among other prominent regional trade regimes, NAFTA covered 35 percent, Mercosur 20 percent, and the Andean Community 16 percent, respectively, of their participating states' imports (Teh et al. 2007: 81–82).

[8] Note that today's European Union began as the European Economic Community in 1958, and was renamed the "European Union" by the Maastricht Treaty signed in 1992. For convenience, this book tends to use the description "European Union" for the whole period.

> of European Union (1992), the creation of a European Central Bank and a single European currency (2002), and a Constitutional Treaty (2004)—Europeans belong to... what? This ostensibly simple, ontological question provokes considerable scholarly disagreement and political controversy.
>
> (Morgan 2005: 30)

And economic historian Robert Skidelsky:

> The European Union is a new political contraption... Is it a federal state in the making? Is it a confederation plus? I suggest that is an experiment in a form of governing a group of countries for which we have not yet found a name.
>
> (Skidelsky 2006: 55)

Former judge of the German Constitutional Court, Dieter Grimm:

> As a matter of political taxonomy, the European Community is still a novelty in want of a convincing label.
>
> (Grimm 1997: 229)

Finally, Jacques Delors, once President of the European Commission, is said to have wittily described the EU as an "unidentified political object" (Thibaud 1991: 47; Marks et al. 1996: 1).

Certainly, there are also many efforts to describe the EU in more specific terms. Descriptions of the EU merely as an "international organization," or as an example of "international integration," however, are not so much incorrect, as insufficiently precise. On the other hand, more precise descriptions of the EU do not always fulfill the simplifying and clarifying role to which social science aspires. Philippe Schmitter, for example, has described the EU as "a 'post-national, unsovereign, polycentric, non-coterminous, neo-medieval' arrangement" (Schmitter 1996: 26), while Andrew Moravcsik has called it a "unique, multileveled, transnational political system," and contrasts the EU with "weaker, less overtly constitutional" international institutions such as the World Trade Organization (WTO) and the North American Free Trade Agreement (NAFTA) (Moravcsik 1998: 1, 6). Almost everybody describes the EU as "highly institutionalized," and many as a "unique" or—the favored expression in the EU literature—"*sui generis*" institution.

The problem with such efforts, and many others like them, to describe the EU as a macro-institution is that they often contribute to, rather than resolve, the widespread intellectual confusion surrounding discussions of the EU in international relations scholarship. After all, the scholar or student working on mainstream topics in international relations would usually be hard-pressed to identify with any specificity what is meant by a "constitutional" international organization, let alone a "neo-medieval" one. Political science scholarship has not yet found a "replacement for proper names" to describe the EU in the generalizable—and easily comprehensible—terms that could potentially be applied to other international organizations (Przeworski and Teune 1970).

To be sure, the EU is a complex international organization that involves a variety of different formal institutions, and which provides a large number of diverse and demanding principles and rules that regulate member-state behavior. For understandable reasons, therefore, introductions to the EU often focus heavily on descriptions and analysis of these institutions—the Council of Ministers, the European Court of Justice, the European Commission, the European Parliament, and so on—as well as accounts of the EU regime's essential obligations, both economic and non-economic. Indeed, much current scholarship is focused, often productively, on particular component institutions or obligations within the EU rather than understanding the EU as a whole in comparative context.[9] However, such disaggregated discussion of institutions and obligations may not identify—and may even obscure—the essential differences between the EU and more common forms of international organization. Here, therefore, we will take a different approach. This chapter will establish the puzzle to be addressed in this book by identifying the essential (relevant to contemporary international relations theory) distinction that underlies the common characterization of the EU as a *sui generis* institution. In other words, it will offer an answer to the question "What, stated in general terms, makes the EU a distinctive form of international organization?"

Inter-State Retaliation and Self-Contained Regimes in International Law

Let us start then, as current approaches to understanding the EU rarely do, with looking at state behavior in other international treaty regimes. International legal theorists, more than international relations scholars, have analyzed the EU in comparative perspective. One of the most acute conceptual characterizations of the EU's distinctive characteristics therefore comes out of theoretical discussions of the differences between the EU's legal regime and general public international law. In public international law, states seek

[9] Examples of recent research on component institutions and obligations in the European Union include: The Council of Ministers: Thomson et al. 2006, Thomson 2011; The European Parliament: Yoshinaka et al. 2010, Lindstädt et al. 2012; The European Commission: Woll 2006, Crombez and Hix 2011; Common Foreign and Security Policy: Krotz 2009, Krotz and Maher 2011; EU negotiations with external actors such as the US: Farrell 2003; Common Agricultural Policy: Knudsen 2009; Parental Leave Policy: Weldon-Johns 2013.

to enforce their legal claims, and to provide incentives for compliance on the part of other states, by taking "self-help" action against the state committing an international wrong (Pescatore 1969: 18).[10] It is inherent to this form of enforcement of international legal obligations that it is essentially bilateral in nature, and traditional public international law has therefore been described as "bilateral-minded."[11] The enforcement measures taken by the state claiming to be suffering an international wrong against the state allegedly committing an internationally wrongful act are referred to variously as "reprisals," "reciprocal measures," or—perhaps the most common contemporary term—"countermeasures."[12] The use of inter-state countermeasures and reciprocity is consistent with the general approach of international law that states are only obliged to fulfill their treaty obligations to the extent that their treaty partners are fulfilling theirs in return (*quid pro quo, do ut des*).

Public international law's reliance on, and authorization of, the use of inter-state reciprocity and countermeasures, on the principle of "self-help," is pervasive and longstanding. The centrality of these mechanisms has been recognized by scholars at least from the time of de Vattel, the eighteenth-century philosopher of international law, and contemporary scholars describe them as "the most effective sanction in public international law" (Weiler 1985: 294), "the importance of which can hardly be overestimated" (Simma 1981: 29–30; see also de Vattel 1916 [1758]: 228; McNair 1961: 578; Elagab 1988: 44; Simma 1994a). Examples of these principles in action in treaty politics can be seen in a wide range of contexts. In 1978, when French authorities refused to permit *Pan Am* flights from the United States to Paris with a "change of gauge" in London, an arbitral tribunal found that the United States was entitled as a response to impose restrictions on *Air France* flights between Los Angeles and Paris via Montreal.[13] When in the 1970s decisions by Swiss political authorities no longer permitted Austrian citizens to acquire property in Switzerland as agreed in the Swiss-Habsburg treaty of 1875, Austria suspended the rights of Swiss citizens to acquire property in Austria (Simma 1978). When a number of Germans taken prisoner

[10] Note that, as this statement indicates, even inter-state countermeasures authorized by international law or international institutions are characterized as "self-help" behaviors. See also Weiler's description of the apparatus of state responsibility and countermeasures as "a creature of the self-help horizontality of international law" (Weiler 1991: 2422 ft 42) or Brewster's statement that trade retaliation is the primary remedy in the WTO system "because it is a self-help mechanism" (Brewster 2011: 147).

[11] Simma 1994b: 230; see also "Third Report on State Responsibility," *Yearbook of International Law Commission*, 1982, vol. 2, Part 1, 38.

[12] The use of these different terms is not necessarily consistent among legal scholars. This book will use the expressions "countermeasures," "reciprocal measures," and "reprisals" interchangeably to cover all forms of "self-help" measures adopted by states to enforce international legal obligations and which would otherwise be contrary to international law.

[13] *France v. United States*, 18 RIAA 417.

in the 1942 Dieppe Raid were discovered to have had their hands tied contrary to treaty requirements, German soldiers responded by tying the hands of the Commonwealth prisoners they captured, and Britain then in turn retaliated by adopting a similar policy in its treatment of German prisoners (Morrow 2001: 982). The British Admiralty justified its use of mines in the North Sea in 1914 as retaliation for prior German use of maritime mines contrary to the 1907 Hague Conventions and customary rules of international law (Phillipson 1915: 372–391). When in 1713 England considered removing trade advantages granted to Portuguese wine under the 1703 Treaty of Methuen, the Portuguese envoy implied that this might result in the removal of trading opportunities granted to England's wool trade (Duguid 2003: especially p. 30). When a new emperor of Byzantium, John Comnenus (ruled 1118–1143), refused to honor trading privileges granted to Venice in a treaty of 1082, the Venetians retaliated militarily from 1122 until their privileges were restored in 1126 (Norwich 1995: 70). These are examples of states taking or threatening retaliatory or reciprocal measures in response to other states' treaty violations, but of course the availability of these mechanisms is also relevant to many international political situations where reprisals are not employed or even explicitly threatened.

The behavior of the EU as a whole, as a member of the WTO, also provides examples of this behavior, as the EU makes use of threats of countermeasures in the form of trade sanctions in its trading relations with states outside the EU (Devereaux et al. 2006). Inter-state reciprocity incentives can also be used to promote order in international politics even in the absence of formal treaty agreements, for example in states' public commitments to "no first use" of weapons of mass destruction (Simma 1981: 31). (If the reciprocity element in such commitments is not immediately apparent, it may help to compare a "no-first-use" policy with a hypothetical "no-second-use" alternative.)

Such basic principles of public international law often remain intact even in highly institutionalized international regimes. The WTO, for example, which in 1995 replaced the General Agreement on Tariffs and Trade (GATT) as the global trade regime, specifies rules and procedures for the settlement of disputes between WTO members. Where WTO members persist in selectively pursuing WTO-inconsistent policies even after the decisions of the WTO's tribunals, the WTO regime authorizes the member which has suffered "impairment" to suspend "equivalent" "concessions" (that is, impose proportionate trade sanctions in retaliation).

In the words of the WTO's Dispute Settlement Understanding:

> If the Member concerned fails to bring the measure found to be inconsistent with a covered agreement into compliance therewith or otherwise comply... any party having invoked the dispute settlement procedures may request

> authorization from the DSB [Dispute Settlement Body] to suspend the application to the Member concerned of concessions or other obligations under the covered agreements.
>
> The level of the suspension of concessions or other obligations authorized by the DSB shall be equivalent to the level of the nullification or impairment.[14]

Examples of WTO-authorized countermeasures include retaliatory US tariffs on adhesives, chocolate, and pork imported from the EU during a EU–US dispute caused by the EU's refusal to allow imports of hormone-treated beef (Devereaux et al. 2006: 73, including ft 112). Similarly, after a dispute settlement panel found that US restrictions on cross-border trucking services were contrary to its NAFTA obligations, Mexico imposed retaliatory tariffs on cat food, dishwashing machines, and tableware imported from the United States.[15] As the NAFTA example illustrates, dispute settlement systems with the potential to authorize "suspension of concessions" or trade retaliation mechanisms are also a regular feature of regional or bilateral trade agreements (Chase et al. 2013: 36ff).[16]

Even within these highly developed international regimes, therefore, a fundamental incentive for compliance is based on the possibility of reciprocal measures adopted by other states. As much scholarship has shown, the WTO's enforcement mechanisms are affected by the same problems associated with the inter-state enforcement of general international law, such as inequalities in retaliatory power and harm to "innocent" firms and individuals affected by retaliatory actions (Charnovitz 2001; Bown and Blonigen 2003; Lawrence 2003). There may even appear to be something intrinsic and inescapable to international law's reliance on inter-state countermeasures as enforcement mechanisms for costly obligations. Unlike decisions of international dispute settlement processes that require the target state to make its policy conform with treaty requirements, inter-state countermeasures can be imposed by the injured state even if the target state does not cooperate in the acceptance of the penalty (Lawrence 2003: 81; Brewster 2011: 147).

[14] Art. 22.2 and Art. 22.4, "Understanding on Rules and Procedures Governing the Settlement of Disputes," Annex 2 of WTO Agreement. See also Art. 3.7: "The last resort which this Understanding provides to the Member invoking the dispute settlement procedures is the possibility of suspending the application of concessions or other obligations under the covered agreements on a discriminatory basis vis-à-vis the other Member, subject to authorization by the DSB of such measures."

[15] The panel decision was taken in 2001; Mexico imposed trade sanctions in 2009 after the United States Congress refused to renew a pilot program allowing a limited number of Mexican trucks to haul freight in the United States. The list of products included in Mexican retaliation is listed in "Mexico Retaliation: NAFTA Trucking Dispute," a document available on the website of the International Trade Administration, United States Department of Commerce. See also "A Small and Dangerous Spat," *New York Times*, March 18, 2009.

[16] Note that many joint members of regional trade agreements nonetheless prefer to pursue trade disputes through the WTO's dispute settlement mechanisms rather than those provided for in regional trade agreements.

In the 1980s, however, leading legal theorists were inspired by elements of a decision of the International Court of Justice (ICJ) to consider the possibility of an international legal regime which would reject the use of inter-state countermeasures as an enforcement mechanism. The ICJ decision itself related to a dispute between Iran and the United States over Iran's detention of US diplomatic and consular staff in Tehran after the Iranian revolution of 1978, which Iran justified as a response to the US' policy of supporting the previous government of Iran. The ICJ decided that, even if the claims of Iran were correct and even if Iran had suffered an international wrong on that account, because the rules of diplomatic law constituted a "self-contained régime," it was not possible for such countermeasures to be adopted in relation to diplomatic and consular representatives.[17]

Reflecting on the ICJ's reasoning, Simma developed a conceptual definition of a "self-contained regime" as one where states would accept international obligations but where the application of international law's normal mechanisms at the disposal of an injured party—inter-state countermeasures in some form or another—would be excluded (Simma 1985; Simma and Pulkowski 2006). States would follow the rules of such an international regime without use of the inter-state incentives normally considered essential to this outcome. Whether international legal regimes of this type are feasible or desirable remains the subject of considerable debate.

Having demonstrated that the incentives provided by inter-state countermeasures and reciprocity are recognized as a longstanding and central feature of international law, and having defined a self-contained regime as a treaty regime which, despite this, operates *without* the use of inter-state reciprocity and countermeasures, we can now apply this concept to the EU. The essential theoretical difference between the European legal order and general international law is that the EU can be characterized as just such a self-contained regime.

In the words of J.H.H. Weiler:

> [O]ne may speculate about the most profound difference between the Community legal order and international law generally. The combined effect of [European law doctrine and remedies] results, in my view, in the removal from the Community legal order of the most central legal artifact of international law: the notion (and doctrinal apparatus) of exclusive state responsibility with its concomitant principles of reciprocity and countermeasures. The Community legal order, on this view, is a truly *self-contained legal regime* with no recourse to the mechanism of state responsibility, at least as traditionally understood, and therefore to reciprocity and countermeasures, even in the case of actual or

[17] *United States Diplomatic and Consular Staff in Tehran*, ICJ Reports (1980). For discussion, see e.g. Simma and Pulkowski 2006: 491.

> potential failure. Without these features, so central to the classic international legal order, the Community truly becomes something "new."
>
> (Weiler 1991: 2422, emphasis added; similarly, see Pescatore 1969: 18; Weiler 1985: 294)

As the authorship of this passage by one of the leading scholars of European law demonstrates, understanding the European legal order as a "self-contained legal regime" is entirely compatible with mainstream European law scholarship. Weiler's identification of the EU as a self-contained regime, and the ECJ cases on which this claim is based, however, have not been followed up in the international relations scholarship on the development of the European legal order (and may perhaps be described as somewhat neglected, even in legal scholarship).[18]

The EU's rejection of the use of reciprocity and inter-state countermeasures between its member states was established in a series of foundational judgments by the ECJ.

These include, first and foremost, the 1964 case *Commission v. Luxembourg and Belgium*, where the ECJ stated that:

> In [the defendants'] view,...international law allows a party, injured by the failure of another party to perform its obligations, to withhold performance of its own...However, this relationship between the obligations of parties cannot be recognized under Community law...[t]he basic concept of the treaty requires that the Member States not take the law into their own hands. Therefore the fact that the [other party] failed to carry out its obligations cannot relieve the defendants from carrying out theirs.[19]

Subsequent decisions include *Essevi*, where the Court stated that:

> Above all, it must be pointed out that in no circumstances may the Member States rely on similar infringements by other Member States in order to escape their own obligations under the provisions of the Treaty.[20]

[18] Political science discussions which come closest to emphasizing this aspect of the EU (but do not offer an explanation of this outcome as an alternative to bilateral reciprocity) include Wallace's reference to the EU as a "diffuse formal regime," and Zürn and Joerges's comparison of compliance outcomes in the EU and WTO (Wallace 1983: 403; Zürn and Joerges 2005). For a study of variation in the *initial design* of international dispute settlement systems, contrasting inter-state retaliation and direct effect mechanisms, see McCall Smith 2000 (note, however, that inter-state retaliation was not necessarily ruled out in the initial design of the Treaty of Rome). For the recognition of the EU's rejection of inter-state countermeasures in general international law scholarship, see e.g. Partsch 1981: 202; Zoller 1984: 110, 113; Elagab 1988: 89, 166–167. For a discussion of the European legal order emphasizing the "revolutionary" nature of *Commission v. Luxembourg and Belgium*, see Gradoni and Tanzi 2008.

[19] Cases 90 and 91/63 *Commission v. Luxembourg and Belgium* [1964] ECR 625. Note that the particular details of the case in *Luxembourg and Belgium* related to the claim that the European institutions themselves had failed to perform their obligations, but the ECJ's reasoning in this and other cases disallowed this behavior between all parties to the treaties, including between the various member states.

[20] Cases 142 and 143/80 *Amministrazione delle Finanze dello Stato v. Essevi* [1980] ECR 1413.

And similarly *Guy Blanguernon*:

> [A]ccording to settled case law, a Member State cannot justify failure to fulfil its obligations...by the fact that other Member States have also failed to fulfil theirs....Under the legal system laid down by the Treaty the implementation of Community law by Member States cannot be subject to a condition of reciprocity.[21]

The fundamental principles of the EU regime as elucidated by the ECJ in *Essevi* and *Guy Blanguernon* run in complete opposition to the fundamental principles of the WTO regime, because infringements by other members *do* indeed allow WTO members to escape their own obligations ("to suspend the application to the Member concerned of concessions or other obligations under the covered agreements," as is stated in the WTO Agreement cited above). In that sense, the WTO reflects an institutionalization of the general approach of international law, while the EU breaks with that approach to insist that its member states adopt a "no-second-use" policy in relation to national measures inconsistent with EU obligations.

The EU's rejection of inter-state countermeasure and reciprocity mechanisms therefore differs qualitatively from situations where states merely de facto do not use the reciprocity mechanisms that treaties may formally provide to them (for example, where states do not pursue GATT violations within the WTO dispute settlement system), as well as from situations where states *do* use inter-state countermeasures even where treaty arrangements do not explicitly provide for them.

The wording of *Guy Blanguernon* suggests the need for precision about the nature of the EU's rejection of the principle of reciprocity. After all, the EU member states benefit from each others' policies of trade liberalization, and perhaps the ECJ's most famous decision—*Costa v. ENEL*—describes the European legal system as being accepted "on a basis of reciprocity."[22] Nevertheless, the reciprocity of obligations among EU member states is quite different from the reciprocity of obligations in general international law. The reciprocity between member states of the EU is an "all-or-nothing" reciprocity where all member states must comply with all compulsory and automatically applied EU obligations addressed to them without the possibility of using the non-fulfillment of obligations by other member states to authorize or validate their own failure to comply (Weiler 1981: 297). It

[21] Case C-38/89 *Ministère Public v. Guy Blanguernon* [1990] ECR I-83.

[22] Case 6/64 *Costa v. ENEL* [1964] ECR 585: "The integration into the laws of each Member State of provisions which derive from the Community, and more generally the terms and the spirit of the Treaty, make it impossible for the States, as a corollary, to accord precedence to a unilateral and subsequent measure over a legal system accepted by them on a basis of reciprocity."

is thus an obligation that is *not conditional* on other states' behavior.[23] The EU therefore involves states in a reciprocal bargain not to use retaliatory trade sanctions as an enforcement mechanism.[24] On the other hand, the reciprocity of public international law, and the reciprocity between the members of the WTO, is a *conditional*, "only-to-the-extent-that-others-do" reciprocity, where states can justify their non-fulfillment of treaty obligations on the basis of their partner's non-fulfillment.

The reciprocity and countermeasures outcome—and the associated disruption of international trade—that the EU *avoids* is vividly described by Weiler and Haltern:

> Consider...the pragmatic nightmare that would ensue in a treaty as long, complex, and, by its own terms, open-textured as the European Treaties if such an interpretation were adopted. State *A*, in the face of an unfavorable judicial decision, unilaterally abrogates Treaty provision *x*...The international law principle of reciprocity would mean that the particular obligation would cease to be operative between *A* and all the other Parties *B–Z*. So now there would be two co-existing regimes in relation to provision *x; x* is applied as among Parties *B–Z*, but inapplicable in the relationship of *B–Z* with *A*. Now imagine that State *B* abrogates, on the same grounds, Treaty provision *y*, and that State *C* does likewise with Treaty provision *z*....Garry Kasparov would, we think, have difficulties in sorting out the permutations.
>
> (Weiler and Haltern 1996: 432, emphasis in the original; see also Schilling 1996).[25]

If the EU's obligations were organized on this sort of reciprocal basis, it is unlikely that the EU would ever have been described as an "unidentified political object." It is precisely the rejection of this sort of inter-state relationship that is the EU's remarkable distinction. This qualitative change in inter-state relations has something of the same profound significance as the comprehensive rejection of the use of armed force as a means of dispute

[23] The term "self-contained regime" is therefore used in this book to refer to treaty regimes that reject the use of inter-state countermeasure and reciprocity mechanisms, in line with the conceptual definition developed by Bruno Simma (Simma 1985). For the avoidance of confusion, it may be helpful to state that this "self-contained regime" is not identical with the concept of a "self-enforcing agreement" commonly used in international relations scholarship. A self-enforcing agreement is one in which two or more parties adhere to the agreement as long as each gains more from continuing the agreement than from defecting from it, and where the agreement is enforced by the parties themselves, not by third-party sanctions (Simmons 2010: 275). Many international agreements are self-enforcing, however, because states make use of inter-state countermeasure and retaliation mechanisms that are incompatible with an international agreement being described as a self-contained regime (e.g. Bown 2009 on the WTO).

[24] One could say that the EU requires reciprocity but forbids "reciprocal measures."

[25] For the relative stability of trading opportunities within the EU compared to other international trade regimes, see Gray and Slapin 2012.

resolution between states belonging to international "security communities" (Deutsch et al. 1957; Adler and Barnett 1998).[26]

To conclude this section, therefore, general international law is a system for organizing the relations between states which is dependent on the use of inter-state countermeasures and reciprocity mechanisms, whose application is guided and organized by general principles, or at times by detailed treaty procedures. The EU, however, is a self-contained regime, operating in costly and demanding issue-areas such as trade, which functions without the use of countermeasures and reciprocity mechanisms characteristic of—and apparently vital to—public international law, and multilateral trade regimes such as the WTO and NAFTA.

International Trade Agreements and Trade Remedies

The EU's rejection of inter-state retaliation mechanisms is not its only distinction. Again, looking at other international trade regimes draws out another difference. International trade agreements of course contain reciprocal obligations for their member states to reduce tariff and non-tariff barriers to trade, as well as dispute settlement procedures. However, they also contain a variety of legal mechanisms by which the participating states can unilaterally re-impose trade barriers, to allow *ex post* management of demanding trade integration at the discretion of national policy-makers. In the WTO, for example, Article VI of the GATT treaty provides states with the right to impose trade barriers where it believes that an established industry is being damaged by imported goods being sold at less than the normal value of the products. Such goods are described as being "dumped," and the trade barriers being imposed are described as "anti-dumping duties." Article VI of the GATT also provides states with the right to impose trade barriers to offset any GATT-non-compliant subsidies that other states have provided their industries. Trade barriers of this second kind are described as "countervailing duties." Article XIX of the GATT provides states with the option to take emergency action to increase trade barriers relating to imports of particular products where these are causing or threatening serious injury to domestic producers. Trade barriers of this third kind are described as industry "safeguard measures."

Anti-dumping duties, countervailing duties, and safeguard measures provided for in international trade regimes are often referred to as the three ordinary forms of "trade defense mechanisms" or—the term we will use

[26] For the suggestion that the EU's break with the use of inter-state countermeasures as a means of enforcing treaty obligations might be worthy of a Nobel Peace Prize, see Phelan 2013b.

here—"trade remedies." The use of trade remedies by states to manage their international trade obligations is pervasive and longstanding, and the centrality of these mechanisms to the politics of trade is widely acknowledged among trade politics experts (Kravis 1954: 319; Rosendorff and Milner 2001; Schropp 2009: 3). They are used extensively by members of the WTO, including by the EU as a whole vis-à-vis its non-EU trading partners.

The reliance on trade remedies often remains important even in trade agreements where states mutually agree to go beyond their WTO obligations by further lowering trade barriers to favored trading partners. NAFTA, for example, provides for the US, Canada, and Mexico to impose anti-dumping and countervailing duties and safeguard measures, vis-à-vis each other (albeit with more specific procedural provisions than ordinary WTO rules), while Mercosur (the regional trade agreement between Brazil, Argentina, Uruguay, and Paraguay) permits anti-dumping and countervailing duties, but not safeguard measures (Teh et al. 2007). Even well-institutionalized international trading regimes, therefore, commonly provide states with legal instruments to escape their trade obligations where these impose severe costs on domestic industries. Partners in regional trade agreements cannot typically agree on liberalization beyond "most favored nation" levels without having trade remedies to fall back on (Voon 2010: 647).

Having therefore demonstrated that trade remedies are a central feature of the politics of international trade agreements, we can now return to the EU. An essential distinction between the EU and other international trade regimes is that the EU does not provide its member states with these legal mechanisms to unilaterally escape their previously assumed trade obligations to each other. The founding treaty of the EEC, the Treaty of Rome, did provide that, during a transitional period ending in the 1960s, the member states could complain to the European Commission about "dumped" imports from other states, and the Commission could authorize the state to adopt protective measures, but since the passing of the transitional period no such mechanism remains available.[27] Nor do the European treaties provide state policy-makers with the option of using countervailing duties or safeguard mechanisms to save particular industries from adjustments imposed by intra-EU trade.[28] The EU requires that its member states maintain an open international market between themselves without making use of such instruments.

[27] Art. 91 of the Treaty of Rome.

[28] The Treaty of Rome also provided for an industry safeguard mechanism of sorts only during the initial, transitional stage: see discussion in Chapter 3. For a survey of a broader range of flexibility mechanisms in the European treaties—including, for example, the exclusion of territories such as the UK bases in Cyprus, and derogations allowing, for example, the then West Germany to maintain its system of inter-German trade with the then East Germany—see Hanf 2001.

The distinctive nature of the EU's rejection of these three trade remedy instruments in intra-EU trade is well validated in comparative research. Teh, Prusa, and Budetta, for example, in their review of trade remedies in seventy-four regional trade agreements, conclude that "only one [regional trade agreement], the European Communities, has managed to abolish all three forms of trade remedies on members' trade" (Teh et al. 2007: 26). Similarly, Voon, in her review of the provision of trade remedy mechanisms in more than 150 regional trade agreements, concluded that only the EU Treaty had abolished all three forms of trade remedies among its members: anti-dumping, countervailing, and safeguard measures (Voon 2010: 647). The Treaty of Rome, signed in 1957, has, in this respect, been described as more "advanced" than more recent forms of international trade integration (Wooton and Zanardi 2002: 22). One study of the role of escape mechanisms in trade politics noted that, when looked at in contrast with the WTO system, policy-makers in the EU member states appear to have "virtually no instrument" to temporarily protect their home markets against intra-regional imports (Roitinger 2004: 207).[29]

There is an obvious connection between the EU as a self-contained regime that rejects the use of inter-state countermeasures, and the EU as an international trade regime that does not provide state policy-makers with trade remedy instruments. Both reflect the EU's prioritization of reliable trading conditions in the European common market over autonomous national policy-making and "self-help" behavior by the participating states. Furthermore, inter-state retaliation mechanisms are often threatened or used in the context of other states' use of trade remedy instruments. In terms of their relative importance, trade remedies are much more commonly employed in many trade regimes, including the WTO, than inter-state retaliation mechanisms. Nevertheless, the rejection of inter-state countermeasures is arguably the more fundamental distinction, because the ability to defect (at the risk of becoming a target of inter-state countermeasures) is international trade law's all-purpose escape mechanism, and the imposition of inter-state countermeasures is general international law's all-purpose enforcement mechanism. The rejection of inter-state countermeasures is therefore directly relevant to the fundamental organizing principles of international law. By contrast, the rejection of trade remedy instruments in the EU is merely a prohibition of particular (if important) types of behavior. However, the rejection of inter-state retaliation and the rejection of trade remedies can, and should, be seen in combination with

[29] Note that use of the Treaty of Rome's balance of payments safeguard mechanism, as well as exchange rate policy by the member states, falls outside the scope of this book.

inter-related characteristics of the EU as a distinctive form of international trade organization.[30]

Conclusion

This identification of the EU as an international trade regime that imposes ambitious policy obligations but rejects the use of inter-state countermeasures and trade remedies sheds new light on previous discussions of the *sui generis* nature of the EU. Compared to characterizations of the EU as a "highly institutionalized" regime, this discussion makes clear that the EU's institutionalization—unlike, for example, those of the WTO or NAFTA—has resulted in a decisive departure from the use of inter-state countermeasures and trade remedies. The EU's rejection of inter-state countermeasures and trade remedies is a matter of sufficient significance that it can plausibly be described as a vital "qualitative difference" between the EU and many other international regimes. This is a description "without proper names" which does not in any way disguise—indeed, it reveals—what is extraordinary about the EU as a form of international trade organization.

Although the description of the EU as a self-contained international regime may be new to many political scientists specializing in EU-related topics, it is a description which is derived from an intimate knowledge of the law and politics of the EU. Use of this term by leading scholars such as Weiler demonstrates that this understanding of the EU is entirely compatible with orthodox scholarly approaches to European law. Furthermore, it builds directly on the distinctions between European law and general international law that the ECJ itself has emphasized.

Above all, however, this approach removes the EU from the opacity of "unidentified political object" debates to reveal a readily recognizable political economy puzzle. It allows the ordinary student of international relations, who often learns a basic version of reciprocity-and-retaliation arguments for state behaviors early in their studies, to quickly grasp what is different about the EU. The same holds even more true for the professional scholar of international relations, who is well aware of the steady stream of new publications about retaliation-based dispute settlement mechanisms, and trade remedies, particularly within the context of the WTO. Using this definition, the EU's distinctive form of international organization becomes a clearly identified—if as yet unexplained—phenomenon.

[30] On the need to consider trade regimes' enforcement and flexibility mechanisms together as a whole, see Roitinger 2004 and Schropp 2009.

A few preliminaries are in order before we proceed to considering possible explanations for this outcome.

Even in an attempt to explain the distinctive nature of the EU as an international organization in aggregate (as a "macro-system" or "macro-institution"), it is still necessary to define the scope of the EU activities that this book will address. This book will focus on the EU as a system for producing compulsory and automatically applied obligations for the EU member states.[31] It thus excludes a wide range of topics such as treaty restraints on national deficits in member states that have adopted the European single currency (the Euro), as well as EU obligations known as "directives," which—unlike those EU obligations which must be *automatically* applied at the national level—require transposition or implementation by a national legislative or regulatory act.[32] While these limitations are significant, to focus on the EU's compulsory and automatically applied obligations is to focus on essential features of the EU that have been present from the early years of the EEC until the present day.

This book also focuses primarily on the EU as an international trade regime, facilitating the free movement of goods and services between the member states. EU obligations include many important trade-related requirements that change relative prices and facilitate cross-border trade, therefore imposing a stream of adjustments on organized interests within the member states. Certainly, this is a somewhat limited view of the contemporary EU, because the economic freedoms provided for by the EU also include free movement

[31] For the more technical reader, "compulsory and automatically-applied obligations" refers here to obligations that benefit from European law's claims to direct application/direct effect in the national legal orders. Note that the scope of policy covered by the EU's compulsory and automatically applied obligations has been enlarged over time, particularly through revisions of the European treaties such as the Single European Act in 1986 and the Maastricht Treaty in 1992, but right from the EU's beginnings in 1958 included substantial obligations relating to trade between the EU member states.

[32] Because "directives" require transposition by national authorities, the late, or incorrect, transposition of EU obligations contained in Directives *may* offer policy-makers "escape" mechanisms that are not available in the case of automatically applicable EU obligations—that is the obligations that enjoy direct effect or direct applicability. This book's focus on explaining the politics of automatically applicable EU obligations is therefore focusing on the politics of the management of the *most* stringent and demanding of EU obligations. By providing an explanation of policy-makers' ability to manage those EU obligations which provide national policy-makers with the *least* flexibility and escape options, however, we necessarily also provide an explanation for the EU member states' ability to manage EU obligations which may provide policy-makers with *more* flexibility and escape options. It also focuses on EU obligations where the EU's distinction from more common forms of international organization is clearest. For this reason, existing explanations of the development of the European legal order also correctly focus on the politics of directly effective EU obligations, rather than on the politics of transposition of Directives (e.g. Weiler 1991; Burley [Slaughter] and Mattli 1993; Alter 2001). To be sure, the extent to which the ability to transpose Directives late or incorrectly is a useful "escape" mechanism for national policy-makers may be exaggerated, and to the degree that certain European obligations contained in Directives may enjoy direct effect in national courts, as the ECJ has established, EU obligations in the form of Directives are included in the scope of our analysis here.

of workers and the right of business establishment, and the scope of the EU's competences has increased over time to include, for example, environmental, educational, social, and even human rights obligations. The EU never was, and certainly is not today, merely a trade regime.

However, there are advantages to focusing on the EU as an international trade regime, because organizing the market between the EU member states has been one of the EU's vital goals from its earliest days, and because this approach connects the EU most directly to wider discussions of international organization in international relations theory, where the scholarship on international trade regimes is highly developed. Furthermore, any explanation of the EU as a macro-institution must *at least* contain an explanation for the EU's ability to provide an open international market between its member states without the use of inter-state countermeasures or trade remedy mechanisms. Facilitating the intra-European market is the central obligation of membership for all EU member states, whereas in certain other prominent issue-areas—the "Schengen Agreement" on internal border controls, or participation in the European single currency—individual member states may opt out to varying degrees (Jensen and Slapin 2012). Moreover, it may well turn out that an explanation for the EU as a self-contained regime in the trade politics issue-area may also go a long way toward explaining the EU's ability to effectively regulate many non-trade issues as well.

For the sake of clarity it may also be worth setting out some questions that this book is not attempting to answer. It does not, for example, attempt to offer a new explanation for why states engage in international cooperation or create international organizations. It accepts the common arguments of existing scholarship that interdependent states engage in international cooperation when their policy-makers can obtain better outcomes by coordinating their behavior with other states than are available through unilateral decision-making behavior (Keohane 1982). Where states' expectations converge around a set of principles, norms, rules, and decision-making procedures, this is known as an "international regime" (Krasner 1982: 186). Where states benefit from coordinated state behavior, but face international collective action problems of choosing standards or preventing defection, they have incentives to form international institutions to reduce transaction costs, fill in incomplete contracts, and monitor state behavior for non-compliance with previous agreements (Stein 1982; Keohane 1984). *Legalized* international institutions can provide increased precision and coherence, and greater delegation of interpretative authority to third parties, in such monitoring procedures and dispute resolution mechanisms (Goldstein et al. 2001). Where states face strong incentives to defect from prior agreements, perhaps most prominently from interest groups facing adjustment costs, such international interactions are often modeled as an inter-state Prisoners' Dilemma, where repeated interactions and retaliatory threats, or "trigger strategies," can provide incentives for states to fulfill their obligations (Axelrod 1984; Keohane 1984; Dai 2002: 405). Where policy-making outcomes are particularly affected by the behavior of neighboring states in a geographical region, states have incentives to form regional international organizations that are particularly focused on the management of policy-making interdependencies and externalities in that particular region (Moravcsik 1998; Mattli 1999). These basic elements of modern rationalist approaches to explaining international organization are not disputed, but rather are accepted as a foundation for this particular research project, which attempts to explain why the EU has developed a particular form of legal obligation and dispute settlement mechanism, distinct from those of other international trade regimes.

Finally, this book does not attempt to offer a new explanation for variation in outcomes *within* the EU legal regime. To be sure, in today's EU some member states, more than others, are found by the ECJ to have failed to fulfill their European obligations, some national court systems submit more questions about European law ("preliminary references") to the ECJ, and important outcomes in the EU legal system also vary across time and across issue-areas. This book, however, is offering an explanation for the distinctive features of the EU's legal regime taken as a whole—indeed for the fundamental organizational structure of the EU as a macro-institution—not for variations in legal outcomes within that regime. At the moment, there is an extensive scholarship explaining variations in outcomes *within* the EU, which consistently rejects the use of inter-state countermeasures and trade remedies, on the one hand, and an extensive scholarship explaining variation in outcomes *within* trade regimes, most prominently the WTO, that rely on inter-state countermeasures and trade remedies.[33] This book, by contrast, offers an explanation of *cross*-regime variations, explaining why the EU, unlike most international trade regimes, rejects the use of inter-state countermeasures and trade remedies.

How, then, can the EU's remarkable rejection of inter-state countermeasures and trade remedies be explained? That is the project of the rest of this book.

[33] For recent examples of work explaining outcomes within the EU legal regime, see Conant 2002; Nyikos 2006; Cichowski 2007; Malecki 2011; and Larsson and Naurin 2013. For recent examples of work explaining outcomes within the WTO legal regime, see Allee 2004; Bown 2005b; Davis and Shirato 2007; and Davis 2012.

2

The European Legal Order

We will turn to two scholarly literatures to see what answers they offer to the puzzle of the EU's rejection of inter-state trade sanctions and trade remedies. This chapter looks at the EU-specialist literature on the development of the European legal order, while the next looks at the generalist international relations scholarship on enforcement and escape in international trade politics.

This chapter proceeds in three parts. The first part serves as an introduction to the special features of law and dispute settlement in the European Union, including the role of national courts, aimed particularly at the generalist reader with little background knowledge of the EU or the European legal order. It describes the supremacy and direct effect doctrines of European law, and provides a summary of how the European legal order has developed over the years. The second part describes the most influential explanations for the development of the European legal order, focusing particularly on the period from the Treaty of Rome through to the mid-1990s, giving the reader an overview of the most important issues raised and debated by leading scholars. The particular puzzle addressed by this book, however, is explaining the EU's ability to reject the use of inter-state countermeasures and trade remedy instruments. The third section demonstrates that current scholarship on the European legal order has not attempted to explain this outcome, and offers a series of inter-connected criticisms of current scholarship on the European legal order that undermine its ability to provide such an explanation. Above all, this scholarship has not attempted to provide an explanation for why state policy-makers, or adversely affected interest groups, would behave in ways compatible with the highly binding constraints of the European legal order. The chapter finishes by drawing conclusions relevant to constructing a new explanation of why the EU rejects the use of WTO-style trade sanctions and trade remedies.

The European Legal Order Then and Now

When the Treaty of Rome was signed on March 25, 1957, as well as declaring that the member states were determined to lay the foundations for "an ever-closer union among the peoples of Europe," and setting out various obligations, institutions, and decision-making procedures, the Treaty provided for a Court of Justice to "ensure that in the interpretation and application of this Treaty the law is observed."[1]

With that ringing declaration, the Treaty set out the various ways in which the Court of Justice, now universally known as the European Court of Justice (or "ECJ"), with its seat in Luxembourg, could be involved in settling disputes. Both the member states and the European Commission were entitled to bring member states before the ECJ for failing to fulfill their treaty obligations.[2] If the ECJ found a member state had failed to fulfill its obligation, that State would be "required" to take the necessary measures to comply with the judgment of the ECJ.[3] These legal arrangements were very much *international* procedures, available for use only by the *governments* of the member states, or—a notable provision—by the European Commission acting as the EU's international secretariat.

However, the *preliminary reference* procedure, contained in Article 177 of the Treaty of Rome, was something different. It provided that, where it was relevant to a legal dispute, *courts* within the member states could directly communicate with—make a "preliminary reference" to—the ECJ, by asking a question about the interpretation of the Treaty, or the validity and interpretation of EU Regulations and other rules ("acts of the institutions of the Community").[4] Recall that the Regulations issued by the European institutions are required to be "directly" (that is to say, automatically) applicable in the legal orders of the EU member states, and thus disputes over their interpretation and application were likely to arise in disputes involving private parties in national courts. Article 177 therefore potentially provided a mechanism by which the ECJ could offer guidance to national courts on

[1] Art 164 of the Treaty of Rome. The essential provisions of the Treaty of Rome have continued to exist, although they have been renumbered several times as the European Treaties have been amended by subsequent treaty amendments to the original treaties. For the sake of simplicity, we will use the article numbers from the original Treaty of Rome. Note that the European Court of Justice itself was first established by the European Coal and Steel Community treaty, the Treaty of Paris.

[2] Art 169 and Art 170. [3] Art 171.

[4] "The Court of Justice shall have jurisdiction to give preliminary rulings concerning: (a) the interpretation of this Treaty; (b) the validity and interpretation of acts of the institutions of the Community; (c) the interpretation of the statutes of bodies established by an act of the Council, where those statutes so provide. Where such a question is raised before any court or tribunal of a Member State, that court or tribunal may, if it considers that a decision on the question is necessary to enable it to give judgement, request the Court of Justice to give a ruling thereon...."

how they should interpret EU Regulations when making their judgments. On one reading, therefore, which became widely accepted as time went by, the national courts were not to freely interpret the Treaty of Rome, or the Regulations it produced, in litigation before them, but were instead to refer such questions of interpretation to the ECJ.

Most commentators claim that Article 177 was not originally created as a compliance mechanism—that is, to ensure that the application of EU obligations in the national legal orders was guided by the ECJ's interpretation of contents of the Treaty of Rome and the Regulations produced by the European institutions (Moravcsik 1998: 155–156; Alter 2001: 9–10, 12–13).[5] Over time, however, as we shall see, the Article 177 mechanism greatly assisted the uniform interpretation and application of EU obligations in the national courts, and became an important element in the EU's system of ensuring national compliance with EU obligations.

These, then, are the various procedures set out in the Treaty of Rome by which the member states and the European Commission could complain about the member states' non-fulfillment of their obligations, and a procedure, perhaps originally of limited purpose, by which the national courts could submit legal questions about the interpretation of EU obligations to the ECJ. Given subsequent developments, however, the Treaty of Rome is as remarkable for its omissions as for its contents. Nothing in the treaty either authorized or forbade the use of inter-state countermeasures or reciprocal measures as an enforcement mechanism between the member states. The Treaty contains no provision proclaiming that signatory governments recognize the supremacy of Treaty obligations, or the Regulations issued by the Treaty institutions, over the national laws of the EU member states. And, although the Treaty did provide that the Regulations agreed by the European institutions were to be directly applicable in the national legal orders of the EU member states, the Treaty did not provide that provisions of the Treaty itself were to be directly effective in the national legal orders. Unusually, however, the treaty did fail to provide the EU member states with unilateral legal escape mechanisms, such as anti-dumping, although various safeguards were provided, particularly during the early transitional stage.

If the provisions of the Treaty of Rome provide a formal account of the European legal order as it was established in 1958, fifty years later these legal institutions and procedures are being extensively used. In 2010, the ECJ made 370 decisions, and national courts in the member states made 385 new

[5] Some observers noted, however, even early on, the similarities between the Art 177 provisions and the question-submitting procedures for ensuring uniformity of constitutional interpretation across courts and jurisdictions in certain constitutional court systems (Lenhoff 1962–1963: 321, ft 600).

requests for preliminary rulings (European Court of Justice 2012: 96, 101, 116). The ECJ today makes decisions on a wide range of disputes, including the protection of consumers' rights when flights are delayed (Kelemen 2011: 1ff), the rights of unions to strike against the use of workers posted from other member states,[6] the rights of individuals targeted for sanctions by decisions of the United Nations Security Council,[7] and an almost limitless range of intra-EU trade-related controversies. Some of the most interesting recent work on the politics of European law explores how this changed litigation environment may perhaps, over time, be transforming European politics (Kelemen 2011).

How did today's European legal order emerge from the relatively unpromising provisions set out in the Treaty of Rome? Two doctrinal developments—"direct effect" and "supremacy"—are widely agreed to have been crucial. The ECJ first elaborated the concept of "direct effect" in its 1963 *Van Gend en Loos* decision, where it claimed that certain obligations contained in the European treaties themselves should also be automatically applied as law in the courts of the member states in disputes involving private parties, without the need for any corresponding national legal act.[8] As the *Van Gend en Loos* judgment stated, these obligations were to be applied "independently of the legislation of the member states." The significance of the *Van Gend en Loos* decision was that the ECJ gave itself the power to add unilaterally to the treaty obligations and EU rules that were to be automatically applied, even without any national implementing act, in the national legal orders, where they could be relied upon by private parties.[9]

The European law doctrine of supremacy was, in turn, first elaborated by the ECJ in its 1964 decision, *Costa v. ENEL*.[10] The supremacy doctrine claims that, where there is an irresolvable conflict between national law and European law, it is the European legal obligation, not the national law obligation, that must be applied, even if the national law is enacted more recently, or *"later in time,"* than the European obligation,[11] a scenario which the ECJ referred to as a "unilateral and subsequent measure."

[6] Case 438/05 *International Transport Workers' Federation v. Viking* [2007] ECR I-10779 and Case 341/05 *Laval v. Svenska Byggnadsarbetareforbundet* [2007] ECR I-11767.

[7] Cases 402/05 and 415/05, *Kadi v. Council of the European Union* [2008] ECR I-6351.

[8] Case 26/62 *Van Gend en Loos v. Nederlandse Administratie der Belastingen* [1963] ECR 1.

[9] Recall that the Treaty of Rome already provided for the "direct applicability" of EU Regulations, meaning that Regulations agreed by the member states in the Council would be applied as law in the national legal orders without any national legal act to ratify, transform, or incorporate them into national law. The direct effect of treaty obligations should therefore be understood as somewhat similar to, and a development of, the existing direct applicability of EU Regulations. See e.g. Hartley 2007: 198ff for a skeptical discussion about the importance of differences between direct effect and direct applicability.

[10] Case 6/64 *Costa v. ENEL* [1964] ECR 585.

[11] In many legal systems, a common rule for reconciling conflicts between laws is that obligations set out in newer, "later-in-time" legislation prevail over obligations contained in older

As the ECJ stated in *Costa*:

> By contrast with ordinary international treaties, the EEC Treaty has created its own legal system which, on the entry into force of the Treaty, became an integral part of the legal systems of the Member States and *which their courts are bound to apply*. By creating a Community of unlimited duration, having its own institutions, its own personality, its own legal capacity and capacity of representation on the international plane and, more particularly, real powers stemming from a limitation of sovereignty or a transfer of powers from the States to the Community, the Member States have limited their sovereign rights, albeit within limited fields, and have thus created a body of law which binds both their nationals and themselves. The integration into the laws of each Member State of provisions which derive from the Community, and more generally the terms and the spirit of the Treaty, make it impossible for the States, as a corollary, to accord precedence to a *unilateral and subsequent measure* over a legal system accepted by them on a basis of reciprocity....
>
> The transfer by the States from their domestic legal system to the Community legal system of the rights and obligations arising under the Treaty carries with it a permanent limitation of their sovereign rights, against which *a subsequent unilateral act* incompatible with the concept of the Community cannot prevail... [emphasis added]

The EU legal system therefore differs from many other international legal systems. Other international tribunals, such as WTO panels, may declare the illegality in international law of the result of national measures where these are contrary to treaty obligations. Importantly, however, these tribunals may not require that states cease to apply the measures in question. It remains for policy-makers in the state concerned to change their internal measures, or—as they choose—not. The EU legal system, by contrast, claims not only to determine the legality of national measures in relation to the European treaties, but also that EU law requires national courts to apply EU obligations where national law is contrary to European law. In other words, EU law requires that European obligations are applied as law by national courts, whether national law provides for it or not.

As the doctrine of direct effect suggests, the ECJ is not the only court that applies EU law. Where European law obligations enjoy direct effect or direct application, national judges apply European law in national courts in litigation open to private parties, such as ordinary citizens and businesses. So, in addition to the possibility of litigation in the ECJ initiated by other member states and by the European Commission, national courts have come to

legislation. This is referred to as the "*lex posterior*" criterion, in line with the legal maxim *lex posterior derogat legi priori*, that new laws displace the effect of earlier laws. See discussion of European law's *lex posterior* problem in Phelan 2010.

provide an extensive and decentralized monitoring and sanctioning system for national failures to comply with costly EU obligations. The national courts are guided by the preliminary reference system by which national judges refer questions of European law to the ECJ and then pronounce their own judgment after the ECJ has decided on the interpretation of European law: so, the Irish judge in Cork and the German judge in Bremen directly apply European law in their courts. Indeed, because national courts have come to routinely apply European law in their disputes, including when making significant adjustments to national law, without necessarily making a preliminary reference to the ECJ, the actual decisions of the ECJ represent only the "tip of the iceberg" of the European legal order.[12] The ECJ and the national courts of the member states are thus integrated into a unitary system of judicial review, so that national judges apply European law in the many disputes that come before them, both with and without involving the ECJ through the preliminary reference procedure (Weiler 1994: 515).

This, then, is the "constitutional" legal regime of the European Union, where EU law claims supremacy over national laws, where national courts apply directly effective European law in place of contrary national law at the suit of private parties, and where the preliminary reference system from national courts to the European court functions somewhat like an appeals system to ensure the uniform interpretation and application of European law across the member states' jurisdictions. As a result of these legal doctrines and processes, the member states appear to face an "all-or-nothing" environment for compliance with EU obligations quite unlike the selective compliance frequently offered to obligations of other treaties or international institutions (Weiler 1981).[13]

It should be obvious that the supremacy and direct-effect doctrines of European law attempt to radically reduce the ability of the member states unilaterally to act contrary to their EU obligations. J.H.H. Weiler, in a seminal article on the "transformation of Europe," argued that, while the ECJ—like other international courts—can only make a declaratory judgment which a state can always ignore, the enforcement of European law by national courts makes it "impossible" for member states to disregard EU obligations (Weiler 1991: 2421). Weiler concluded that this participation by national courts hinders the common practice of "selective exit" from costly international legal obligations:

[12] The *Acte Clair* doctrine of the ECJ discourages national courts from referring issues to the ECJ that relate to settled legal issues: Case 283/81 *CILFIT v. Ministry of Health* [1982] ECR 3415. For examples of ambitious national court applications of European law without use of a preliminary reference to the ECJ, see Anthony 2002: 92; Obermaier 2008: 744.

[13] For a detailed analysis of the supremacy doctrine, see e.g. Phelan 1997: 98–120.

> The judicial doctrine of direct effect...provides the following presumption: Community legal norms that are clear, precise and self-sufficient...must be regarded as the law of the land in the sphere of application of Community law...
>
> The doctrine of direct effect might not strike all observers as that revolutionary, especially those observers coming from a monist constitutional order in which international treaties upon ratification are transposed automatically into the municipal legal order and in which some provisions of international treaties may be recognized as "self-executing."...
>
> In light of supremacy the full significance of direct effect becomes transparent. Typically,... [*a*] *national legislature unhappy with an internalized treaty norm simply enacts a conflicting national measure and the transposition will have vanished for all internal practical effects.* By contrast, in the Community, *because of the doctrine of supremacy, the E.C. norm,* which by virtue of the doctrine of direct effect must be regarded as part of the Law of the Land, *will prevail even in these circumstances.* The combination of the two doctrines [direct effect and supremacy] means that Community norms that produce direct effects are not merely the Law of the Land but the "Higher Law" of the Land. Parallels to this kind of constitutional architecture may, with very few exceptions, be found only in the internal constitutional order of federal states.
>
> (Weiler 1991: 2413–2415, emphasis added)

Simply put, direct effect and direct application automatically place EU obligations "in" the national legal orders, and supremacy prevents those EU obligations from being taken "out" again by conflicting national law. Together they create a remarkably binding system for the enforcement of EU obligations.

The full functioning of today's European legal order only emerged over time. The number of ECJ decisions increased from 20 in 1962 to 138 in 1979 and 203 in 1993. More and more national courts asked for the ECJ's opinion through the preliminary reference procedure, rising from 32 in 1970 to 141 in 1990 and 249 in 2004 (European Court of Justice 2012: 115–118). The ECJ's case law developed decision-making principles that regulated national measures for impermissible barriers to trade between the member states with increasing intensity. For example, the Treaty of Rome included in Article 30 a prohibition on quantitative restrictions on imports and "all measures having equivalent effect." The ECJ interpreted this article in its *Dassonville* decision to mean that "all trading rules enacted by member states which are capable of hindering, directly or indirectly, actually or potentially, intra-Community trade, are to be considered as measures having an effect equivalent to quantitative restriction" (Gormley 1985: 21).[14] The ECJ used this logic to restrict the use of quality standards tied to particular territories, requirements for souvenir goods to be labeled if they were "foreign" products, publically

[14] Case 8/74 *Procureur du Roi v. Dassonville* [1974] ECR 837.

sponsored publicity campaigns calling for the consumption of domestically produced goods, and even legal restrictions on advertising where these were understood to restrict trading opportunities (Gormley 1985).

One of the best-known of the ECJ's judgments was the *Cassis de Dijon* decision, taken in 1979, which introduced the requirement of "mutual recognition."[15] In the *Cassis de Dijon* dispute, an importer of French fortified wine found that they were prevented from selling their goods on the German market because German regulations prevented the sale of fruit liqueurs of that particular strength. The importer claimed that this sort of regulation was a disguised barrier to trade, even though the German regulation applied equally to alcoholic drinks produced in Germany and in the other EU member states.

In its decision, the ECJ decided that the German regulation was, indeed, a disguised barrier to trade, and, as such, contrary to the European treaties. Its reasoning, however, went beyond that specific result to suggest that the member states could not prevent by regulation the marketing and sale of goods where these met the standards of regulation and marketing in the home market of another member state. In other words, the member states were obliged to "mutually recognize" each others' regulatory standards, so long as such regulations had a "parallel function" (Weiler 2000: 218–223). Although the implications of this principle for the sale of other goods and services were developed and modified in later litigation, *Cassis de Dijon* is a much discussed example of the ECJ's ambitious approach to restricting the impact of non-tariff barriers to trade between the EU member states.

The other important *type* of legal decisions that must be mentioned at this stage are the decisions by national courts that have recognized, at least in part, the direct effect and supremacy doctrines of European law. Thus, the courts of the legal orders of each of the EU member states have produced a set of canonical decisions describing, and often limiting, their accommodation of these European law doctrines. For Germany, whose constitutional court decisions on this question are perhaps the most discussed of all the national legal orders, the most prominent cases include *Solange I* in 1974, *Solange II* in 1986, and the *Maastricht-Urteil* on the constitutionality of the Maastricht Treaty in 1993.[16] The content of these national court decisions often addresses the question of the relationship between European law and

[15] Case 120/78 *Rewe-Zentral v. Bundesmonopolwaltung fiir Branntwein* [1979] ECR 649.

[16] *Solange I*: 37 BVerfGE 271, Oppenheimer 1994: 419–460; *Solange II*: 73 BVerfGE 339, Oppenheimer 1994: 461–495; *Maastricht-Urteil*: 89 BVerfGE 155, Oppenheimer 1994: 526–575. Each of the member states has similar cases, however, including *Thoburn* in the United Kingdom, *Crotty* in Ireland, and the Maastricht constitutionality decision of the Danish Constitutional Court. *Thoburn*: [2003] QB 151, [2002] 4 All ER 156. *Crotty*: [1987] IR 713, [1987] ILRM 400. *Danish Maastricht case*: Danish Supreme Court Decision of 6 April 1998, reported UfR 1998, p. 800, Oppenheimer 2003: 175–192.

the protection of human rights—or, to be more exact, between European law and the fundamental rights protected by national constitutions. In the *Maastricht-Urteil*, the German Constitutional Court insisted that EU obligations that conflicted with the rights protected by German constitutional law would be inapplicable in Germany, while the Danish Constitutional Court's decision on the Maastricht Treaty made a similar declaration about the inapplicability in Denmark of European law obligations that conflicted with the rights protected by the Danish constitution.[17] Perhaps for this reason, as we will see, explanations of the development of the European legal order by both lawyers and political scientists often focus on the possibility of conflicts between the ECJ and national courts over the protection of the fundamental rights of individuals.

Explaining the European Legal Order

We now turn from describing the European legal order to discussing the scholarly work that has attempted to explain it. This assessment and review will offer extensive criticisms of the current scholarship addressing this question, so we should start by acknowledging its virtues. Even now, many years after their initial publication, Weiler's wonderful account of the "transformation of Europe," Garrett's debates with Burley and Mattli, Stone Sweet's statistical analysis of the preliminary reference procedure, and Alter's narrative of the maneuverings between German courts and the ECJ remain essential reading for all those who want to understand the EU's system of dispute settlement. This literature, taken together, has introduced many to the study of the politics of European law, a contribution that must be gratefully acknowledged by anyone interested in the European legal order.

The reader should note that this scholarship largely concentrates on the foundational period from the signing of the Treaty of Rome to the mid-1990s, and that will also be our focus here, although such explanations remain relevant to understanding the power and influence of today's European legal order.

[17] *Maastricht-Urteil* of the German Constitutional Court: "A European policy decided under Title V or VI of the Union Treaty, involving an encroachment upon basic rights by the German sovereign power, consequently cannot restrict the protection of basic rights by the German courts. To that extent, exactly the same applies as in the case of a conventional international agreement: if its implementation nationally would violate basic rights, it is prohibited by constitutional law" (Oppenheimer 1994: 548). Maastricht decision of the Danish Constitutional Court: "Article 20 [of the Danish Constitution] did not permit an international organization to be entrusted with the promulgation of measures which were contrary to provisions in the Constitution, including its rights and freedoms" (Oppenheimer 2003: 177).

In recognition of his enormous influence on subsequent scholarship, we will begin by discussing the writings of Joseph Weiler. Weiler was among the first to emphasize the essential enforcement role of *national* courts in the development of the European legal order. While a decision of the ECJ in Luxembourg could, like that of any international tribunal, always be disregarded by national governments *in extremis*, so Weiler argued, the same could not be said for the decisions of national courts, who were involved in the enforcement of European law through the preliminary reference system. He put this argument succinctly: "A state, in our European democracies, cannot disobey its own courts" (Weiler 1991: 2421; also 1985: 297).

Subsequent political science scholarship has offered a variety of explanations for the European legal order, but many have shared Weiler's special emphasis on the cooperation of national courts with European law in the enforcement of EU obligations. A wide range of scholars accept that the essential difference between the EU and other regimes is that the *national* courts enforce the supremacy of European law against potentially unwilling elected politicians. Karen Alter's description is typical: "National courts would not let politicians ignore or cast aside as invalid unwanted decisions. Nor could politicians veto ECJ decisions through a national political vote, because [European] law was supreme to national law.... [N]ational court legitimacy forced the [member state] government to find legally acceptable solutions to accommodate the jurisprudence of the ECJ.... In the European Union,... governments cannot selectively opt out of the European legal system..." (Alter 1998: 133, 144; similarly, e.g., Alter 2001: 219; Pollack 1997: 118; Stone Sweet 2004: 25; Stone Sweet and Brunell 1998a: 66; Conant 2002: 42; Helfer and Alter 2008–2009: 873–874).

Why were these national courts so positively responsive to the developing European legal architecture (Weiler 1991: 2425)? On this vital question, Weiler put forward a series of influential, if admittedly speculative, answers (Weiler 1991: 2425).[18] First, the national courts may have been influenced by the legal legitimacy associated with the ECJ's role in "upholding the law." Second, through a process *"transnational incrementalism"* the national courts in the various member states slowly came to copy one another in accepting more and more of the new European legal construct (Weiler 1991: 2425). Third, this legally driven "constitutional revolution was a narrative of plain and simple judicial empowerment," whereby national courts, particularly "lower" national courts, gained a de facto power of judicial review over national legislation (Weiler 1991: 2426). In other words, the constitutionalization of the

[18] "The most fascinating question in this regard is how to explain the responsiveness of the Member State courts to the new judicial architecture.... Due to its nature, reply to the question must remain speculative."

European legal order involved a strengthening of the judicial branch against the political branches of government *within* the member states. Finally, the human rights jurisprudence of the ECJ reassured national courts that the constitutionalization of the European legal order would not lead to violations of fundamental rights. As Weiler said, "Accepting supremacy of Community law without some guarantee that this supreme law would not violate rights fundamental to the legal patrimony of an individual member state would be virtually impossible. This especially would be true in member states like Italy and Germany where human rights enjoy constitutional protection" (Weiler 1991: 2418). By promising *itself* to protect the rights of individuals, the ECJ helped to persuade national constitutional courts to accept the supremacy of European law (Weiler 1991: 2417–2418, 2426 ft 52).

Weiler's discussion of the political context of the constitutionalization of European law went beyond the politics of courts, however. He emphasized the interaction between these important legal changes and the political and institutional interests of political decision-makers in the form of the national governments of the member states. As Weiler explained, "Legal and constitutional structural change has been crucial, but only in their interaction with the Community political process" (Weiler 1991: 2407). Weiler therefore put forward two reasons why these profound changes occurred with a minimal measure of political opposition by the member states (Weiler 1991: 2428–2429). First, that the increasing constitutionalization of the European legal order coincided with the insistence of national governments on "unanimity" or "consensus" decision-making (that is, under the shadow of national vetoes) in the Council, rather than the majority voting provided for in the Treaty of Rome.[19] So, the member states were willing to accept the constitutionalization of the Treaties because the national governments of these member states were, at the same time, taking real control of the European decision-making process (Weiler 1991: 2429). The constitutionalization of the treaties also brought domestic advantages to these national executives. After national executives had agreed on new European regulations in their Council negotiations, these decisions were now "constitutionalized" in ways that reduced the ability of their own national parliaments to "have second thoughts" or control their content at the national level (Weiler 1991: 2430).[20] These diverse elements made up Weiler's "law in context," or "law and politics," approach to explaining the "quiet" development of the European legal order (Weiler 1991: 2409; 1994).

[19] This was associated with the struggle over EU decision-making rules initiated by De Gaulle's France which led to the so-called "Luxembourg Compromise," with its emphasis on de facto national veto rights over the creation new EU rules and policy, in early 1966.

[20] This argument proved influential—see e.g. Moravcsik 1994. For a detailed empirical criticism, see Phelan 2002; also Lindseth 2010: e.g. 117–118.

At around the same time as Weiler was writing about the transformation of Europe through national courts' participation in the enforcement of European law, Geoffrey Garrett was developing a more state-centric explanation of the role of the ECJ—which eventually led to a celebrated exchange of views on the role of states and courts in the development of the European legal order.[21] Garrett started by acknowledging that certain aspects of the European legal order were difficult to reconcile with ordinary understandings of the role of international institutions—where enforcement institutions merely provide information, after which states *themselves* punish violations by retaliatory and reputational mechanisms—and therefore that it was necessary to move "beyond the approaches prevalent in the international relations literature on cooperation" (Garrett 1992: 535–537). Nevertheless, for Garrett, the mere assertion of direct effect and supremacy by the ECJ could not explain the effectiveness of the European legal system, so the critical question was why the member states *acquiesced* in the ECJ's new legal order (Garrett and Weingast 1993: 196). Garrett's answer was that the ECJ addressed the monitoring and incomplete contracting problems confronting EU member states (Garrett 1992: 556–557; Garrett and Weingast 1993: 197ff). Given incentives to defect on international trade agreements, mutual monitoring was necessary, and given the difficulty of anticipating all possible disputes, including interpretation in the light of specific circumstances, the ECJ's role was consistent with the interests of the EU member states (Garrett 1992: 556–558). In particular, the European legal system forced member states that defected on their obligations to do so in a "very public way" (Garrett and Weingast 1993: 198).

At the same time, Garrett argued, the ECJ would be responsive to the states that make up its political environment: "It is thus reasonable to expect that the justices would choose not to act in ways that powerful political actors in the EC would disapprove," including avoiding the possibility that a state would choose to ignore or not to comply with a ruling that it deems to violate its fundamental interests (Garrett 1992: 558). The EU system accommodates this problem, so Garrett claimed, by excluding some matters from majority decision-making, and by allowing member states to evade ECJ by appealing to legitimate public policy goals, such as environmental or health and safety concerns, to justify trade barriers (Garrett and Weingast 1993: 198–199, including ft 55). Furthermore, the outputs of judicial policy-making should reflect the interests of the EU's most powerful states. "[I]t seems that the principles governing the decisions of the European court and hence governing

[21] Some of Garrett's papers were co-authored with Weingast, Kelemen, Schulz, and Tsebelis. (Garrett 1992, Garrett and Weingast 1993, Garrett 1995, Garrett et al. 1998, Tsebelis and Garrett 2001).

those of domestic courts following its rulings are consistent with the preferences of France and Germany" (Garrett 1992: 558).[22] Garrett supported this claim by arguing that the ECJ's judgment requiring "mutual recognition" of other states' regulatory standards (in the famous 1979 *Cassis de Dijon* case) was consistent with France and Germany's interest in lowering trade barriers, while excluding from this approach issues sensitive to these member states, such as financial regulation (Garrett 1992: 559).

In a direct response to Weiler and Garrett's attempts to explain the European legal order, Anne-Marie Burley and Walter Mattli set out to explain the penetration of European law into the domestic law of the member states—or, more precisely, the construction of a functioning legal system in which national courts both referred cases to the ECJ and complied with the resulting judgments as part of a legal process that privileged EU over national law (Burley [Slaughter] and Mattli 1993: 43; Mattli and Slaughter 1998: 184).[23] Here Burley and Mattli drew interestingly on Ernst Haas's "neofunctionalist" theory of international integration. Haas had argued that progress in international integration would occur not only as the result of inter-state diplomatic bargains, but also through the interactions of supranational actors and domestic actors other than the national governments, who would be persuaded to shift their loyalties to the supranational institutions (Haas 1958). Burley and Mattli applied this argument to legal integration, identifying the ECJ as the supranational actor interacting with subnational actors within the member states, particularly the national courts.[24] These national courts had incentives, as Weiler had explained, to use European law to obtain greater rights of judicial review over national legislation. Others at the national level, including practicing lawyers and law professors specializing in European law, and individual litigants benefitting from European law rights, had similar incentives to promote European law through the use of the preliminary reference procedure (Burley [Slaughter] and Mattli 1993: 59, 62–64; Mattli and Slaughter 1998: 180). The interactions between the ECJ and its wider legal audience were not only formal, however, as the European judges built a constituency of national judges and lawyers through "seminars, dinners, [and] regular invitations to Luxembourg" (Burley [Slaughter] and Mattli 1993: 62; similarly, Alter 2001: ix).

Furthermore, the "nominally apolitical" nature of international *legal* integration, according to Burley and Mattli, made the expansion of the ECJ's role hard to resist. It attracted national courts, whose participation in a

[22] Indeed, in a later publication Garrett suggested that the ECJ had tended to act as a "de facto agent of the German government" (Garrett 1995: 176).

[23] See also Helfer and Slaughter 1997.

[24] On the special role of the ECJ "single-handedly" transforming the Treaty of Rome, see Burley [Slaughter] and Mattli 1993: 70.

dialogue with the ECJ depended in part on their perception of it as a court like themselves, as a fellow member of a "community of law" (Mattli and Slaughter 1998: 196). Law also acted as a "mask and a shield," requiring actors to respond to the ECJ by counterarguments on legal terms (Burley [Slaughter] and Mattli 1993: 72–73). Thus, they claimed, the primary mechanism for the expansion of European law had been the ECJ's cooptation of judges and lawyers in the member states, thereby creating a community of actors above and below the state (Mattli and Slaughter 1995: 183–184). Burley and Mattli claimed that the ECJ had created

> a one-way ratchet by permitting individual participation in the system only in a way that would advance community goals... Citizens who are net losers from integrative decisions by the council or the commission cannot sue to have those actions declared ultra vires. But citizens who stand to gain have a constant incentive to push their governments to live up to paper commitments.
>
> (Burley [Slaughter] and Mattli 1993: 60, 62)

Burley and Mattli criticized Garrett's view that the ECJ's rulings were "consistent with the preferences of France and Germany" as "simply wrong," pointing out that Germany's lawyers had argued *against* the result of the *Cassis de Dijon* decision that Garrett had claimed reflected Germany's preferences (Burley [Slaughter] and Mattli 1993: 51).[25] As Burley and Mattli explained,

> What we know is that at the time a particular case is brought [to the ECJ], different governments strongly disagree as to its outcome. Over time, however, they tend to accept the Court's position and regard the path chosen as inevitable. *It is precisely this process that needs to be explained.* Here... Neofunctionalism is in its element.
>
> (Burley [Slaughter] and Mattli 1993: 51, emphasis in the original)

They concluded: "The answer can only be that the Court does have the power to pursue its own agenda, and that the personal incentives in the judicial and legal community, as well as the structural logic of law, favor integration" (Burley [Slaughter] and Mattli 1993: 74).

Garrett responded to Burley and Mattli's challenge by accepting that the EU legal system had developed in ways that were not foreseen by the state signatories to the Treaty of Rome, and by not contesting the claim that the mechanism for this expansion was the cooptation of member-state lawyers and judges by the ECJ (Garrett 1995: 173–174). Garrett refocused his argument on explaining the outcome that Burley and Mattli insisted that only

[25] They also criticized Garrett's neglect of non-state actors: Burley [Slaughter] and Mattli 1993: 50.

neofunctionalism could explain—that is, where governments strongly disagree with the outcome of an ECJ decision, but nonetheless comply with the decision, and even come over time to accept the Court's position. Garrett argued that in such cases rational states could weigh the costs of accepting the ECJ's decision against the benefits derived from having an effective legal system in the EU (Garrett 1995: 172). In other words, Germany's *general* economic interests could overlay its specific sectoral ones (Mattli and Slaughter 1995: 188). Looking again at the *Cassis de Dijon* decision, Garrett pointed out that while a "tiny part" of the German economy—producers of a type of fortified wine—might have been adversely affected, Germany had a more general interest in the liberalization of European trade that could lead it to accept the result. However, where the domestic political costs were high and the benefits of trade liberalization were weak, then states would be more likely to ignore the ECJ's decisions (Garrett 1995: 176–177). Garrett also pointed out that the treaty provisions allowing the member states to balance trade liberalization against other public policy purposes (health and safety, consumer protection, etc.) gave the ECJ ample room to make decisions that reflected the balance of state power in particular cases (Garrett 1995: 178–180; replicating the argument in Garrett and Weingast 1993: 199).

Burley and Mattli, in reply, persisted in their disagreement with Garrett (Mattli and Slaughter 1995). They reiterated that legal reasoning and legal constituencies at the national level allowed the ECJ to depart significantly from member-state preferences in case after case (Mattli and Slaughter 1995: 186–187). Empirically, they criticized Garrett's renewed discussion of the *Cassis de Dijon* case, an element in his general argument that states would ignore ECJ decisions if it were to impose costs on a large enough constituency. While the segment of the fortified wine industry facing new competition as a result of *Cassis* was indeed small, Burley and Mattli noted that Germany also accepted a later ECJ decision that removed non-tariff barriers, and thus increased imports, affecting the much larger beer industry (Mattli and Slaughter 1995: 188).[26] Furthermore, while provisions of the European treaties do allow the balancing of trade liberalization against other public policy purposes, these do not provide an all-purpose escape mechanism, and indeed the ECJ did not allow Germany to benefit from such "balancing" claims in the *Cassis* case. In general, the ECJ followed legal, rather than political, reasoning in allowing the use of such exceptions, building their decisions on the basis of legal texts and prior cases, as well as the purposes of the treaty (Mattli and Slaughter 1995: 186–187). As long as the ECJ preserved sufficient adherence to legal reasoning to persuade "its audience of national

[26] Case 178/84 *Commission v. Germany* [1987] ECR 1227.

courts," so Burley and Mattli maintained, it enjoyed a significant advantage over the member states (Mattli and Slaughter 1995: 187). Because of weaknesses in Garrett's empirical claims, and perhaps because Burley and Mattli declared that Garrett now agreed with most of what they had set out to prove in their original article, Burley and Mattli are often regarded as having come off best in this exchange.[27]

Alec Stone Sweet and Thomas Brunell enriched this discussion by contributing a more empirical analysis of the use of the preliminary reference procedure set out in Article 177 of the Treaty of Rome (Stone Sweet and Brunell 1998a; see also Stone Sweet and Brunell 1998b; Stone Sweet 2004). They argued that European legal integration—the construction of a supranational constitution—was driven by the interaction of transnational market exchange, the demand for third-party dispute resolution, and the production of new legal norms. In particular, growth in the use of the preliminary reference procedure was best explained by growth of trade between the member states in goods and services. Stone Sweet and Brunell agreed in large part with Weiler and Burley and Mattli that the ECJ was an independent legal actor, operating in a permissive legal environment because it required unanimous action by the member states to overturn its decisions (Stone Sweet and Brunell 1998a: 74; Stone Sweet 2004: 25). More generally, they claimed, European integration was driven by transnational activity and the efforts of the European institutions to reduce transaction costs, behavior that the national governments of the member states could react to but did not control (Stone Sweet and Brunell 1998a: 63). Stone Sweet and Brunell's work on the use of the preliminary

[27] Burley and Mattli claimed that "[Garrett] now agrees with our claim that the primary mechanism for the expansion of European law has been the court's co-optation of judges (and lawyers) in the member states, thereby creating a community of actors above and below the state." (Mattli and Slaughter 1995: 183–184). However, Garrett's 1995 discussion of this point had merely stated that while judges in the member states often support the ECJ, they do not always do so, and space prevented a fuller discussion of this complex issue (Garrett 1995: 173–174). Furthermore, while Burley and Mattli said that Garrett had originally described "the European Union legal system as a straightforward implementation of Member State wishes" (Mattli and Slaughter 1995: 193), Garrett's 1995 paper had accepted that the EU's legal system had developed in ways not foreseen by the state signatories to the Treaty of Rome, and Garrett and Weingast's 1993 chapter had already argued for a distinction between the ECJ's role in making "path-breaking" legal decisions and the "critical question" of why the EU member states "acquiesced" in that outcome (Garrett and Weingast 1993: 196; Garrett 1995: 173–174). In a later publication, Mattli and Slaughter, building on work by Pollack, put forward a way of synthesizing their neofunctionalist and Garrett's intergovernmental approaches to the ECJ (Mattli and Slaughter 1998: esp 182; see also Pollack 1997). This suggested synthesis, however, restricted national policy-makers' mechanisms of control of the ECJ to *collective* action by the member states in, e.g., the Council of Ministers, whereas Garrett's scholarship had stressed the need for an explanation for why national policy-makers acquiesced in European law's restrictions on their *unilateral* policy-making (e.g. Garrett 1992: 558, 1995: 172). Subsequent criticisms of Garrett's scholarship have tended to focus most particularly on his claim that ECJ decisions reflected the preferences of France and Germany as the EU's dominant member states, as well as his neglect of national judges and litigants (Alter 2009a: 12–13; Stone Sweet 2004: 116–117).

reference procedure inspired an important subsequent literature (e.g. Nyikos 2006; Wind et al. 2009).

Perhaps the next influential contribution was Karen Alter's "historical institutionalist" explanation of the development of the European legal order, which drew on theoretical work by Paul Pierson (Alter 2001: ix).[28] In a well-written full-length account, *Establishing the Supremacy of European Law,* Alter set out to explain why national judges and politicians in Germany and France accepted the ECJ's bold assertion of the supremacy of European law (Alter 2001).[29] Alter's special focus was on inter-court judicial rivalry, and "doctrinal negotiations," in the development of the European legal order. These rivalries and negotiations were both between the ECJ and the national courts, and between *different* national courts with divergent interests (constitutional courts, lower courts, courts with various distinct jurisdictions). These judicial politics, with both winners and losers, had, Alter argued, been left out of neofunctionalist approaches to explaining the politics of European law (Alter 2001: 3, 45–53). Whereas Burley and Mattli had described the European legal order as a "one-way ratchet" of mutual judicial empowerment, Alter argued that the national courts varied in their cooperation with the ECJ, with some courts at times becoming *less* cooperative and creating greater limits to the national application of European law, according to their interests (Alter 2001: 41–43, 64–66).

In an extended case study on Germany, Alter followed the various decisions of the German Constitutional Court—*Solange I, Solange II,* the *Maastricht-Urteil,* and so on—as well as other German courts that indicated the fluctuating legal rationales on which German courts were prepared to accept the supremacy of European law in Germany (Alter 2001: 64). On the issue of whether the German courts should protect the human, or fundamental, rights of individuals from potential violation by European law, German legal doctrine changed repeatedly, and inconsistently, over time, with both "warming" and "cooling" periods. By the end of the 1990s, however, and despite German lawyers continuing to view European law as a type of international law, so Alter wrote, it was "absolutely clear" that European

[28] Pierson discussed the ECJ, and the "constitutionalizing" of the European polity, in his broader historical institutionalist analysis of European integration. Pierson emphasized institutional rules that allowed the ECJ to make decisions by a simple majority of its judges, and provided secrecy for internal decision-making (neither internal votes nor dissenting views are made public) in ways that sheltered ECJ judges from member-state and popular pressures. Furthermore, efforts to overturn judicial decisions required unanimous agreement among all the member states, which would often not be available, and efforts to restrict the power of the Court might jeopardize the single-market project (Pierson 1996: esp 133–134, 143, 146).

[29] Alter admitted that legal outcomes in the EU were likely to be consistent with neofunctionalist narratives, but at the same time emphasized flaws in neofunctionalist explanations (Alter 2009a: 16).

law took precedence over conflicting German parliamentary law (Alter 2001: 73–74, 118).

As far as national politicians were concerned, Alter suggested that political actors had short time horizons that could be "played on" by the ECJ in making bold doctrinal decisions with minimal immediate financial and political consequences (Alter 2001: 188). Then, once ECJ doctrine was accepted by national judiciaries, so that national courts would not let national politicians ignore unwanted ECJ decisions, the ECJ became bolder (Alter 2001: 190, 192). Admitting that there are "relatively few examples" of national politicians trying to get national courts to reverse their acceptance of European law supremacy, Alter argued that politicians apparently "lacked the will" for a struggle with national courts (Alter 2001: 192–195).

Alter's account has become an influential standard introduction to the politics of the European legal order. With its emphasis on how European and national courts clashed over fundamental rights questions, it also set the agenda for later archival work on Germany's relationship with European law (e.g. Davies 2012).

Leslie Goldstein's contribution was to bring an ambitious comparative perspective to a scholarship dominated by discussions of the EU and its member states alone (Goldstein 1997; Goldstein 2001).[30] Goldstein pointed out that the first fifty years of the EU had seen much less EU member-state defiance of EU "federal authority" than the first fifty years of the "American Union"—that is, the United States—had seen defiance of US federal authority. She observed that outright legislative rejections of federal supremacy by state-level elected politicians had been common in the early US, but as good as non-existent in the early EU. Defiance of ECJ doctrine tended to be found more in the courts of the EU member states—for example, in the German courts' decisions on fundamental (or human) rights questions—whereas defiance in the states of the early US often included important roles for elected politicians, who intermittently disrupted previously routine acceptance of US federal authority (Goldstein 2001: 19–21, 33–42).

Goldstein looked for an explanation for the "rarity and softness of tone" of member-state resistance to the ECJ compared to the frequency of overt state defiance of federal authority in the early US (Goldstein 2001: 15). She found that the US comparison cast doubt on many of the arguments put forward in the EU-specific literature. Contrary to Alter's claims, Goldstein found that the ECJ's sometime practice—of establishing new legal principles, but strategically not applying them to the case immediately at hand—had failed

[30] Goldstein compared the European Union not only to the early United States, but also to the early Dutch and Swiss federations. For a more recent comparison between the early United States and the early European Union, see Glencross 2009.

to prevent state resistance to expansive decisions of US federal courts (Alter 1998: 131–133; Goldstein 2001: 50–51). Contrary to Weiler's argument that the acceptance of the ECJ's authority was induced by "transnational incrementalism" or "transnational judicial cross-fertilization," Goldstein shows that cross-state influence could work in either direction (Weiler 1991 24–25; Goldstein 2001: 58; also Burley [Slaughter] and Mattli 1993: 67). In the early US, states copied each others' *defiance* as much as they copied their obedience to federal authority. Contrary to Weiler's emphasis on the "force of legal formalism" and Burley and Mattli's "logic of the law" in the EU case, the widely held respect for "the law," and for the US Supreme Court, did not prevent repeated state resistance to US federal law (Burley [Slaughter] and Mattli 1993: 65–74; Weiler 1993: 423–427; Goldstein 2001: 59). Contrary to Garrett and Weingast's argument that states' general interests in accepting the ECJ's authority, even if it might go against the interest of a state in an occasional instance, might explain their acceptance of ECJ rulings, Goldstein showed that this sort of incentive failed to prevent chronic outbreaks of state resistance to federal authority in the early US (Garrett 1995: 172; Goldstein 2001: 60–61). Finally, contrary to the suggestion of Alter and others that the ECJ was able to get powerful states to do its bidding because of the difficulty in obtaining unanimous member-state agreement to overturn ECJ decisions, Goldstein showed that a similar situation in the early US federation did not prevent the states from openly and unilaterally flouting the authority of the US Supreme Court (Alter 1998: 136–140; Goldstein 2001: 61–62; see also Scharpf 1988). In short, Goldstein convincingly put a query over the significance of many of the arguments emphasized by the scholarship that had discussed the EU in the absence of any comparative context, and raised the question of whether there were wider environmental factors that facilitated the development of the European legal order.[31]

Three more recent contributions to this debate deserve special attention. First, Peter Lindseth's *Power and Legitimacy: Reconciling Europe and the Nation-State* tied the development of the European legal order into broader trends in European governance over the twentieth century. He argued that

[31] It was perhaps not surprising that the influence of neofunctionalist mechanisms did not hold up well in comparative perspective. Weiler had originally described the possible influence of many of these mechanisms as "speculative" answers to questions about the development of the European legal order, and while Burley and Mattli's discussion of similar mechanisms did not contain this caveat, they provided little empirical evidence, for example, to support the claim that national court judges believed they were "empowered," or for the importance of "law as a mask," or that national courts' "loyalties" had changed, in the development of the European legal order (Weiler 1991: 2425–2426, Burley [Slaughter] and Mattli 1993: 62–65, 72–73, 64, and 67). Burley and Mattli's 1993 neofunctionalist paper drew its influence from its stimulating theoretical conjectures, and perhaps also from the weaknesses identified in Garrett's alternative approach, rather than from a solid empirical foundation for the claims it advanced. For an earlier criticism on these lines, see Kilpatrick 1998.

the delegation of rule-making power to European institutions must be seen as part of a general reconciliation of the forms of parliamentary democracy with administrative governance across the European nation states in the post-war period. Looking particularly at France, the UK, and Germany, Lindseth showed how national courts conceive of the institutions of European governance (including the ECJ) as *administrative* forms of governance, whose authority is still ultimately derived from historically constituted bodies of representative government on the national level, rather than autonomously constitutional authorities with plenary powers in their own right (Lindseth 2010: 1).[32] National courts and parliaments therefore balance the functional demands for international integration with continuing attachment to the nation state as the primary locus of democratic and constitutional legitimacy. On this basis, European integration is but one part of the deeper history of "the extensive shift in normative power to the executive and technocratic sphere with the establishment of the welfare state after 1945," and the need for mechanisms of "oversight" and legitimation of administration outside parliamentary control (Lindseth 2010: 42). By stressing that the choice for supranational delegation was not a choice "outside of time" (or place) (Lindseth 2010: 54), Lindseth reminded us that legal institutionalization of the EU therefore took place in a Europe that was "already institutionalized" in distinctive ways at the national level (Lindseth 2010: 57): "The willingness of the Member States, and more particularly their parliaments, to bind themselves to norms produced by relatively autonomous regulatory agencies at the supranational level (at least in certain specified domains) was a direct consequence of this political-cultural environment on the national level" (Lindseth 2010: 60).

Second, Karen Alter and Laurence Helfer renewed the debate from a fresh direction by revealing that a regional integration agreement in Latin America, the "Andean Community of Nations," or "Andean Community," had deliberately imitated many institutions of the European treaties, making the ECJ in particular a model for its dispute settlement tribunal, the Andean Tribunal of Justice (ATJ) (Helfer and Alter 2008–2009; Helfer et al. 2009; Alter and Helfer 2010, 2011; Alter et al. 2012). The ATJ incorporated the key ECJ doctrines of the supremacy and direct effect of Community law, and Andean treaty provisions allowed national courts in the Andean states to submit preliminary references to the ATJ on matters of Andean law. Furthermore, considered in terms of the number of decisions rendered, the ATJ is the third most active international court today, with well over 1,000 decisions (Alter and Helfer 2010). Because the ECJ and ATJ were "structurally identical international courts," so Alter and Helfer argued, they provided a natural experiment to

[32] On this logic, the European Parliament, despite being a directly elected institution, is also a delegated, administrative form of governance.

test alternative explanations of international judicial lawmaking (Alter and Helfer 2010: 563).

The experiment was an interesting one because, on closer inspection, the resemblance between the ATJ and ECJ faded somewhat. Alter and Helfer showed that the ATJ had been unable to secure national courts' regular use of the preliminary reference system or acceptance of the supremacy and direct effect of Andean law. While apparently enjoying insulation from state policy-makers similar to the ECJ, the ATJ had tended—in a most un-ECJ-like way—to respect the discretion that Andean law leaves to state policy-makers (Helfer et al. 2009: 37; Alter and Helfer 2010: 565, 568–569, 580–581). Furthermore, 97 percent of all preliminary references to the ATJ related to just one issue-area—intellectual property—where the ATJ system was effective at obtaining preliminary references and enforcing its judgments, even against member-state resistance (Helfer et al. 2009: 14). Outside of that "island" of effective international adjudication, the ATJ has not obtained the same obedience (Helfer et al. 2009).

Alter and Helfer explained the general ineffectiveness of Andean law by a variety of factors, including the limited commitment of the member states to Andean integration,[33] the limited specificity of Andean market rules, and the lack of compliance constituencies such as national judges and—particularly—the pro-integration jurist advocacy groups that had supported the creation of the European legal order. The success of the ATJ in intellectual property disputes was due, by the same logic, to the tribunal's connection with a constituency of national intellectual property agencies that used the ATJ to manage appeals and defend cross-Andean standards. Alter and Helfer noted that the Andean case suggested that the preliminary reference procedure had played a less decisive role in the development of the European legal order than previous scholarship had emphasized, and perhaps differences in broader social and political forces, such as the lack of pro-integration jurist advocacy networks in the Andean Community, might better explain the regional differences (Helfer and Alter 2008–2009: 876, 920, 927 (on jurist advocacy networks); see also Alter 2009b).

Finally, focusing on legal questions in particular, we should mention the recent emergence of detailed empirical studies by historians such as Anne Boerger-De Smedt, Bill Davies, and Morten Rasmussen, as well as sociologists such as Antoine Vauchez (e.g. Rasmussen 2010; Boerger-De Smedt 2012; Davies 2012; Vauchez 2012).[34] Boerger-De Smedt has looked in detail at the

[33] The Andean states' largest trade markets were outside the Andes, in the United States for example, and the Andean states made limited amounts of secondary legislation compared to the EU member states (on the latter, see Alter and Helfer 2010: 583).

[34] See Davies and Rasmussen 2012 on the growing historical scholarship on European law.

negotiation of the dispute settlement provisions of the Treaty of Rome, as well as its predecessor, the Treaty of Paris that established the Coal and Steel Community (Boerger-De Smedt 2012). Davies has drawn impressively on German government archives to produce a detailed empirical history of Germany's reception of European law, revealing, for example, that German *policy-makers* did not share the opposition of German *government lawyers* to the ECJ's decisions in *Van Gend* and *Costa* (Davies 2012: e.g. 157–158). Davies's study also expanded the scope of how we should think about national reception of European law by including analyses of the German media and public opinion.

Much of this recent scholarship, however, has focused on examining the role of legal elites and bureaucrats in the generation, reception, and celebration of the ECJ's constitutional decisions. Vauchez, for example, has argued that transformation of the *Van Gend en Loos* decision into its now mythical status was achieved not by the ECJ itself, but by the collective authorship of legal entrepreneurs and networks acting through judicial decisions, academic conferences, and parliamentary debates (Vauchez 2010). Building on letters and archives from the early period of European integration, Rasmussen has described in detail the involvement of Michel Gaudet, director of Legal Service of the EEC Commission, in the ECJ's decisions on direct effect and supremacy (Rasmussen 2010). With a narrative immediateness (e.g. Rasmussen 2010) and a focus on specific individuals, this scholarship has generated new objects of study, such as the socializing role of *Festschriften* (collected volumes of essays by friends and colleagues) for retiring ECJ judges, and reinvigorated old ones by bringing in-depth analysis to the networks of pro-European lawyers whose role had previously been much emphasized but rarely empirically studied. Despite these achievements, however, this scholarship has not yet advanced a new answer to the great puzzles of European legal integration—such as how the ECJ managed to "transcend" state sovereignty—but has rather brought attention on new puzzles, such as how the ever-increasing number of new ECJ judges are socialized into the constitutional doctrines of European law (Vauchez 2012: 67). Tacitly at least, however, the logic of this scholarship on networks of European lawyers tends to support a neofunctionalist, "politics-of-lawyers" explanation of the development of the European legal order.[35]

We should also mention the work of a less legally focused scholar, Andrew Moravcsik, whose book *The Choice for Europe* is perhaps the most prominent work of social science on the European Union as an international organization

[35] This scholarship is not, however, much focused on the interactions that induced the *national* courts to participate in the European legal order (e.g. Cohen and Vauchez 2011: 420; but see Davies 2012).

(Moravcsik 1998). Influenced by the economic historian Alan Milward, *Choice for Europe* sets out a policy-maker-centric explanation of treaty negotiations in the European Union, where national governments, under the influence of various interest groups facing the opportunities and risks of international economic interdependence, agree to delegate or "pool" authority in international institutions to solve credible commitment problems (Milward 1984; Milward et al. 1992; Moravcsik 1998: 4, 87–88). Moravcsik's work is sweeping, covering the negotiation of European "grand bargains" from the Treaty of Rome in the 1950s to the Maastricht Treaty in the 1990s. Given this panoramic ambition, it is understandable that the role of the ECJ, and the development of the European legal order, does not receive much consideration.[36]

When Moravcsik does discuss the role of the ECJ in *Choice for Europe*, it is in the context of a very general discussion of delegation as a solution to credible commitment problems:

> Pooling and delegation may raise the visibility of non-cooperation... Once sovereignty has been pooled or delegated, any attempt to reestablish unilateral control... may require governments to launch costly and risky renegotiation of the institutions, perhaps involving a suspension of cooperation.... Finally, international institutions may help establish reputations for member governments, reputations easily damaged by noncompliance in a few areas.[37]

This bland discussion, supported by a reference to leading institutionalist scholar Robert Keohane's argument about reputation incentives, would be applicable—as it certainly was for Keohane—to the GATT, or perhaps almost any other international organization (Keohane 2005: xi). Despite stating that the ECJ is "a constitutional court in some ways more powerful than those of many national systems" (Moravcsik 1998: 67, also 86), and noting that the original negotiators of the Treaty of Rome did not appreciate the later significance of the Article 177 procedure (Moravcsik 1998: 155–156), *Choice for Europe* offers little identification of—or explanation for—the *relative* effectiveness of dispute settlement in the EU compared to other trade regimes.

Moravcsik did offer a more detailed discussion of the European legal order in an earlier paper (Moravcsik 1995). Here he developed an "intergovernmental theory of supranational autonomy," which he used to compare the relative autonomy of the ECJ and the European Commission. Drawing in particular on work by Burley and Mattli, Pierson, and Weiler, Moravcsik argued that prior member-state approval of European legislation made it less

[36] Moravcsik admits to the relative neglect of "the dynamics of legal dispute resolution" in *Choice for Europe* (Moravcsik 1998: 500).

[37] Moravcsik 1998: 74, with ft 107 referring to Keohane's *After Hegemony* (Keohane 1984: 105–106). See also Moravcsik 1998: 68, ft 93, referring to Burley [Slaughter] and Mattli 1993; Moravcsik 1995.

likely that they would object to any ECJ rulings; that the ECJ's autonomy was strengthened by its relatively longer time horizon; that "legal language" could increase the autonomy of the Court by masking its true intent; that, via the preliminary reference procedure, the ECJ enjoyed privileged links with national judges, who enjoy the autonomy provided by rule-of-law ideologies; and that the ECJ could make decisions that changed the policy *status quo*, and challenge the member states to attempt to overrule it through unanimity or supermajority procedures (Moravcsik 1995: 623–624, 622, 625). Perhaps surprisingly, given his emphasis on the importance of state policy-makers and inter-state relationships in explanations of other aspects of European integration, Moravcsik's discussion of the ECJ emphasized similar mechanisms to those elaborated by neofunctionalist and historical institutionalist scholars of the European legal order.[38]

Criticisms of Current Explanations

This scholarly literature has made many contributions to our understanding of the development of the European legal order. The particular puzzle addressed by this book, however, is explaining the EU's ability to impose a stream of demanding policy adjustments on its participating states while rejecting the use of inter-state countermeasures and trade remedy instruments. This section advances a series of inter-connected criticisms of current scholarship on the European legal order that undermine its ability to explain this outcome.[39]

No Focus on Explaining the EU's Rejection of Inter-State Countermeasures and Trade Remedies

Any effort to use existing explanations of the development of the European legal order to explain the EU as a self-contained regime runs into an immediate difficulty. This scholarly literature does not identify the EU as a self-contained regime, nor does it discuss the leading cases, such as *Luxembourg and Belgium*, *Essevi*, and *Guy Blanguernon*, where the ECJ rejected the

[38] Moravcsik stressed, however, that these purported mechanisms of European legal integration remained "hypothetical," still requiring empirical testing (Moravcsik 1995: 625, but see Moravcsik 2005: 363). Note, in relation to the argument developed later in this book, that Moravcsik minimized the possible role of domestic welfare states in explaining the development of European integration, at least as relates to the outcomes addressed in *Choice for Europe* (Moravcsik 1998: 4, 6 ft 6, 40 ft 35, 496).

[39] This chapter draws on an earlier publication, addressing the scholarship of Burley and Mattli, Alter, and Stone Sweet only, by this author in *Journal of European Public Policy* (Phelan 2011b).

"reciprocal-measures-as-last-resort" approach so central to the functioning of general international law. Instead, this scholarship often emphasizes the EU's distinction from other forms of international treaty only in vague and general terms, instead of the specific contrast discussed here.[40] Nor do these explanations of the development of the European legal order mention the EU's distinctive rejection of the three most common forms of trade remedies (Voon 2010). Attempting to use this scholarship on the development of the European legal order to explain why the EU rejects the use of inter-state countermeasure mechanisms, as well as trade remedies, is therefore an effort at "retrofitting" this material to generate an explanation for an outcome that this scholarship did not identify, or claim to explain.[41] The tendency of explanations of the European legal order to proceed without explicit contrast to more common forms of international organization and international dispute resolution is, no doubt, partly responsible for the limited integration of this literature with wider international relations scholarship.[42]

This omission is a fundamental difficulty with existing explanations of the European legal order. The examples of general international law, and the practices of the WTO and many other regional trade agreements, demonstrate that the concrete alternative to the EU's special outcome is a trade regime that makes use of inter-state countermeasures, together with anti-dumping and other trade remedies. Once the novelties of the EU's dispute settlement system are identified in such comparative terms, the most compelling dependent variable for explanations of the development of the European legal order is not therefore variation in the degree to which the courts of the member states accept the ECJ's supremacy doctrine as it relates to human rights, or variation in the number of preliminary references from different EU states, or even variation between the dispute settlement provisions of the Treaty of Rome and the European legal order as it eventually developed— but variation

[40] For example, Alter describes the EU's legal system as "in clear contrast to the typical weakness of international law and international courts," Stone Sweet writes that the ECJ had displaced the "state-centric, 'international regime'" of international relations scholarship, and Burley and Mattli characterize the EU in classic *sui generis* terms as "well short of a federal state, but far more than an international organization" (Burley [Slaughter] and Mattli 1993: 41; Alter 2001: ix, 1, 211; Stone Sweet 2004: 1). Research on variation in dispute settlement design in regional trade regimes does at times recognize, without much further elaboration, that direct effect and inter-state retaliation systems are clear alternatives (e.g. McCall Smith 2000: 142); however, this is not the research design pursued in leading explanations of the development of the European legal order.

[41] A stimulating paper by Keohane, Moravcsik, and Slaughter does discuss the EU and WTO dispute settlement systems in comparison (Keohane et al. 2000). Similarly to previous work by Slaughter [Burley], however, the paper focuses on the independence of judges and the role of private actors in the EU system, rather than on the EU's remarkable rejection of inter-state countermeasures (Phelan 2012: ft 31).

[42] See discussion in Chapter 1.

in whether or not international trade regimes make use of inter-state countermeasures and trade remedies.[43]

Recent work on the Andean Community provides a good example of the limited recognition by current scholarship of the significance of the EU's rejection of inter-state countermeasures. Yes, the Andean Community treaty, like the Treaty of Rome, provides for a preliminary reference procedure, and the ATJ has incorporated supremacy and direct-effect doctrines into its decisions. Nonetheless, while we should be grateful that Alter and Helfer have brought the Andean Community to wider scholarly attention, the ECJ and ATJ are not best considered "structurally identical international courts" with "no clear differences" in their judicial design features (Alter and Helfer 2010: 563).[44] If, as we have argued, the essential distinctive feature of the European legal order is understood to be its rejection of inter-state countermeasures as an enforcement mechanism, then on this fundamental issue the ATJ is not at all designed like the ECJ.

Article 27 of the Treaty establishing the ATJ contains the following provision:

> If that Member Country fails to fulfil the obligation..., the Court,...shall establish the limits within which *the claimant country* or any other Member Country *may restrict or suspend, in whole or in part, the benefits obtained by the Member Country* at fault under the Cartagena Agreement.[45] [Emphasis added]

This provision, of course, makes use of the "self-help" reciprocity and countermeasures mechanisms that the EU has persistently rejected (Weiler 1991: 2418–2419, 2422 including ft 42). These intra-Andean retaliation mechanisms are regularly used in practice: a report of the Andean Community's Secretary-General's office in 2006 recorded that intra-Andean sanctions had been authorized in twenty-three cases, and actually applied in thirteen of those (Secretaría General 2006: 26).[46] The Andean Community also permits its member states to make use of trade remedies, including anti-dumping, countervailing duties, and intra-Andean safeguard measures (e.g. Finger and Nogués 2006: 161 on Colombia [including the intra-Andean safeguard], 271–272 on Peru). The Andean Community's similarities with the European

[43] Alter 2001 focuses, particularly for the German case, on variation in national court acceptance of European law's supremacy doctrine as it relates to human rights. Stone Sweet and Brunell 1998b focus on variation in the use of the preliminary reference mechanism.

[44] Alter and Helfer did at times note that the ATJ also possessed an inter-state retaliation system, e.g. Alter and Helfer 2010: ft 21; Alter et al. 2012: 649–650, but this aspect was not given prominence in their analysis.

[45] Art 27 of the Treaty Creating the Court of Justice of the Cartagena Agreement (Amended by the Cochabamba Protocol), available on the Andean Community's website at: <http://www.comunidadandina.org/ingles/normativa/ande_trie2.htm>.

[46] Intra-Andean trade retaliation is sometimes applied for only brief time periods, however.

institutions therefore co-exist with important continuing affinities with the escape and enforcement mechanisms of more ordinary forms of international trade regime.[47]

Weiler's famous essay on *The Transformation of Europe* is the great exception in this literature. It contains the following passage of great importance:

> It is at this juncture that one may speculate about the most profound difference between the Community legal order and international law generally. The combined effect of constitutionalization and the evolution of the system of remedies results, in my view, in the removal from the Community legal order of the most central legal artifact of international law: the notion (and doctrinal apparatus) of exclusive state responsibility with its concomitant principles of reciprocity and countermeasures. The Community legal order, on this view, is a truly *self-contained legal regime* with no recourse to the mechanism of state responsibility, at least as traditionally understood, and *therefore to reciprocity and countermeasures*, even in the face of actual or potential failure. Without these features, so central to the classic international legal order, the Community truly becomes something "new."
>
> (Weiler 1991: 2422, emphasis added)[48]

Nonetheless, it is fair to say that even Weiler's famous essay is not truly focused on explaining the EU's rejection of inter-state countermeasures. Indeed, the very next sentence downplays the importance of this question:

> At the end of the day the debate about the theoretical difference between international law and Community law may have the relevance of some long-lasting theological disputes—i.e. none at all.

This final comment may partly explain why political science scholars, who have found Weiler's *Transformation* essay so influential in other respects, failed to concentrate on this distinction between the EU legal order and general international law. To scholars working on wider topics in international organization, such as WTO dispute settlement, however, the ability of the EU

[47] The discussion of the inter-state retaliation system in the Andean Community should therefore be more prominently integrated into any comparison between the EU and Andean Community legal systems (compare Alter and Helfer 2010: ft 21; Alter et al. 2012: 649–650). For further discussion, see Phelan 2013a.

[48] Weiler refers to ECJ cases such as *Luxembourg and Belgium*, *Essevi*, and *Guy Blanguernon* as support for this conclusion, and to Simma 1985 as the origin of the "self-contained regime" concept. See also "International law is as uncompromising as Community law in asserting that its norms are supreme over conflicting national norms. But, international law's horizontal system of enforcement, which is typically actuated through the principles of state responsibility, reciprocity and countermeasures, gives the notion of supremacy an exceptionally rarified quality, making it difficult to grasp and radically different from that found in the constitutional orders of states with centralized enforcement monopolies." (Weiler 1991: 2418–2419). The EU's rejection of inter-state countermeasures is also emphasized in Weiler 1985.

to so persistently reject the logic of inter-state countermeasures may appear of very practical relevance.

The scholarship of Geoffrey Garrett is also a partial exception. In one of his early papers, Garrett introduced his discussion of the European legal order by observing that the fact that the EU member states themselves do not punish other states' treaty violations challenged common approaches to explaining international cooperation (Garrett 1992: 535–536). Despite this promising introduction, however, Garrett did not follow up this insight to offer an explanation of why the EU rejected the use of inter-state countermeasures that seem to be so vital to other treaty regimes.

The fact that previous scholarship on the European legal order has not focused on explaining the puzzle of the EU's rejection of inter-state countermeasures and trade remedies no doubt explains why much of the material this scholarship discusses is not always very pertinent to explaining this outcome. As we will see, some of the most studied aspects of the European legal order are not necessarily the most relevant to explaining the EU's ability to reject the use of inter-state countermeasures and trade remedies, while other important aspects of the political environment of European integration have perhaps been unnecessarily neglected.

An Overfocus on the Question of Human, or Fundamental, Rights

One notable feature of current scholarship on the European legal order is its persistent focus on the relationship between EU obligations and human rights—or, more precisely, between EU obligations and the fundamental rights of individuals protected by their national constitutions. As stated above, European law's supremacy doctrine is a conflict resolution rule requiring that directly effective European law must be applied regardless of conflicts with contrary national law. The most vital obligation, emphasized in the ECJ's foundational supremacy decision, *Costa v. ENEL*, is that European law obligations must be applied even if in conflict with a new, "later-in-time," national statute. The supremacy doctrine as elaborated by the ECJ, however, requires that European law obligations must be applied regardless of *any* conflict with national law.

One such conflict would occur where a EU obligation conflicted with a right protected by a national constitution—for example, where an EU Regulation restricting certain economic activities might conflict with a national constitutional "right to property."[49] EU law might therefore potentially require

[49] E.g. Case 11/70 *Internationale Handelsgesellschaft v. Einfuhr- und Vorratsstelle für Getreide* [1970] ECR 1125, a case about the potential conflict between a European Regulation and the "right to property" protected by the German Constitution.

citizens to behave in ways that violated their national constitutional rights. Current explanations of European law supremacy place considerable emphasis on this scenario. Alter's extended case study on Germany, for example, focuses overwhelmingly on explaining variation in German courts' doctrines on the relationship between European law and the rights protected by the German Constitution, in the famous *Maastricht-Urteil* decision and other cases. Alter considers the politics and struggle of European law's supremacy in relation to German constitutional rights at much more length than its relationship to ordinary German statutes and regulations (Alter 2001: 64–123).[50]

This concentration on national constitutional rights is likely to be misplaced, however, if the EU's legal system is recognized as an alternative to the bilateral retaliation arrangements, and trade remedy instruments, employed by many other international trade regimes. Disputes over treaty obligations in such regimes, and the use of inter-state countermeasures in them, are overwhelmingly the result of ordinary national legislation/regulation that fails to meet treaty obligations, often as the result of narrow interest group lobbying. Any explanation for the EU's rejection of inter-state countermeasures and trade remedies should therefore focus equally on the relationship between European law and ordinary laws and regulations, rather than on the relationship between European law and national constitutional rights.

[50] Other scholars adopt similar approaches. Stone Sweet discusses the German case in relation to German constitutional rights but does not give equivalent consideration to conflicts with "ordinary" German legislation (Stone Sweet 2004: 87–91). Burley and Mattli rely on e.g. Mancini, to support their argument that the ECJ depended on the support of the national courts (Burley [Slaughter] and Mattli 1993: 63). In turn, Mancini emphasizes the management of that relationship in relation to national constitutional rights (Mancini 1989: 608ff). A similar emphasis on fundamental rights questions, and the relative marginalization of the question of conflicts between European law and "later-in-time" national legislation, can be found in recent work such as Davies 2012. Alter's empirical treatment of the problem of conflicts between EU obligations and German constitutional law fundamental rights also arguably exaggerates the importance of such conflicts. Alter writes that in German law, treaty obligations enacted by the German parliament were subject to the "same constitutional constraints" as national law (Alter 2001: 72). This is an accurate description of the fundamental doctrinal attitude of German courts to the constitutionality of treaty obligations. However, in practice, the German Constitutional Court does not subject treaty obligations to the "same constitutional constraints" as national law. Instead, while insisting on its right to review treaty obligations against the German Constitution, the Court has repeatedly demonstrated itself prepared to make decisions that allowed the constitutionality of treaties that contained obligations that might otherwise conflict with fundamental rights protected by the German Constitution, so long as these were not incompatible with the most fundamental commitments of the German constitutional order. See, for example, the German Constitutional Court's decision on the Saar Treaty, BVerfGE 4, 157, described by one scholar as the Court adapting a "a rigid legality to the exigencies of foreign policy" (Münch 1957: 290–291). For a more extensive discussion, see Phelan 2013c. For a compatible view on the relationship between European law and the protection of human rights by national constitutions, see Lindseth 2010: 177–178.

Limited Attention on the Possibility of Unilateral National Acts to Disapply EU Law

What of issues more directly relevant to international economic disputes, such as ordinary national legislation and regulation that conflicts with treaty obligations?[51] Here, the point to note is that current scholarship tends to neglect a full and careful discussion of how exactly national political and legal systems have addressed the problem of conflicts between European and national legal obligations, particularly national legislation enacted *after* the European obligation has been imposed.[52] This is a technical issue, but an important one, which we will therefore deal with at some length.

The supremacy claim of European law requires, as we have seen, that national courts apply European law in place of contrary national legislation, particularly national statutes enacted "later in time"—that is, subsequent to the European obligation. The national courts of the EU member states have come, in fact, to apply European law in these circumstances. A critical question, however, is whether national courts would apply European legal obligations if a national parliament deliberately decided to remove or restrict the domestic application of an EU obligation, for example by unmistakably amending the national laws (or, where relevant, constitutional provisions) that authorize the execution of European law in the national legal orders.[53]

[51] This section draws on an earlier publication in *European Law Journal* by this author (Phelan 2010).

[52] For example, two leading accounts of the relationship between German law and the development of the European legal order devote little attention to this topic (Alter 2001; Davies 2012; cf. Phelan 2011b).

[53] It is essential to recognize that, despite the ECJ's claims to the contrary, national courts continue to derive their application of European Community law, including its supremacy and direct effect, from the provisions of their national legal orders that authorize and permit the application of Community law. As Hartley writes, "If direct effect is given to a provision of Community law, that provision is applied by the national court as part of the law of the land. No rule of national law *specifically* referring to it is necessary.... [H]owever, a rule of national law making general provision for direct effect *is* necessary" (Hartley 2007: 192, emphasis in the original). For further discussion, see, for example, Hogan and Whelan 1995: 8, 9–10; Phelan 1997; Craig and de Búrca 2008: 377; Hartley 2010: 260, 259–286; De Witte 2011: 46. In a fundamental sense, therefore, national courts reject the ECJ's claim in *Van Gend en Loos* that directly effective European law is applied "independently of the legislation of the Member State," or, in this author's own formulation, "The paradox of Community law is that the jurisprudence of national courts on the application of Community law in the national legal orders relies on the very national laws that Community law distinctively claims to have freed itself from" (Phelan 2010: 256). Note that deriving the domestic application of European law from national constitutional arrangements does not necessarily imply that the domestic application of European law is a national *constitutional obligation*. In the cases of Denmark, Ireland, and Germany (discussed here), the better view is that national constitutional arrangements *allow* the domestic application of European law, but the *obligation* on national courts to apply European law is derived from a national statute, and could be removed or selectively restricted by a deliberately conflicting national statute (Phelan 2010). Of course, where the national obligation to apply European law is directly derived from national constitutional law, that national constitutional law itself could be subject to unilateral national amendment and restriction.

This possibility, if available, would reopen the option that European law's supremacy doctrine claims to foreclose, allowing a national legislature "unhappy with an internalized treaty norm" (to use Weiler's expression, *cited earlier, p. 34*) to unilaterally remove its application within their state. It turns out that national law does appear to offer opportunities of this sort in several, at least, of the member states.

For the Danish legal order, Due described such a scenario as follows:

> Should the Danish Parliament pass an act withdrawing some of the powers unilaterally, Danish authorities, including the courts, will have to consider future Community acts within the area concerned inapplicable in Denmark, although this will be contrary to international law.
>
> (Due 1999: 329, also 315)

Hartley described a similar scenario, where the British Parliament (deliberately and unmistakably) amends the British legislation that gives force to European law in the United Kingdom, the European Communities Act 1972:

> After the new Act comes into force, a Frenchman arrives at Dover with a consignment of lamb destined for the British market. Customs officials turn the consignment back. The importer brings proceedings in the English courts claiming that, notwithstanding the Act, he has a right to import the lamb. Can it seriously be asserted that the courts would find in his favour? They could not do so on the basis of Community law, because the relevant rules of Community law would have no legal effect in the United Kingdom: The only basis on which they could have effect—the European Communities Act 1972—would expressly exclude them. The courts could not lawfully refer the matter to the European Court, since the provisions allowing or requiring such references would no longer have any effect in the United Kingdom. If they did, or if the European Court somehow took it upon itself to give a ruling anyway, its ruling would have no legal validity in the United Kingdom. In short there would be no legal ground for granting the importer a remedy. It might be said that, because Britain has joined the Community, Parliament is bound by the Community Treaties and cannot legislate against them…It is, however, well established that Parliament *can* legislate contrary to a Treaty that is binding on the United Kingdom.
>
> (Hartley 1999: 176–177)

For the Irish case, D.R. Phelan writes:

> The legislation [the European Communities Act 1972, an Irish statute] has the same problems *vis-à-vis* subsequent legislation as the European Community [*sic*] Act in the United Kingdom.[54] So, for example, if a subsequent statute enacted by the democratically elected Oireachtas [the Irish Parliament] specifically

[54] This is the UK legislation Hartley is referring to in the immediately preceding passage.

> derogated from a European Community rule, could this 1972 Act be invoked against it? There is no existing doctrine to say it could. There is nothing in Irish law to weaken the effectiveness of a statute saying "European Community law shall not be part of the domestic law of the state" or, "European Community law shall not be part of the domestic law of the state so far as it conflicts with fundamental rights protected under the Constitution." European Community law has a similar status in the Irish hierarchy of norms as a statute, the status being conferred by a statute which benefits from a jurisdictional immunity of debated extent. European Community law does not have a status superior to [Irish] constitutional law, rather the interaction of the 1972 Act and [provisions of the Irish Constitution] generally preserves its application.
>
> (Phelan 1997: 333–334, also 352)[55]

Such a "specific derogation" by statute could equally remove the application in Ireland of *any* Community law obligation.

The same can be argued for Germany. The German courts have emphasized, repeatedly, that (as the Constitutional Court stated in the *Maastricht* decision) "European Community authority derives from the Member States and can have binding effect on German sovereign territory only by virtue of the German implementing order.... The validity and application of European law in Germany depend on the implementing order contained in the Law Approving the Treaty" (Oppenheimer 1994: 557). The emphasis on this German *statute*, and not the German Constitution itself or the doctrines of the ECJ, as the basis for the application of European law in Germany has been an essential thread running through the major decisions of the German courts (Mayer 2005: 9). Furthermore, the German Constitutional Court has also emphasized that the application of the European law is "dependent upon the Member States constantly breathing life into the treaty" and that the "implementation and development of the Treaty have to be sustained by the Will of the Contracting Parties" (Oppenheimer 1994: 565). On the logic of the German Constitutional Court, the supremacy and direct effect of European law in Germany could therefore be ousted or restricted by an unmistakable repeal or amendment of that German statute, or by a German legislator deliberately refusing to continue to "breathe life" into particular EU treaty obligations.

To repeat, the courts of Denmark, the United Kingdom, Ireland, and Germany, like the courts in other EU member states, routinely allow conflicts between European law and "later-in-time" national law to be resolved in principle by the application of European law, under the guidance of the preliminary reference procedure. However, that everyday acceptance of European

[55] See also Phelan 2008a.

law supremacy does not mean that the national parliaments of these member states do not retain unilateral options to selectively oust the domestic application of European law if they chose to so insist.[56] National courts, loyal to their national polities, accept the supremacy of European law only because they can maintain that national parliaments *want* them to.[57] Thus neither the doctrines of supremacy and direct effect nor the ECJ's preliminary reference procedure have prevented national politicians from unilaterally and selectively removing the automatic application of EU obligations in their domestic courts. Instead, the courts of the member states may accept only a "limited" version of European law supremacy, and have not needed to create understandings of the relationship between national and EC law which would restrain an express national attempt to legislate contrary to European law.[58]

The incomplete and ambiguous "supremacy" that such national courts *do* acknowledge to European law is more than sufficient to ensure the secure application of directly effective EU obligations by national courts, however, as long as national parliaments continue to behave in ways that support this approach to resolving conflicts between European and national law.[59] The "all-or-nothing" application of European law in the national legal orders that is the distinction of the European legal order is therefore created not by national court doctrine alone (that is to say, national court doctrine accepting a version of European law's doctrines of supremacy and direct effect), but by that national court doctrine *in combination with* compatible behavior by national policy-makers.[60]

[56] The generalist reader may already find the legal analysis set out here sufficient, but for an extended analysis of this issue for the four member states of Denmark, Ireland, the United Kingdom, and Germany, see Phelan 2008a, 2010. The examples discussed refer to the state of the law in the 1990s, demonstrating that the supremacy of European law over subsequently enacted national legislation in these member states was limited and contingent decades after the apparent "constitutionalization" of the European treaties.

[57] Or, where relevant, that national constitutions want them to.

[58] For this reason, it can be argued that national courts in several member states have not, in the fundamental sense, accepted the ECJ's claim in *Costa v. ENEL*, nor has the flourishing of the European legal order required them to do so (Phelan 2010: 268).

[59] Although there is considerable evidence that national courts in several member states would straightforwardly let their national parliaments deliberately legislate to disapply the domestic legal application of EU obligations, the argument works also with a more modest version of this claim: that is, the courts of the member states have never needed to develop legal rules or principles that would restrain a deliberate, express national political effort to selectively oust the application of EU law of the sort described in the passages above from Due, Hartley, and D.R. Phelan. Even that more modest version undermines the claim that it is national courts that are *forcing* national governments to live up to their EU obligations. To dispute the argument advanced here would require a demonstration that national courts in the UK, Ireland, Denmark, and Germany have developed national legal doctrines to apply directly effective EU obligations even where national parliaments, or, where relevant, national constitutional legislators, explicitly and unmistakably legislated to selectively remove their application in the domestic legal order. Such a demonstration would not be easy. See Phelan 2010: 268–269 and throughout.

[60] "Instead of the two distinct scenarios described [by Weiler 1991: 2413–2415, cited p. 34 in this volume], there is clearly a third scenario, whereby national courts apply treaty obligations

That the solution to conflicts between European law and national legislation is comprised of *both* national legal doctrines *and* accommodative national policy-maker behavior strikes at the heart of explanations for the supremacy of European law based on the idea that national judges "would not let politicians ignore or cast aside as invalid unwanted decisions" (Alter 1998: 133).[61] The unused unilateral options remaining to the member-state governments also undermine the logic of claims that the ECJ is an independent legal actor operating in a permissive legal environment because it would require hard-to-obtain unanimous action by the member states to overturn ECJ decisions (e.g. Stone Sweet and Brunell 1998a: 74; Stone Sweet 2004: 25). Individual member-state governments retain instruments by which they could *unilaterally* overturn the applicability of the ECJ's decisions in their own courts, and in the process reduce the ECJ's influence

even in the place of subsequent contrary national legislation because they assume that is the will of the national legislator.... This national method of legal interpretation, when combined with the persistent restraint of the national legislatures for their part, is sufficient to provide the secure application of European treaty obligations in the EU Member States in place of [subsequent contrary national legal] obligations" (Phelan 2010: 270, 268 [clarification inserted], also 255). "All-or-nothing": Weiler 1981: 297.

[61] On this vital question, neofunctionalist and historical institutionalist scholarship on the European legal order tends to be ambiguous and contradictory. Prominent authors at times proceed on the basis that the EU member states have *no* unilateral options to remove the application of EU obligations from the national legal orders, while at other times they adopt an alternative approach—that the member states do retain such unilateral options, these just remain unused. Burley and Mattli, for example, in their 1993 publication that launched the neofunctionalist approach to European law, acknowledge the scholarly claim that "if a national legislature decided to limit the effect of a Communities regulation, or to nullify it, and if this intention was made plain to the national courts by the legislature, the national courts would not apply Communities law" (Burley [Slaughter] and Mattli 1993: 49; see also Taylor 1983). In their follow-on publication, however, a list of possible constraints on the ECJ omits any mention of the possibility of such national legislative unilateralism, mentioning only the constraints of consistent legal doctrine, information asymmetry with the member states, the rules of collective decision-making in the EU, and public attitudes (Mattli and Slaughter 1998, e.g. Table 1, p. 187). Similarly, Stone Sweet, writing on "Constitutional Dialogues in the European Union," notes that national jurisprudence, while normally accommodating the supremacy of directly effective EU obligations, left open the possibility of national legislation explicitly designed to unilaterally and selectively remove the application of European law obligations from the national legal system (Stone Sweet 1998: 317 (UK), 323 (Italy)). Nevertheless, in a later publication, Stone Sweet proceeds on the understanding that EU law doctrines necessarily deprive the member states of their unilateral options to act contrary to directly effective EU obligations (Stone Sweet 2004). In *Establishing*, Alter writes "Originally national governments could simply pass new legislation to avoid an ECJ decision. Once national courts had accepted European law supremacy, they refused to allow their governments to avoid European legal obligations by relying on national legislation" (Alter 2001: 219; similarly, Alter 1998: 133, 144). In a passage at the end of *Establishing*, however, Alter recognizes the possibility that the member states could indeed attempt to unilaterally legislate to overturn national court decisions recognizing European law supremacy (Alter 2001: 193–194). In short, the neofunctionalist and historical institutionalist scholarship does not demonstrate that national courts prevent deliberate national legislative unilateralism contrary to apparently "supreme" EU obligations. Indeed, these authors tend at times to acknowledge that policy-makers in the EU member states may not be constrained by national courts in this way, but these acknowledgments are not followed up by a reconsideration of these authors' "politics of lawyers" approach to explaining the development of the European legal order.

within their states to that more commonly enjoyed by international tribunals. What needs to be explained is why national policy-makers so persistently refuse to do so.

A related, but somewhat different, observation may be made about the work of scholars such as Garrett, who emphasize that national governments of the member states have the power to "ignore" or "refuse to comply with" decisions of the ECJ, perhaps where the ECJ decision would impose severe adjustment costs on an important domestic interest group. This literature tends not to distinguish between *two* very different scenarios.

The first scenario would be where the national government "ignores" or "refuses to comply with" the ECJ's decision by not fully adjusting national policy to meet the EU obligation, or perhaps by complying in relation to the immediate case only but refusing to change its policy for similar cases or future legal conflicts. In this case, to be sure, the litigant—or broader class of possible beneficiaries—may not immediately obtain the policy change to which European law has declared that they are entitled. However, as with other forms of litigation, after a favorable initial judgment, particularly against public authorities, the way remains open for such litigants, and others with similar claims, to continue to pursue their European law rights before the ECJ and national courts, in an environment where national courts accept that EU obligations as interpreted by the ECJ are directly effective and supreme over contrary national law. In those circumstances, "ignoring" or "refusing to comply with" the ECJ's decision may, if the litigants are determined and have the resources to pursue the issue, result in a stream of further litigation seeking to obtain the benefits that the ECJ had declared the litigants eligible to obtain. Detailed case studies show that recalcitrant governments, trying to limit the impact of ECJ decisions by administrative means, can be forced by continued litigation in national courts to end legal uncertainty by legislating to provide for the European law rights.[62] Thus EU member states "ignoring" or "refusing to comply with" ECJ decisions in this way face a very different environment from WTO members "ignoring" the outcomes of WTO dispute settlement, because the outcomes of WTO dispute settlement panels are not automatically enforceable in national courts. This is what Weiler refers

[62] "In conclusion, the national judiciary was the sword of the ECJ in implementing the *Kohll/Decker* jurisprudence. This article clearly indicates that national courts are a key variable for understanding and explaining national implementation: they are able to accelerate implementation. As soon as national courts accept and apply the doctrines elaborated by the ECJ, governments face accomplished facts. Such national rulings in combination with contradicting legislative provisions and other more reluctant courts created legal uncertainty in the Member States. The domestic legislator was, therefore, forced to implement the ECJ rulings and to change the law on the books in order to decrease this uncertainty." (Obermaier 2008: 751–752; similarly, but noting the organizational challenges of public interest litigation to enforce EU environmental obligations, Slepcevic 2009).

to when describing violations of EU law as taking place within an ethos of domestic rather than international law (Weiler 1991: 2464).

However, that is not the only scenario. As we have just described, it would also be open to a member state to unilaterally restrict part of the automatic application of European law, including its supremacy and direct effect, within their national legal order, for example by amending the national legal provisions that provide for the national application of European law. In the "import of lamb" scenario that Hartley describes, the disappointed litigant would no longer be able to rely on national courts to enforce the European obligation, and, in effect, the violation of European law would revert to taking place within a context of *international*, rather than domestic, law (Weiler 1991: 2464). These two scenarios are different and clarity on distinguishing them is at the heart of understanding the special nature of the European legal order. Yes, member states may attempt to ignore EU obligations and ECJ decisions, but they can only do so in a manner constrained at least to some important degree by the continued automatic application of EU obligations by their national courts, *unless* they are willing to unilaterally remove the obligation on their courts to automatically apply EU obligations even if in conflict with national law.

Little Discussion of Incentives for Policy-Makers

This discussion of the limited, and potentially removable, restraints that national court acceptance of EU law supremacy imposes on national policy-makers brings us, in turn, to current scholarship's limited development of explanations for state behavior compatible with the effectiveness of the European legal order. Perhaps the most common approach in contemporary international relations scholarship, when offering explanations for outcomes relating to the effectiveness of international trade regimes, is to lead with explicit elaborations of the incentives for state policy-makers to behave in ways compatible with the outcomes observed, taking into account the possibility of interest group resistance. However, political science explanations of the European legal order tend not to proceed in this way. Rather, these studies elaborate the EU's dispute settlement system, particularly the roles of the ECJ and national courts, and the doctrines of supremacy and direct effect, with the implication that the European legal constraints are so binding that an extensive elaboration of incentives for state policy-makers to behave in a way compatible with this outcome is not required.[63]

[63] Indeed, the neofunctionalist and historical institutionalist scholarship developed in part as an explicit rejection of state-centric approaches to explaining the European legal order. In particular, Garrett's attempt to explain the European legal regime as a response to incentives for defection and incomplete contracting issues was criticized, compellingly, by these scholars

For example, Burley and Mattli's discussion of incentives for governments to accommodate the outcomes produced by the neofunctional processes of European legal integration reads as follows:

> What role is there for governments? According to neofunctionalism, government's role is "creatively responsive." As holders of the ultimate political power, governments may accept, sidestep, ignore, or sabotage the decisions of federal authorities. Yet, given their heterogeneity of interests in certain issue-areas, unilateral evasion or recalcitrance may prove unprofitable if it sets a precedent for other governments. Thus governments may either choose to or feel constrained to yield to the pressures of converging supra- and subnational interests.
>
> (Burley [Slaughter] and Mattli 1993: 54)

Alter, writing on incentives for state policy-makers to avoid unilaterally removing European law supremacy from their national courts, writes that:

> [T]here is concern that intimidating national actors because they are faithfully implementing European law can create unwanted consequences. It can be seen as illegitimate: an authoritarian strategy inappropriate in a democratic system. And it can antagonize other European states.... Perhaps most importantly, it is usually easier for governments to find creative ways to lessen the impact of a contested decision than it is to forge ahead with fights in parliament over the national judiciary.
>
> (Alter 2001: 192–195)[64]

If, however, an explanation for why the WTO might operate without its bilateral trade sanctions enforcement system were to rest on brief claims that this could result from state policy-makers becoming aware that defection sets bad precedents, or becoming concerned about antagonizing other WTO members, such arguments would hardly be accepted as sufficient. Yet the neofunctionalist and historical institutionalist scholarship on the European legal order rests on just such modest accounts of incentives for

for suggesting that ECJ decisions in individual cases reflected the preferences of France and Germany as the most powerful member states (similar criticisms in Burley [Slaughter] and Mattli 1993: 50–51; Mattli and Slaughter 1995; Stone Sweet 2004: 116; Alter 2009a: 12–13). However, if national courts only accept the supremacy of European law on the basis that the national parliaments (and/or national constitutions) intend them to do so, as much evidence suggests, then explanations of European law supremacy need, in addition to a discussion of legal politics, an explanation of the incentives for policy-makers in the EU member states to behave in a compatible manner. Davies's recent history of Germany's acceptance of European law does place a new emphasis on the German *government*'s behavior, separate from that of courts and lawyers (Davies 2012). Davies's emphasis on national policy-makers is much to be welcomed, but it does not identify, or attempt to explain, the EU's rejection of WTO-style trade retaliation and trade remedies.

[64] Even Alter's arguments about incentives for state policy-makers remain "politics of law" orientated. Note the secondary emphasis on the responses of other states.

state policy-makers to accept the automatic application of European law in the national legal orders. We therefore know little about the incentives for state policy-makers to behave in ways compatible with the automatic application of European law in their domestic courts.

Garrett's discussion of the European legal order was much more grounded in explicit discussions of incentives for state behavior. Garrett saw the role of the European legal order as to solve problems of incomplete contracting and monitoring that always arise where states cooperate in issue-areas where there are incentives to defect on costly obligations. Nevertheless, Burley and Mattli's reply to Garrett remains telling: yes, the member states need an international court to help with resolving disputes, filling in missing contract terms, and holding parties to their world, but this general observation does not help us explain the remarkable *relative* effectiveness of the European legal order compared to other international dispute resolution mechanisms (Mattli and Slaughter 1995: 184–185). In the terms employed in this book, Garrett's emphasis on the problems of monitoring and incomplete contracting does not explain why the EU addresses these problems through a "self-contained regime" rather than through a WTO-style regime. An adequate explanation would require much greater specificity in relation to the outcome being explained, compared to the alternatives.[65] Garrett employs a generalist approach to explaining incentives for states in international relations that is not well adapted to explaining the EU-specific outcome. A better approach would match a policy-maker-focused explanation with the EU's distinctive outcome.[66]

[65] Similarly, "reputation" as a mechanism cannot be an adequate explanation for the supremacy outcome, e.g. Pollack 1997: 118, because much more common styles of state behavior—such as common forms of state behavior within the WTO—are also frequently explained by reputation incentives. For general limits to such reputational arguments, see Phelan 2009. The claim that states are deterred from evading ECJ decisions because such a government "would be punished by other governments for ignoring the ruling" (Carrubba 2005: 685, repeated in Carrubba et al. 2008) also fails to offer an explanation for why this threat produces a supremacy-of-treaty-obligations outcome in the EU but only a WTO-style bilateral reciprocity outcome in other multilateral trade regimes.

[66] A reverse critique—a failure to make arguments about EU-specific outcomes compatible with broader claims in international relations scholarship—can be applied to aspects of historical institutionalist scholarship. Pierson and Alter argue that the ECJ was able to manipulate national governments, because the high discount rates of national politicians made them especially value the short-term material outcome of ECJ decisions even where the latter made doctrinal decisions with profound long-term consequences (Pierson 1996; Alter 2001). However, the scholarship on international organization, in line with Prisoners' Dilemma models of cooperation in anarchy, emphasizes by contrast that it is states that especially value the future—that is to say, with *low* discount rates—that are most likely to achieve the deepest international cooperation (Axelrod 1984; Keohane 1984). Because of these authors' limited engagement with wider scholarship on international cooperation, this tension is not discussed.

Discussion of a Limited Range of Actors and Institutions

Current explanations of the development of the European legal order have one further element in common: they tend to discuss a limited range of actors and institutions. Weiler's account of the legal transformation of Europe, for example, is a discussion of a continent whose actors include the European institutions, democratic states, independent courts, "lower" courts seeking greater autonomy from their national legal hierarchy, and national executives seeking to exert more control over national policy-making. In Burley and Mattli's account, Europe is made up of states, the ECJ, national judges, litigants, and the pro-European community of professors and propagandists. In Alter's book, Europe consists very largely of national governments, diverse national courts, and the European institutions.[67] The most recent historical work on the activities of European legal elites is focused, if anything, on an even narrower cast of characters, such as friends and correspondents of Jean Monnet (e.g. Rasmussen 2010).

We hope that the reader will not be too surprised to learn that the populations of the postwar European states were not comprised entirely of lawyers, and that there are many important institutions in the EU member states other than court systems and national governments. The neofunctionalist and historical institutionalist explanations of the European legal order tend to focus above all on only two sorts of interaction—those between various lawyers (and litigants), and those between the ECJ and the other European institutions, including the member states as decision-makers in the Council of Ministers. Such scholarship is "law in context," to be sure, but it can also be fairly described as "law in a little bit of context." It is "law and politics," but without any connection to the broader context of mass politics in post-1945

[67] Alter's book introduces her account by emphasizing that she will look at the losers, as well as the winners, from European legal integration. Her focus, however, is above all on the *courts that lose*, as well as the courts that win, from European legal integration, not on organized interests in national civil societies (Alter 2001: 3, 45–52, but see e.g. 43 for a reference to firms opposing liberalization). Alter's more recent work expands this circle somewhat, to include jurist advocacy networks in the EU case, and national intellectual property agencies (and note the *lack* of jurist advocacy networks) in the Andean case (Helfer and Alter 2008–2009: 927; Alter 2009b). Other historical institutionalist work also discusses a limited range of actors: in Pierson's essay on historical institutionalism and European integration, Europe largely consists of national "Chiefs of Government," and the European institutions, particularly the ECJ (Pierson 1996, albeit with a wider range of actors in its discussion of European social policy). Interestingly, in a concluding passage to a 2009 collection of essays, Alter criticized her own 2001 book for its "incomplete" focus on national courts (Alter 2009a: 296). She then called for further research on possible connections between European legal integration and an extensive list of wider trends in postwar European politics, including—most relevant to our purposes—the "embedded liberalism" compromise of the 1960s, 1970s, and early 1980s, as well as Alan Milward's argument for how European integration helped states deliver that compromise (Alter 2009a: 296–301).

Europe.[68] There are other national institutions that may have an important role in explaining the development of the European legal order.

The scholarship of Garrett and Lindseth provides exceptions to this general trend. Garrett's contributions have always paid close attention to the potential problem of a member state facing an adverse decision of the ECJ that imposes considerable costs on a powerful organized interest group. By including the *adversely affected interest group* among his important actors, Garrett directly linked the study of the European legal order to more mainstream approaches to international trade politics, where the problem of import-competing interest groups facing adjustment costs (or the opposition of interests to trade-related regulatory burdens) is a central focus of analysis.[69] The exclusion of such groups from many analyses of the development of the European legal order is an important omission.

Lindseth's scholarship, by contrast, emphasizes a wider range of domestic institutions at the member-state level. In particular, many European states had come to accept a certain form of parliamentary government that combined considerable discretion and autonomy in administrative politics with the persistence of the fundamental legitimacy of national parliaments. Lindseth persuasively demonstrates that such domestic institutions were highly compatible with the forms and legitimacy requirements of European integration. Lindseth does not directly connect these institutions to the EU's distinction as an international regime that rejects the use of inter-state countermeasures and trade remedies, but he offers a much richer view of the domestic institutional environment that underlay the development of the European legal order.

With the exceptions of Garrett and Lindseth, therefore, the scholarship offering explanations for the development of the European legal order tends to discuss a narrow range of actors and institutions. Many variables whose influence on state behavior is widely recognized in trade politics scholarship are entirely left out of these discussions. These include important domestic politics

[68] Davies similarly criticizes Weiler for restricting his discussion of "law and politics" to "high politics and diplomacy" (Davies 2012: 212–213). Davies's own account includes analyses of debates about the ECJ among German legal scholars, in the German media, and within the German government, and constitutes a considerable advance on previous scholarship. The interaction of domestic political institutions and international trade law can, however, involve a wider range of actors and institutions than, for example, the inter-departmental meetings of lawyers and state secretaries that are Davies's primary focus in his account of the West German government's response to European law (Davies 2012: 139–179).

[69] Burley and Mattli, by contrast, do not focus on the problem of adversely affected interest groups pressing for unilateral actions contrary to EU obligations in their 1993 paper. They do discuss this problem in their 1995 response to Garrett—where their response is mostly to demonstrate that ECJ decisions *do* put pressure even on significant interest groups in powerful states, rather than to consider how this is politically acceptable—but they omit it from their discussions of constraints on the ECJ in their 1998 paper (Burley [Slaughter] and Mattli 1993; Mattli and Slaughter 1995; Mattli and Slaughter 1998, including table of constraints on ECJ on 187).

variables such as variation in democratic constitutional structures—the design of electoral systems and legislative institutions—and variation in the generosity of social insurance systems. They also include variables related to distinctive types of international economic exchange. Thus the findings of much of the EU-specialist scholarship on the development of, and effectiveness of, the European legal order may suffer from "omitted variable bias"—that is, biased findings resulting from the omission of important causal factors. By bringing these variables back in, it may be possible to offer a substantially revised and multicausal explanation of the development of the European legal order.[70]

Assessment and Conclusion

The most important comment about the existing scholarship on the development of the European legal order is that it has not attempted to explain

[70] Three important comments on this literature are more technical and can be addressed in a footnote: first, there is sometimes a tendency to underplay the fact that EU Regulations already enjoyed the somewhat similar status of "direct applicability" as provided for in the Treaty of Rome when discussing the ECJ's declaration of the "direct effect" of treaty obligations in *Van Gend en Loos*. Burley and Mattli's 1993 paper, for example, states that "The history of the 'constitutionalization' of the Treaty of Rome, and of the accompanying 'legalization' of community secondary legislation, is essentially the history of the direct effect doctrine" (Burley [Slaughter] and Mattli 1993: 60). Omitting a discussion of the direct applicability of Regulations as provided for in the Treaty tends to exaggerate the ECJ's role in the creation of the European legal order. Second, some scholars have attempted to produce a precise count of the number of occasions on which the national courts have defied the obligations of European law. Goldstein, for example, counts twenty-five incidents of member state defiance of European Community authority between 1958 and 1994, including rejections of ECJ doctrine that EC law is supreme over national law (Goldstein 2001: 21). However, the better view may be that the national courts in many member states have consistently derived the authority for the supremacy and direct effect of European law from national legal sources, and for this reason such national court systems as a whole exist in a permanent state of defiance of the most all-encompassing version of the supremacy doctrine as the ECJ has elaborated it. See references in footnote 53 in this chapter. A more comprehensive count of the instances of rejection of the ECJ's doctrine that EC law is supreme to national law might therefore include a very large number of national court decisions relating to European law since the ECJ's elaboration of the supremacy and direct effect doctrines. Third, scholarship sometimes has a tendency to draw conclusions about the role of the ECJ from analyses situating the ECJ only within the context of other European institutions (the European Commission, the Council of Ministers, etc.). Conclusions from such analyses are not always persuasive when viewed in the light of comparisons between the ECJ and other international tribunals. Moravcsik, for example, writes that the member states are less likely to object to ECJ rulings than to European Commission proposals, because the ECJ is making decisions on policies to which the member states have already, in most cases, given prior approval (Moravcsik 1995). Looked at in a wider perspective, however, it is clear that WTO members often object to WTO dispute settlement outcomes (and even the *use* of the WTO dispute settlement procedures), even though the WTO members are also only being held to WTO obligations to which they have already given prior approval. Similarly, Weiler's claim that the member states acquiesced in the "constitutionalization" of European law because they were exercising real control, by national vetoes, over EU policy-making can only be a partial explanation of this outcome, because the ordinary situation in international trade regimes is that states maintain *both* a national veto over new trade obligations *and*, after trade obligations have been agreed, the right to selectively exit at the risk of trade retaliation/the right to use trade remedies (Weiler 1991: 2429).

the EU as a self-contained regime, or its rejection of trade remedy instruments. The neglect of this central question no doubt explains why much of the material discussed by this literature is only of tangential relevance to this puzzle. Its overfocus on human rights issues, relative neglect of interest groups adversely affected by EU obligations, and limited integration with wider international relations theory all limit its ability to answer the question being addressed by this book.

This discussion of previous explanations of the European legal order does, however, allow us to draw two important conclusions relevant to any new explanation of the EU's rejection of inter-state countermeasures and trade remedies, and connect them to some of the best contributions advanced in earlier debates.

The first is that any explanation of the European legal order as a self-contained regime must meet what we may call "Garrett's challenge": the need to identify an explanation rooted in interests and incentives for policy-makers in the EU member states. The need for an explanation focused on policy-makers' incentives is re-doubled by the recognition that national courts in several, at least, of the member states accept only a "limited" version of the supremacy of European law, but that compatible behavior by state policy-makers has allowed the European legal order to thrive nonetheless. Ideally, such an explanation would be a transparent development of more generalist explanations of state behavior in international relations theory, including the common use of inter-state Prisoners' Dilemma models in explanations of international trade organization (Axelrod 1984; Keohane 1984; Dai 2002: 405).

The second is that any explanation of the European legal order as a self-contained regime must also meet what we might call "Burley and Mattli's challenge." Thus any account that emphasizes, in line with wider scholarly approaches to international organization, that the ECJ helps the member states in the resolution of disputes, filling in missing contract terms, and holding parties to their word, must go further to offer an explanation of the remarkable *relative* effectiveness of the European legal order compared to other international dispute resolution mechanisms (Mattli and Slaughter 1995: 184–185). Only by responding to *both* these challenges can a satisfactory explanation of the EU as a self-contained regime be developed.

3

Enforcement and Escape in International Trade Politics

If previous scholarship on the European legal order does not attempt to explain the EU as a "self-contained regime," and cannot be persuasively "retrofitted" to generate a convincing explanation of the EU's rejection of inter-state countermeasures and trade remedies, then it makes sense to look elsewhere. The most obviously relevant scholarship is the well-developed and important literature on enforcement and escape in international trade politics. This literature may appear, at first sight, extremely well suited to address the puzzle of the EU as a self-contained regime. After all, the EU imposes a stream of trade-related market and policy adjustments on organized narrow interests—exactly the conceptual problem addressed by the scholarship on the enforcement of obligations in the World Trade Organization, for example. As we will see, however, this scholarship rarely directly addresses the possibility of an international trade regime that rejects the use of both inter-state trade sanctions and common forms of trade remedy.

The chapter starts with a discussion of the World Trade Organization (WTO), its dispute settlement system, and the extensive scholarship that it has inspired. The next section demonstrates that scholarship on dispute settlement in the WTO tends to assume that the enforcement of international trade obligations requires inter-state retaliation mechanisms of the sort that the EU rejects. The final section discusses the literature on *escape* mechanisms—or "safety valves"—in international trade politics, of which WTO-style dispute settlement processes are only one, and the limited engagement of this scholarship with trade politics within the EU.

The World Trade Organization and its Dispute Settlement Understanding

The WTO came into being in 1995, but its history really begins in the postwar period that saw the creation of so many of today's international institutions, including the United Nations and the North Atlantic Treaty Organization. Before 1945, and particularly before 1914, international trade had not been extensively regulated by international organizations. After 1945, powerful figures in US and British politics believed that an organized international architecture providing for reciprocal reduction in trade barriers would help prevent the trading instability of the 1930s. A relatively small group of like-minded governments therefore entered into extensive negotiations to establish international economic institutions, which eventually produced an agreement on the General Agreement on Tariffs and Trade (GATT) in 1947.

The GATT created a structure that facilitated mutual trade liberalization between its members. In a series of so-called "trade rounds," GATT members negotiated with each other to exchange mutual reductions in trade barriers. The most important negotiations often took place bilaterally between countries that were already engaged in intensive economic exchange, so that GATT members were exchanging clearly identified export opportunities in known products. However, the rules of the GATT required that any trade concessions granted to one GATT member should be extended to all other GATT members on a "most-favored-nation" basis. Thus mutual concessions between trading partners contributed to the growing liberalization of international trade among all GATT members.

The GATT is best understood as a *framework* for trade liberalization. GATT members can maintain significant trade barriers, tariffs as well as non-tariff barriers, in their trade with other GATT members. However, the GATT process nonetheless encouraged states to reduce their trade barriers by creating incentives for reciprocal deals to facilitate exports. In the area of non-tariff barriers, GATT's basic rule is—simply put—"national treatment," which requires that GATT members' domestic regulations treat goods and services produced by other GATT members no less favorably than goods and services produced by their own domestic industries (e.g. Van den Bossche 2005: 326–364). "National treatment" is a powerful rule inhibiting regulatory discrimination against imported goods and services, but it also has considerable limits. A GATT member might ban the use of a particular product, for example on health-and-safety grounds, and so long as the ban applies equally to nationally produced goods as well as goods imported from other GATT members, such a ban would be GATT-compliant, even if such regulation tended to indirectly favor domestic industries. GATT members therefore preserve considerable domestic regulatory autonomy within the context of the "national treatment" rule.

The GATT has of course developed over the last several decades. Tariff barriers between GATT members are much lower now than they were in the early postwar period (Roitinger 2004: 14). The importance of non-tariff barriers in trade negotiations has risen. The GATT framework for trade in goods has been supplemented by the General Agreement on Trade in Services, as well as by an Agreement on Trade-Related Aspects of Intellectual Property, an Agreement on Government Procurement, and an agreement regulating states' policies on food safety and animal and plant health. Over time, the GATT's membership grew to 128 members by 1994 (today's WTO, in 2012, has more than 150 members).[1]

The formal institutions of the GATT had relatively limited roles. All new obligations had to be agreed by the state parties themselves (often bilaterally) in the "trade rounds," so an important role of the GATT secretariat was to facilitate and organize those discussions. It had no policy development or legal prosecution role to parallel the role of the European Commission set out in the EU treaties. Of most interest here, GATT practice over time came to provide for a dispute settlement procedure.[2] GATT members could complain about policies adopted by other members that failed to provide the trading opportunities that had been agreed in earlier trade rounds. Such complaints could be heard by a dispute settlement panel, and if, following an adverse decision, the GATT member refused to change its policy to make it GATT-compliant, the complaining member was entitled to "suspend the application of concessions"—that is, impose retaliatory trade restrictions. The GATT's dispute settlement arrangements therefore potentially provided for a relatively well-developed process for the assessment of complaints and enforcement mechanisms, but it was limited in its practical effectiveness by procedural restrictions. GATT rules provided that all GATT members, including the member whose measures were the subject of a complaint, had to agree to permit the use of, and progress in, GATT's dispute settlement procedure. Thus all GATT members needed to consent to establish a dispute settlement panel, to adopt the report of a panel, and to authorize any retaliation if a contracting party maintained rules inconsistent with a panel report (Barton et al. 2006: 69). These procedures may have reduced the degree to which dispute settlement under the GATT could impinge on national policy-making,

[1] Dates that GATT and WTO members joined the organization can be found on the WTO website at <http://www.wto.org/english/thewto_e/gattmem_e.htm and http://www.wto.org/english/thewto_e/whatis_e/tif_e/org6_e.htm>.

[2] As Pescatore 1993 explains, the GATT treaty itself contained very little in the way of dispute settlement procedures, but these were worked out over time by practice and subsequent agreements.

but they also reduced the effectiveness of international dispute settlement in the global trade regime (Barton et al. 2006: 68–69). In the 1970s, only 32 disputes were dealt with by the GATT secretariat, a number that rose to 115 complaints filed in the 1980s (Barton et al. 2006: 69).[3]

It is commonly believed that one result of the relative paralysis of the GATT's formal dispute settlement procedures was a growing turn toward unilateral trade restrictions as a mechanism to enforce trade obligations and reduce trade barriers, particularly by the United States. In the 1980s, the United States became well known for threatening other GATT members with trade barriers, often outside the process provided for by the GATT, so as to force the other party to lower barriers to trade in US goods, services, and intellectual property. The United States required that its partners unilaterally liberalized even without any reciprocal concessions from the United States (Bayard and Elliot 1994: 1).[4]

In the late 1980s and early 1990s, the increasing globalization of trade and concerns by other GATT members over the use of unilateral trade restrictions by the United States combined to lead to profound changes to dispute settlement in the world trade regime (Bayard and Elliot 1994: 350–351; Barton et al. 2006: 71). The Uruguay trade round, agreed in 1994, created the WTO that subsumed the previous GATT obligations in a new framework with new institutions. While the role of the WTO secretariat is similar to that of the previous GATT secretariat, the WTO's dispute settlement process is rather different. The WTO's Dispute Settlement Understanding (DSU) removed many of the procedural provisions that limited use of the GATT's dispute settlement process. In particular, WTO members whose policies were subject to complaint could no longer unilaterally prevent the establishment of a dispute settlement panel, or prevent the adoption of the panel's decision. Thus the WTO's DSU is a much more "automatic" procedure than the equivalent under the GATT.

In more detail, the WTO's DSU provides for a state-to-state procedure for assessing the validity of complaints about national "measures" that are alleged not to comply with a member's WTO commitments, and for authorizing inter-state retaliation as an enforcement mechanism. After a required period of consultation, WTO members can ask for a dispute settlement panel to consider their complaint that the benefits they have been granted under the WTO agreements have been "nullified or impaired" by "measures" (that is to say, policies or practices) adopted by another WTO member. The panel,

[3] Retaliation under the GATT's dispute settlement procedure was authorized only once (Davey 1987: 60).

[4] For examples, see Bayard and Elliot 1994: 71, 187–208, 428–430. The unilateral use of trade restrictions absent dispute settlement can also be observed during the WTO era in US trade policy behavior vis-à-vis *non*-WTO members (e.g. Nzelibe 2008: 337) .

consisting of three "well-qualified" individuals, is required to make an "objective assessment" of the matters before it, and to produce a report containing findings as to whether a measure is consistent, or not, with the WTO agreements.[5] The findings of the dispute settlement panel may be appealed to the permanently established Appellate Body, which may uphold, modify, or reverse the findings of the panel.

Where the panel, or, as the case may be, the Appellate Body, finds that a measure adopted by a WTO member is inconsistent with their WTO obligations, it recommends that the member brings that measure into conformity with the WTO agreements. However, if a member fails to bring the measure in question into conformity with the WTO agreements, and the two parties do not come to a mutually agreeable settlement, the WTO member that initiated the complaint may request authorization from the WTO's dispute settlement body to, in the words of the DSU, "suspend the application to the Member concerned of concessions or other obligations under the covered agreements."[6] In plain English, this is a request for authorization to impose retaliatory trade sanctions.

The WTO's dispute settlement process is therefore highly institutionalized, but in ways that are largely consistent with dispute settlement in general international law. In the WTO, governments of WTO members complain about other members' policies and practices. Non-state actors such as firms and individual citizens have no ability to directly activate the WTO's dispute settlement process to complain that policies or practices in another WTO member are contrary to its WTO obligations, although of course they may lobby their national policy-makers to do so. The outcome of dispute settlement in the WTO is not automatically applied as law within the WTO member's own legal systems. Rather, even after a finding of a panel or the Appellate Body that a national measure is inconsistent with a member's WTO obligations, it is up to the WTO member in question to change that policy, or not, as it so decides. And where a WTO member chooses not to bring

[5] "Well-qualified" Art 8.1 of the WTO DSU. "Objective assessment" Art 11 of the WTO DSU.

[6] The process is more extensive than this brief description allows. The member whose practices have been found inconsistent with their WTO obligations can claim to be in compliance with the findings of the panel or Appellate Body. The complaining member can then ask for a "compliance panel" to evaluate the sufficiency of the respondent state's actions, and the compliance panel's decision can be appealed by either party to the Appellate Body. If the Appellate Body finds that the violation is ongoing, it will require the member to comply with the Appellate Body's ruling within a reasonable period of time. At which point, the complaining member may request the authorization of the suspension of trade benefits to the state found to have violated its WTO obligations. The member whose practices have been found inconsistent with their WTO obligations can then object to the extent and form of the proposed suspension, at which point a panel may be formed to determine the maximum extent and form of the permitted suspension. At that point, the complaining state may begin to apply trade retaliation. For a fuller description, with an emphasis on the long delays before any retaliation is authorized, see Brewster 2011.

its national measure into conformity with the WTO agreements within a reasonable period of time, the complaining member state can impose trade retaliation "equivalent" to the loss caused by the original violation.

Since the WTO came into force in 1995 until the end of 2011, the DSU's procedures have been used in relation to more than 400 disputes (not all of them addressing completely distinct disputes, however). The most active users are the United States, the European Union, Canada, and Brazil, but many other states have been repeatedly involved, including Argentina, China, Chile, Colombia, Thailand, Mexico, South Korea, and Australia. In 2011, there were eight requests for consultations (the first formal step in dispute settlement proceedings), nine new panels were established, and eight panel and five Appellate Body reports were adopted (World Trade Organization 2012: 86). Many disputes are settled before a Panel has been convened, and trade retaliation has seldom been authorized and even more rarely applied in practice. Up until the end of 2010, there have been eighteen instances where the WTO has authorized retaliation, and WTO members have gone forward to implement retaliation in nine of these cases (Davis 2012: 18).

WTO disputes often deal with some of the most important and sensitive issues in international trade politics. In 1996, for example, the US filed a WTO complaint about longstanding EU restrictions on the sale of hormone-treated beef, and, following authorization by a panel, imposed trade sanctions on German pork, French cheese, and Italian canned tomatoes in July 1999 (Devereaux et al. 2006: 31–96, 73). In 2003, when a WTO Panel and the Appeals Body found that the US use of safeguards to protect its steel industry was not compatible with its WTO obligations, the EU threatened $2.2 billion in retaliatory tariffs on US goods—at which point the US withdrew the safeguard measure (Devereaux et al. 2006: 193–233, 228). In 2004, a WTO panel found that US restrictions on internet gambling discriminated against gambling services provided over the internet from Antigua and Barbuda, and in 2007 Antigua and Barbuda requested the authorization to impose retaliatory measures on the United States (Alexander and Soukup 2010: 333–335).

It should be no surprise that the study of WTO dispute settlement occupies a central place in contemporary international relations scholarship. Research has found that WTO members that have larger economies or are more involved in international trade tend to be the targets of complaints (Sattler and Bernauer 2011); that states are more likely to pursue WTO disputes against trading partners who have previously initiated trade disputes with them (Busch and Reinhardt 2002: 464); that states are more likely to violate their WTO obligations vis-à-vis trading partners with weak retaliatory potential (Bown and Blonigen 2003; Bown 2004); that disputes between states with large power differentials tend not to be pursued through the WTO's dispute settlement system (Sattler and Bernauer 2011); that it is highly likely that many violations of WTO obligations are not pursued through the WTO's dispute settlement system (Horn et al. 1999; Davis 2012: e.g. 9, 16);[7] that trade exports are significantly increased after a favorable decision by a dispute settlement panel (Bechtel and Sattler 2012); and that states tend not to pursue trade disputes in the WTO where WTO violations affect research-intensive industries whose rate of innovation is so rapid that they cannot benefit from the WTO's drawn-out process of dispute settlement (Davis and Shirato 2007).

State participation in WTO dispute settlement also varies in line with international political relationships. Research finds that states do not pursue WTO complaints if this would damage an important diplomatic relationship (Japan, for example, tends not to pursue Japanese firms' requests to pursue trade disputes with China through the WTO's dispute settlement system) (Levy and Srinivasan 1996; Odell 2000: 25; Davis and Shirato 2007; Davis 2012: 233–237); that states that are dependent on foreign aid are less likely to pursue WTO complaints (Bown 2005a); and that states are more likely to initiate WTO disputes against states with which they share an alliance (Davis 2012: 92–100). State participation in WTO dispute settlement is also affected by differences in domestic political institutions. Research finds that democracies tend to pursue more disputes than non-democracies (Busch 2000; Davis and Bermeo 2009; Sattler and Bernauer 2011); that democracies with more domestic checks and balances are more likely to pursue disputes through the WTO dispute settlement process, rather than informal negotiations (Davis 2012); that states where policy-makers are chosen by electoral systems that tend to privilege narrow interests tend to violate their GATT WTO obligations more frequently (Rickard 2010; Davis 2012: 90–91); and that WTO members with little domestic experience of highly legalized systems and the rule of law are less likely to initiate disputes (Shaffer 2003; Allee 2008: 10–11; Davis and Bermeo 2009; but see Sattler and Bernauer 2011).

Our understanding of dispute settlement in the WTO is therefore well advanced. It is perhaps the leading object of study in contemporary research in international political economy. Few institutions in international relations are as thoroughly examined as the WTO's DSU.

[7] Bown 2005b notes that some states may prefer to retaliate against WTO-inconsistent trade restrictions through use of anti-dumping measures, rather than the WTO's dispute settlement process.

The EU and Enforcement in International Trade Politics

Looking to this scholarship to find an explanation for the EU's rejection of inter-state trade sanctions, however, immediately runs into difficulties.[8] This international relations scholarship, just like general international law scholarship, turns out to emphasize the importance of inter-state countermeasures and "reciprocal measures" as incentives for states to fulfill costly trade obligations. Kenneth Dam, writing in the 1970s, emphasized this aspect of the GATT:

> The best guarantee that a commitment of any kind will be kept... is that the parties continue to view adherence to their agreement as in their mutual interest.... Thus, the GATT system, unlike most legal systems,... is not designed to exclude self-help in the form of retaliation. Rather, retaliation, subjected to established procedures and kept within prescribed bounds, is made the heart of the GATT system.
>
> (Dam 1970: 80–81)

The importance of the retaliation mechanism is also recognized by GATT staff and government officials. Former GATT Director-General Arthur Dunkel explained in 1981 that governments were restrained from a substantial slippage toward protectionism only by "a kind of balance of terror"—the fear that if they resorted to trade restrictions, these would evoke retaliation, as well as undermining the trading system as a whole (Croome 1995: 11). "Retaliation as a legal remedy is not very effective," writes Huerta-Goldman, working for the Mexican mission to the WTO in Geneva in 2010, "but it is preferable to have a system that offers these mechanisms, as deficient as they may be, rather than not to have any such system at all" (Huerta-Goldman 2010: 296).

The same way of thinking about today's WTO is demonstrated in these passages of a leading recent monograph:

> The mechanism of using something of value as a threat that can be taken away (their export market) is what keeps the whole system functioning....
>
> Although most disputes do not reach the stage of formalizing the WTO-authorized retaliation threats, let alone having countries implement them in practice, to suggest that retaliation threats are irrelevant fails to recognize the importance of economic incentives inherent in the self-enforcing WTO agreements. While it may bubble to the surface only infrequently, an undercurrent of potential retaliation is inherent in every dispute.
>
> (Bown 2009: 44, 131)

[8] This section draws on an earlier publication in *International Studies Review* by this author (Phelan 2012).

The possibility of trade sanctions is therefore always "on the table" in WTO dispute settlement, even when sanctions are not actually being applied at any point in time.

Indeed, scholarship on international trade relationships frequently explicitly rejects the possibility that open international markets can be reliably maintained without inter-state countermeasure mechanisms, emphasizing the need for "direct retaliation" against defections involving demanding obligations, and that relying on "binding international commitments" alone would "reduce incentives for compliance" (Martin 1992b: 771; Lawrence 2003: 79–80). Such assertions are, we may add, consistent with the reciprocity-and-retaliation approach to cooperation under anarchy that dominates rationalist understandings of international institutions (Axelrod 1984; Keohane 1984). Many studies therefore assume that international organization in trade politics requires an inter-state enforcement mechanism that the EU institutions have consistently rejected. As we have seen, as early as 1964, the ECJ declared that self-help retaliatory action by EU member states was not permitted by European law.[9]

The emphasis in this scholarship on the need for GATT-style "suspension-of-equivalent-concessions" retaliation mechanisms in trade politics is reinforced by widespread skepticism that threats of massive retaliation can be used to prevent states from selectively defecting from *part* of a wide range of trade obligations.

The problem of states complying only *partially* with their treaty obligations is often accepted as a central difficulty of treaty politics. After all, complete non-compliance by one party can be met by complete non-compliance in return; the more problematic situation is providing incentives and mechanisms which can address the common problem of states only complying with *part* of their obligations, while *selectively* defecting on others (Weiler 1985). WTO-style reciprocity mechanisms address this problem, in ways that approximate international law's requirements for proportionality in countermeasures, so that states that fulfill only, say, 80 percent of their WTO obligations may only receive approximately 80 percent of the concessions that other WTO members had offered in return ("approximately": Spamann 2006). The rejection of proportional inter-state reciprocity arrangements by the EU would therefore appear to strip the EU of a mechanism for addressing the problem of selective defection.

When the lack of a mechanism to withdraw equivalent benefits from states that selectively defect on EU obligations is pointed out, it is a commonplace in EU-centric discussions to suggest that such EU member states

[9] Cases 90 and 91/63 *Commission v. Luxembourg and Belgium* [1964] ECR 625.

would be obliged to completely depart from the EU. This possibility is sometimes phrased somewhat indirectly. For example, when considering the possibility that states might selectively reject the domestic application of compulsory EU obligations, as is common in other treaty regimes, Weiler writes, perhaps somewhat tactfully, "If a Member State cannot accept these obligations, better that it be allowed to withdraw, even unilaterally" (Weiler 1985: 298). It is certainly an alternative which is frequently raised in debate when the puzzle of why the EU manages without WTO-style sanctioning systems is discussed.

The credibility of such a mechanism finds little support in the scholarship on enforcement in international trade politics. Schelling's classic essay on bargaining argues that massive punishments are so obviously painful to both sides that they are not taken seriously by those to whom such threats are addressed; only step-by-step incremental punishments can be credibly applied (Schelling 1956: 297). In the trade politics issue-area, Davis, discussing the possibility of the WTO substituting a threat of massive retaliation for its use of "equivalent" trade sanctions, writes simply:

> Threatening complete withdrawal from the trade regime (as in the "grim trigger" strategy that upholds cooperation over repeated games) is so costly that it does not represent a credible response to a single act of defection by a trade partner raising a trade barrier....
>
> How do states address individual trade barriers that are significant for an industry but would not justify withdrawal from the regime?... The [WTO's] dispute settlement system addresses this problem.... The moderate level of punitive measures against violations enhances stability in the system by accommodating temporary noncompliance driven by political necessity.
>
> (Davis 2012: 14, 31–32)

As Davis suggests, consideration of massive inter-state punishments often involves discussion of the "grim trigger" strategy in a repeated Prisoners' Dilemma. A *trigger strategy* in a Prisoners' Dilemma specifies both the event which "triggers" a retaliatory punishment, and the type of punishment that is triggered. The type of punishment involved in a *grim* trigger strategy is maximum punishment for an infinite period. It therefore offers the maximum incentive for actors to comply with costly obligations, and therefore, compared to alternative strategies, would appear to be able to sustain the largest possible deviation from pre-cooperative behavior.

However, it is widely accepted that such "grim-trigger" strategies are not optimal policies. Most importantly, because states may be obliged by domestic pressures to selectively defect from their obligations *regardless* of the amount of retaliation threatened, states have little incentive to employ a "grim-trigger" retaliation strategy which may lead to massive mutual costs but nevertheless not prevent defection (Downs and Rocke 1995).[10] For this reason, threats of massive retaliation are generally rejected as a credible substitute for proportionate countermeasures or reciprocity mechanisms. Indeed, in discussions of other international regimes or negotiations, the practicality of such incentives is often dismissed almost out of hand, and, instead, GATT-style "suspension-of-equivalent-concessions" mechanisms are understood to be the only feasible form of trigger strategy. Any appeal to the importance of an "expulsion" or "massive retaliation" mechanism in EU-centered discussions finds little support in the scholarship on enforcement in international trade politics.[11] It is far more likely that such demanding obligations can be imposed on the EU member states without a WTO-style retaliation mechanism because their policy-makers find it politically manageable, as well as beneficial, to accept them.

The EU and Escape in International Trade Politics

This discussion brings us to the central reason why theoretical discussions of trade politics emphasize the need for "suspension of equivalent concessions" enforcement mechanisms in trade regimes. Such "proportional" inter-state retaliation mechanisms are seen as one of *many* legal *ex post* "escape mechanisms" provided by such regimes.[12] The essential point is that WTO rules do not absolutely require that the WTO members fulfill the substantive WTO obligations agreed in previous trade rounds. WTO members may choose not to fulfill their obligations even after an adverse outcome in dispute settlement if, for example, the domestic political cost of fulfillment would be too high. Because this possibility of non-fulfillment is always there, WTO members have a "safety valve" that prevents WTO obligations from impinging too deeply on national political autonomy. But to prevent such non-compliance being over-used as a safety valve, WTO members need to pay a price for doing

[10] WTO-style "proportionate" retaliation, together with other such escape mechanisms, is frequently justified as a superior alternative to requiring (or creating incentives for) states to completely exit from international agreements. See e.g. Rosendorff and Milner 2001; Pelc 2009: 350; Zimmermann 2011: 404.

[11] One could add here that EU states seeking to expel a non-compliant member completely from the EU would face the problem of coordinating the use of this option with each other (Martin 1992a).

[12] Note that the WTO's DSU provides only for "suspension of concessions" as a "temporary measure" and states that "full implementation" of e.g. a panel's recommendation to bring a national measure into compliance with WTO obligations is "preferred" (WTO DSU Art 22.1). Some argue therefore that the WTO requires full implementation of its obligations, with the result that that "accepting retaliation" is not a "legal" escape mechanism within the WTO regime. However, there is no time limit to the "temporary" use of such retaliation, and the better view is that defecting-at-risk-of-retaliation is tolerated as legal practice for members within the WTO regime (see e.g. Lawrence 2003: 41).

so (Rosendorff and Milner 2001). In the self-help world of international politics, that price can be extracted by "equivalent" inter-state trade sanctions. As Richard Morningstar, former US ambassador to the EU (1999–2001), described a WTO dispute concerning an EU ban on the sale of US-produced hormone-treated beef: "The US won the case. The EU basically said, 'Well, we can't comply.'... The US was awarded $120m in sanctions. And what did the EU do? They said, 'Well, okay, we'll live with the sanctions,' because they make the political decision that they couldn't take the risk, the political risk, of complying with the decision."[13]

Perhaps the most influential theoretical treatment of this question is contained in two tightly written and compelling publications, *Optimal Imperfection? Domestic Uncertainty and Institutions in International Relations*, a book by George Downs and David Rocke, and a widely read companion article, *Is the Good News about Compliance Good News about Cooperation?* by Downs, Rocke, and Peter Barsoom.[14] Their arguments build on a basic Prisoners' Dilemma model of inter-state interactions under anarchy, inspired by economic models of firms in price-fixing cartels, where self-help enforcement is provided by firms' threats to damage other cartel firms' profits by reverting to supplying goods at lower prices. Following this logic, the authors argued that as the requirements of trade treaties become increasingly demanding, they would require ever-increasing amounts of inter-state retaliation to serve as effective enforcement incentives.[15] They therefore claimed that many treaties obtain good compliance because they are only "shallow" agreements, requiring little of their participating states.

The authors doubted that transparency, legal obligation, or persuasion provide important incentives for states to fulfill their treaty obligations (Chayes and Chayes 1993), and were particularly critical of the possibility that "transparency" *by itself* would affect state behavior. Here, they followed the logic of Iklé's classic paper, *After Detection: What?*: "A potential violator

[13] Ambassador Morningstar was speaking at Harvard University's International Relations Week, April 16, 2004. See Devereaux et al. 2006: 31–96 for an account of the beef hormone trade dispute.

[14] The similarities in the arguments put forward in Downs and Rocke's 1995 book and Downs, Rocke, and Barsoom's 1996 paper are sufficiently strong that it makes sense to consider them together (Downs and Rocke 1995; Downs et al. 1996).

[15] "Inter-state": Downs, Rocke, and Barsoom write "Self-interest will prevent such cheating only if the consequences of cheating are greater than the benefits. To achieve a situation where this disincentive exists, states must resort to a punishment for defection. In this case, one punishment strategy prescribes that state A begin by observing the treaty, but if B violates it, even modestly, state A should respond by abrogating the agreement (or otherwise reducing its level of compliance) for some specified period of time." (Downs et al. 1996: 384–385). Downs, Rocke, and Barsoom do expand their argument to claim briefly that their arguments apply regardless of whether or not sanctioning occurs in such a decentralized inter-state manner (Downs et al. 1996: 387), but, as the discussion that follows here demonstrates, the logic of their central argument is not applicable to alternative mechanisms that do not use inter-state sanctioning.

of an arms-control agreement will not be deterred simply by the risk that his action may be discovered.... To be effective, a sanction must be applied as a result of governmental decisions by the injured countries" (Iklé 1961: 208, 211). For Downs, Rocke, and Barsoom, the importance of transparency lies in the reaction it provokes in other parties: "this reaction is, of course, the substance of enforcement" (Downs et al. 1996: 393).

While Downs, Rocke, and Barsoom provided several reasons why treaties are likely to be shallow, the most important was that domestic interest-group demands may at times force state policy-makers to adopt protectionist policies regardless of the amount of threatened inter-state retaliation (Downs and Rocke 1995: 89). Where there is uncertainty about interest-group demands (Downs and Rocke 1995: 88), then extreme retaliatory strategies are not very useful, since they may nonetheless fail to deter the targeted behavior, and of course the retaliation itself imposes considerable costs on the state employing it. As a result, states have incentives to employ more modest, GATT-style trade sanctions, which provide a significant but limited deterrent against defection without attempting, in vain, to deter it altogether (Downs et al. 1996: 398–399). The logic of these limited inter-state sanctions is clearest "in a trading world of democratic governments that do not know how much free trade they want to commit themselves to" (Downs and Rocke 1995: 100). This is the reason, according to Downs and Rocke, that GATT-style modest retaliation regimes, employing "equivalent" inter-state sanctions that do not completely deter defection, are the only type of trade enforcement regimes that appears to occur in practice.[16] Indeed, even when only *one* of a pair of states is intermittently subject to such intense domestic interest-group pressures that it invariably capitulates to their demands, it does not make sense even for the state *without* such domestic pressures to employ an excessive retaliation strategy (Downs and Rocke 1995: 91ff). For a variety of interconnecting reasons, therefore, trade regimes will not unconditionally require states to fulfill their trade obligations, but instead permit unilateral defection at the potential cost of incurring GATT-style retaliation.

In short, therefore, both WTO-centered empirical scholarship and more theoretical discussions of the enforcement of demanding obligations in international trade regimes offer little or no consideration of the possibility that a

[16] "In the second case, we would see modest punishments that do not completely deter defection but that allow defection when domestic pressures are high. Only the second case appears to occur in practice. Trade sanctions rarely exceed the compensation standard by a large amount" (Downs and Rocke 1995: 93). "With its compensation principle that promises Pareto-efficient defections and backup remedy of withdrawal of concessions, the GATT discourages protectionist measures but does not harshly sanction them. This modest sanction is enough to keep states from abusing a costless escape clause and helps coordinate the expectations of states in such a way that a trade war of spiraling retaliations and counterretaliations is avoided" (Downs and Rocke 1995: 100).

demanding international trade regime could—like the EU—operate without the use of WTO-style inter-state sanctioning mechanisms.[17] Indeed, one could go further: scholarship on enforcement and escape in international trade politics tends to forego detailed and knowledgeable engagement with the distinctive features of the EU as a trade regime.

The influential scholarship of Downs, Rocke, and Barsoom, which we have discussed above, can again serve here as an example. The authors argue that the use of inter-state retaliation measures has been essential to the effectiveness of the GATT/WTO, and that the authorization of these reversionary sanctions has become more automatic as the costliness of WTO obligations has increased, fitting their claim that as regulatory rules tighten, the magnitude of punishment would need to increase (Downs et al. 1996: 391). They then add that, as *its* obligations became more demanding, the EU *also* strengthened *its* enforcement system, based on the penetration of European law into the domestic law of its member states, by adding a system of fines in the 1992 Maastricht Treaty (Downs et al. 1996: 392; relying on Burley [Slaughter] and Mattli 1993).

This elision of WTO and EU treaty arrangements, however, obscures the importance for their argument of the fact that the EU rejects the use of WTO-style self-help sanctioning mechanisms on which their models are based.[18] The WTO and EU regimes are in this sense *opposites*, because the

[17] Some exceptions that discuss WTO- and EU-style enforcement mechanisms in comparison mostly focus on *access* to dispute settlement: Levy and Srinivasan emphasizes that open access to dispute settlement in trade regimes may require states to pursue disputes even where this may cause political difficulties between the participating states, thus giving states an incentive to restrict access to dispute settlement (Levy and Srinivasan 1996). In his discussion of public versus private enforcement of international economic law, Sykes notes the EU as an exception to the rule that trade agreements tend to only allow public (government actor) enforcement mechanisms, and suggests two reasons: first, that this outcome was "an unanticipated creation of courts" (though Sykes notes that political actors could have reversed this), and second, that *ex post* oversight by the European Commission could "override judicial decisions that political actors find unpalatable" (although Sykes provides no examples, and notes that the Commission's ability to politically discriminate between industries may be restricted) (Sykes 2005: 652–654). In her discussion of the WTO DSU, Davis writes that only against a background of common interests would states allow non-state actors to activate treaty dispute settlement systems, noting that the highest levels of this sort of integration occur in the EU, where "this development has been confined to European states with shared democratic values, economic union, and alliance interests" (Davis 2012: 298–299).

[18] Downs, Rocke, and Barsoom claim that their argument applies regardless of the specific mechanism of enforcement, whether GATT-style institutions, or unilateral sanctions (such as US threats of trade sanctions to enforce environmental treaties), or "by domestic law as in the European Union" (Downs et al. 1996: 387). But this last claim is hard to square with the general logic developed in these publications. The list of "cooperation researchers in the rational choice tradition" with whom these authors associate themselves in Downs, Rocke, and Barsoom (1996: 382, ft 12) all emphasize inter-party/inter-state retaliation and reversionary strategies. That includes the economists writing about noncooperative strategies by firms in collusive cartels (Abreu et al. 1986; Abreu 1988; Abreu et al. 1989; also Green and Porter 1984) as well as the trade politics scholars emphasizing GATT-style inter-state retaliation systems (Sykes 1990: 321–323; Hungerford 1991: 359; Martin 1992b: 771; Staiger 1995: 1500 [Staiger also approvingly cites Dam 1970: 80–81]; Bayard and Elliot 1994 throughout [including US unilateralism pre-WTO]). The

consistent rejection of all forms of decentralized inter-state retaliation or reversionary strategies is the organizing principle of the European Union as an international organization. As Weiler writes,

> This type of sanction [reciprocal reprisals] is unavailable within the Common Market. A differentiated regime of countervailing measures among the Member States in the face of alleged or real violations would not only destroy the basic idea of creating a common marketplace for factors of production, but would also penalize innocent individuals who are among the main beneficiaries of the Common Market. In this respect, a system of reprisals by Member States in the face of a partner's failure to fulfil obligations would be as unthinkable as American states, Swiss cantons, German länder or Canadian provinces introducing countervailing measures against each other.
>
> (Weiler 1985: 294)

If, then, the "substance of enforcement" lies in the response to violations by other parties, the EU, forbidding such responses, does not employ the "substance of enforcement."[19] The EU does not fit the logic of this model, or of the models of firms in price-fixing cartels that inspired it—at least not without much more careful consideration. For the same reason, it is incorrect to suggest that WTO-style retaliation systems are the "only" type of trade enforcement mechanism that "appears to occur in practice" (Downs and Rocke 1995: 93, 100).[20]

A better understanding of the distinctive features of the EU as an international trade organization might have allowed the treatment of the EU as, at least, an interesting anomaly to the general argument, and perhaps even to consider whether the member states of the EU are employing qualitatively

fuller development of the argument of the 1996 paper in Downs and Rocke's 1995 book rests entirely on decentralized trigger strategies, without any claim to its applicability to situations where treaty obligations penetrate into the domestic legal system, or the EU in particular.

[19] The European legal order requires its member states to fulfil their obligations even if other parties do not, which is the negation of any WTO-style reversionary trigger strategy, and seems unlikely to be a successful organizing principle for firms in a price-fixing cartel. Neither before nor after the power to fine member states was introduced by the Maastricht Treaty in 1992 did the EU make use of such self-help enforcement mechanisms. Two additional points should be noted. First, monetary fines are not widely considered to be a plausible substitute for self-help enforcement mechanisms in international law, because the target country must cooperate in the payment of the fine, whereas the complaining state can impose inter-state countermeasures even if the target state does not cooperate in the imposition of the penalty (e.g. Sykes 2005: 660–661). Second, if Downs, Rocke, and Barsoom, by assimilating the EU into their wider argument, contend that either the integration of international law into domestic law or the imposition of fines for treaty violations removes the need for inter-state sanctioning mechanisms in international politics, it would seem to undermine their more general claim that treaties are likely to involve only shallow obligations because that is all that can be enforced by inter-state sanctioning mechanisms.

[20] To be fair, GATT-style retaliation systems or similar mechanisms are certainly common in international trade regimes (Chase et al. 2013: 36ff).

different forms of trigger strategy to the members of the GATT or WTO. As it is, Downs, Rocke, and Barsoom's 1996 article discusses only two distinct trade regimes by name and, contrary to their expectations, it is by all accounts the "shallower" regime—the GATT/WTO—that employs inter-state retaliation as an enforcement mechanism, while it is the "deeper" regime, with the tighter regulatory rules—the EU—that does not (Downs et al. 1996: 391; Gaines et al. 2012).

The limited engagement of the scholarship on enforcement and escape in international trade regimes with trade within the European Union goes beyond discussions of the role of inter-state trade sanctions. The ability of states to accept inter-state retaliation rather than fulfill their obligations is usually considered as just one of many *ex post* "escape mechanisms," "flexibility mechanisms," or "safety valves" that are legally provided for in the WTO regime (Roitinger 2004; Schropp 2009). Other prominent escape mechanisms include anti-dumping duties, countervailing duties, and industry safeguard mechanisms. Anti-dumping duties involve national policy-makers imposing a temporary increase in tariffs on imports of a particular good from another WTO member from where the goods are being "dumped"—that is, sold at a lower price abroad than in their domestic market. Countervailing duties involve national policy-makers imposing a temporary increase in tariffs on goods which are being subsidized in the country of their production, thus harming producers in the importing country.[21] Safeguard measures involve national policy-makers imposing a temporary increase in tariffs on imports of a particular good where an increase in imports is causing, or threatening to cause, serious injury to competing industries in the importing WTO member. All three of these mechanisms allow states to unilaterally provide protectionism to the benefit of organized interests, with a great deal of policy-maker discretion, although each has a different emphasis. Anti-dumping policies are targeted at the behavior of particular foreign *firms*, while countervailing duties involve an allegation against foreign *government policies* (in providing subsidies) and thus countervailing duties are sometimes considered to have more "foreign policy content" (Hoekman 1998: 2, 40). Anti-dumping measures and countervailing duties are applied only against imports from a particular state, while safeguard measures are applied against imports from all other WTO members.

These mechanisms are actively used. Between 1995 and 2006, WTO members launched more than 2,900 anti-dumping investigations, as well as 183 countervailing duty and 155 safeguard investigations (Kucik and Reinhardt 2008: 478 ft 4). To be sure, not all of these investigations leads to

[21] Safeguards are provided for in Art XIX of GATT 1994, and in the Agreement on Safeguards.

the application of increased trade barriers, but many do. Between 1979 and 2001, of 4,633 instances where national governments considered employing anti-dumping or countervailing duties, policy-makers actually imposed the duty about half the time, in 2,045 cases (Allee 2004: 8).[22]

These mechanisms—anti-dumping, countervailing duties, and safeguards—are often considered the most important legal safety valves employed by WTO members. However, the WTO regime provides several other important escape mechanisms. The WTO provides, in Article XXVIII of GATT 1994, that states may unilaterally and permanently withdraw trade commitments made in previous trade rounds, independently of substantive preconditions (without, for example, having to demonstrate that increased imports are damaging a domestic industry). Such states are obliged to negotiate with their trading partners to attempt to make mutually beneficial agreements, but WTO rules give the member an absolute right to unilaterally modify their commitments (Emaus 2008: 14). Other WTO members then have the right to withdraw equivalent commitments in return. Between 1951 and 1994, 42 GATT contracting parties availed themselves of the renegotiation option some 300 times, and, since the replacement of the GATT by the WTO, at least 34 requests for modification of commitments under Art XXVIII have been made (Emaus 2008: 43–44).

If one includes possibilities for unilateral increases in protectionism that are not effectively restricted by WTO rules, then the list of possible escape or safety-valve mechanisms within the WTO is even longer. Many states apply tariff rates at levels far below the "bound" rates they are committed to in the WTO agreements (this is referred to as "binding overhang"), so, entirely consistently with their WTO commitments, states may unilaterally raise their applied tariffs within their "bound" level. Between 2005 and 2006, for example, more than 560 increases to applied tariffs by an amount greater or equal to 15 percent were observed in a sample of 72 WTO members (Davis and Pelc 2013: 6 ft 8). Other aspects of the WTO that can be viewed as "escape mechanisms" include the long period of retaliation-free non-compliance, without retrospective penalties, facilitated by the slow procedures of the WTO's DSU (Brewster 2011), as well as mutual forbearance by WTO members in pursuing disputes with each other. In July 2012, for example, China responded to the EU's indication that it would pursue an investigation of subsidies to, and threaten tariffs against, two Chinese telecoms equipment companies, by indicating that it would respond by investigating subsidies to European agricultural, automotive, renewable energy, and telecoms groups. The *Financial Times* commented that concerns about the Chinese reaction appear to have "put on ice" a case that

[22] There is evidence that trade is disrupted even at the point that states begin the process of *investigating* whether anti-dumping duties should be imposed (Blonigen and Prusa 2001).

once seemed imminent.[23] Lax enforcement is therefore an informal means of achieving flexibility in these agreements (Davis 2012: 12 ft 12).

The use of such escape mechanisms obviously damages the reliability of international trading opportunities. It is widely agreed that such escape or flexibility mechanisms are necessary, however, to encourage states to join demanding trade regimes and to enable them to remain members. A much quoted passage by GATT expert Kenneth Dam lays out the logic:

> The GATT has a special interest in seeing that as many agreements for the reduction of tariffs as possible are made. Enforcement of bindings is important in the GATT insofar as such enforcement gives contracting parties the confidence necessary to rely upon tariff concessions offered by other contracting parties. But because of the economic nature of tariff concessions and the domestic political sensitivity inherently involved in trade issues, a system that made withdrawals of concessions impossible would tend to discourage the making of the concessions in the first place. It is better, for example, that 100 commitments should be made and that 10 should be withdrawn than that only 50 commitments should be made and that all of them should be kept.
>
> (Dam 1970: 80)

Modern scholarship overwhelmingly agrees with Dam. Rosendorff and Milner argue that escape clauses such as anti-dumping and countervailing duties are efficient and make it easier for states to agree on international trade deals (Rosendorff and Milner 2001). Kucik and Reinhardt demonstrate empirically that states that possess domestic institutions capable of investigating anti-dumping complaints are more likely to join the WTO and to commit to lower tariff rates in doing so (Kucik and Reinhardt 2008). In turn, this flexibility is necessary because "[g]overnments face domestic political pressure to violate the terms of agreements. The magnitude of these pressures varies over time and may be so intense that upholding costly international commitments is temporarily impossible" (Kucik and Reinhardt 2008: 480; similarly, Teh et al. 2007: 31–32; Emaus 2008: 7). This is exactly the same justification as that provided for the WTO authorization only of "proportional" inter-state countermeasures, rather than massive retaliation or expulsion strategies (Zimmermann 2011: 388–389). Anti-dumping instruments, and similar escape mechanisms, are therefore a form of "political insurance" for liberalizing policy-makers.[24]

[23] "China raises heat in EU trade dispute," July 9, 2012, *Financial Times*.

[24] Fischer and Prusa argue that political economy reasons may lie behind policy-makers' preference for anti-dumping as opposed to alternative policies to manage the risks of open markets. They suggest that alternative policies of taxation and subsidy are not used for political economy reasons (i.e. the political difficulty of raising taxes) (Fischer and Prusa 2003: 747).

The argument that international trade regimes need trade remedy instruments as unilateral *ex post* escape or flexibility mechanisms is often presented as a finding of general applicability. Rosendorff and Milner write that "many," or even "almost all" international trade agreements have such escape clauses (Rosendorff and Milner 2001: 834, 829).[25] Kravis claims that "some kind of escape provision is, therefore, almost an inevitable feature of any durable international agreement to reduce trade barriers" (Kravis 1954: 319; cited approvingly in Pelc 2009: 351–352).[26] Davis and Pelc write, "Trade remedies such as antidumping and countervailing duties, and safeguards, are standard in modern trade agreements" (Davis and Pelc 2013: 6). Kucik and Reinhardt even suggest that "the idea that [flexibility provisions in international agreements promote cooperation] has begun to dominate theoretical work on international law and politics" (Kucik and Reinhardt 2008: 498–499). None of the leading contributions to this scholarship discusses the possibility of an international trade regime imposing demanding obligations on organized interests that does *not* provide states with the three most common forms of trade remedy flexibility mechanism. Indeed, this literature appears to understand that WTO-type escape mechanisms are the norm.

To be sure, there is a growing literature that attempts to explain *variation* in the design of flexibility and escape mechanisms, and other institutional features, in preferential and regional trade agreements (McCall Smith 2000; Baccini et al. 2011). Research has found that regional trade agreements vary widely in how much they regulate the use of anti-dumping and other escape mechanisms (Hicks and Kim 2012); that "model" designs of trade agreements (such as the "NAFTA model") diffuse in the international system (Baccini et al. 2013); that greater trade interdependence leads to greater levels of institutionalization in regional trade agreements (Haftel 2013); that states make trade-offs between the depth of market integration and the availability of flexibility mechanisms, asking for more escape mechanisms as trade agreements become deeper (Baccini et al. 2012; Johns forthcoming); that higher levels of intra-industry trade—that is, where states trade relatively similar goods distinguished by quality or brand differences—reduce the demand for flexibility mechanisms (Baccini et al. 2012; Kucik 2012); and that the relative balance of export-orientated and import-competing sectors within a state affects policy-makers' demand for rigid or flexible trade agreements, for example anti-dumping rules with more or less stringent evidentiary and procedural requirements (Kucik 2012).

[25] Rosendorff and Milner mention, on page 842, the possibility that domestic institutions may cause variation in the use of such trade remedy instruments.

[26] Kravis 1954 noted as an exception, however, that the new members of the European Coal and Steel Community had surrendered their rights to protect their domestic coal and steel industries against imports from other members of the Community (319, ft 1).

The reader of this book will not, however, need to be reminded that the EU rejects the use of WTO-style trade remedy instruments just as it rejects the use of WTO-style inter-state countermeasures. The European treaties require the member states to maintain an international market between themselves without resorting to such types of legally sanctioned unilateral *ex post* escape or safety-valve mechanisms. The rejection of the use of these trade remedy instruments to manage trade relations between its members is, as we have explained, one of the EU's remarkable distinctions (Voon 2010: 647; Teh et al. 2007: 26; Voon 2010: 647).

The EU's special status in this regard is recognized in scholarly discussions of whether the WTO or regional trade agreements could be reformed to remove provisions relating to anti-dumping, countervailing duties, and industry safeguards. Such scholarship tends to emphasize the disruptions to trade associated with the use of anti-dumping duties and other trade remedy instruments. This scholarship has not, however, put forward well-developed explanations for why the EU is able to do away with such trade remedies, often emphasizing, in effect, the EU's greater ambitions as an explanation for its greater effects. Voon suggests that the EU's ability to remove trade remedies between its members (and the lesser ability of a small number of other trade regimes—such as the Hong Kong–China trade agreement or the Mercosur customs union in Latin America—to restrict the use of some elements of these mechanisms) emphasizes the role of "broader and deeper integration" in eliminating these remedies (Voon 2010: 647). Hoekman notes that the EU is unique in that it involves the complete liberalization of trade in goods, services, labor, and capital, and in the extent of the constraints it imposes on the member states, including enforcement by the ECJ (Hoekman 1998: 14). Wooton and Zanardi argue that it is the goal of creating a single market between states that is the critical element behind the phasing out of anti-dumping provisions (Wooton and Zanardi 2002). Prusa, Teh, and Budetta are skeptical about claims that a common competition policy across the members of a trade regime (as there is in the EU) can explain the removal of anti-dumping instruments, as competition policy is often concerned with protecting consumers, and therefore does not fulfill the essential political function of anti-dumping instruments, that is, protecting producers (Hoekman 1998; Teh et al. 2007: 27–28). De Araujo et al., in a survey of anti-dumping in Latin America, suggest in passing that the EU member states were able to abolish anti-dumping because of the high levels of integration in the EU and because intra-EU redistribution through the "structural funds" eased the economic and political costs (De Araujo et al. 2001: 569–570). These discussions tend to be more focused on the inability of other trade regimes to forego the use of these measures than on explaining the EU outcome.

As for the other escape mechanisms and safety valves emphasized in the WTO literature, these are also much less available to national policy-makers within the EU. The EU member states do not, of course, have the legal right to unilaterally reduce their trade obligations to each other. The direct access of private parties to dispute settlement in the EU means that "escape" is much less likely to be facilitated by mutual forbearance between state policy-makers. Within the EU, the stringency of dispute settlement may be reinforced by, for example, requirements for retrospective damages.[27] And, of course, new EU obligations can be imposed on the EU member states even without their *ex ante* agreement, because of the availability of majoritarian forms of decision-making in the Council of Ministers. Furthermore, the substantive content of the EU's trade-related and regulatory norms is highly intrusive and demanding. In the terminology of current debates, the EU's obligations are therefore both "deep" and "rigid."

The Treaty of Rome that founded today's EU did, of course, contain its own set of "safeguard clauses," which set out procedures by which the member states might under certain circumstances be relieved of their Treaty obligations.[28] The "safeguard clauses" in that treaty are, however, qualitatively different from those contained in more common forms of trade regime. Article 226, for example, provided that, in case of difficulties in a particular sector of the economy, a member state could apply for authorization to take protective measures—including derogations from the rules of the Treaty—in order to rectify the situation and adjust the sector to the economy of the European common market.[29] On first sight, this appears to be a general-purpose industry safeguard mechanism, readily recognizable from other trade treaties. There are at least three important differences, however. First, unlike the most prominent GATT safeguards, this safeguard was not available to be unilaterally used by the member states as internal politics dictated. Rather, its use needed to be authorized, in advance, by an independently established international body, the European Commission.[30] Second, this safeguard

[27] Since Case C-6 and 9/90 *Francovich v. Italy* [1991] ECR I-5357. On the politics of *Francovich*, see Tallberg 2000. For a discussion of how the possibility of damages can affect incentives for policy-makers' use of delays in dispute resolution processes to benefit from acts contrary to treaty obligations, see Schermers 1989.

[28] Kravis 1963: 268–365, esp 297–302 for safeguards in the transitional period; Kapteyn and VerLoren Van Themaat 1973: 227–237.

[29] Art 226 (1) of the Treaty of Rome: "If, during the transitional period, difficulties arise which are serious and liable to persist in any sector of the economy or which could bring about serious deterioration in the economic situation of a given area, a Member State may apply for authorisation to take protective measures in order to rectify the situation and adjust the sector concerned to the economy of the common market" (for an example, see Kapteyn and VerLoren van Themaat 1998: 169).

[30] Unilateralism: Kravis 1963: 377; Gori 1967: 73. Role of European Commission in EU safeguard arrangements: Kravis 1963: 287; Gori 1967: 80. In effect, the direct, *non*-gatekeepered access of non-state actors to the EU's dispute settlement system has its counterpart in the gatekeepered and supervised use of safeguard mechanisms by the EU member states.

explicitly requires the sector in question to adjust to the European common market, which is not a requirement contained in the GATT trade remedy mechanisms.[31] Third, and perhaps most surprisingly, the Treaty of Rome provided this protection-of-industry-sector safeguard *only for the transitional period* when the common market was first being established. Since 1970, the European treaties do not contain a general-purpose industry safeguard clause of this type.[32]

The other safeguard mechanisms in the Treaty of Rome have much the same characteristics. Compared to safeguard clauses in other treaty regimes, they are much less unilaterally available to the member states, being subject to the control of the European Commission or the other member states acting collectively in the Council.[33] They aim to eventually require, rather than prevent, adjustment to the disciplines of the European market. And they were restricted in number and scope after the passing of the Common Market's transitional period in 1970.

One further aspect of the European treaties should also be mentioned, although it is open to question whether it is correctly classified as a "safeguard" mechanism.[34] This is the possibility for member states to justify national regulatory restrictions that impact on the intra-EU free movement of goods and services by reference to public policy, public morality, public or animal health, or the protection of national treasures, under Article 36 of the Treaty.[35] In earlier scholarship on the European legal order, it was sometimes claimed that the ECJ used this mechanism to allow powerful member states to escape their single-market obligations.[36] Detailed examinations of the ECJ's treatment of Article 36 justifications provide little support for such an interpretation. Rather, the ECJ has *both* taken a restrictive perspective

[31] Kravis 1963: 359.

[32] Kravis 1963: 312: "Although there are many clauses providing for derogations from the obligations of the Treaty on one ground or another, the only provision designed specifically to make possible relief for a particular industry in serious difficulties is limited to the transitional period (Article 226)." Similar temporary safeguards were included in instruments of accession as new member states joined the EU (e.g. Kapteyn and VerLoren Van Themaat 1989: 358). Similarly, Art 91 of the Treaty of Rome allowed for investigations of, and remedies for, allegations of dumping, but only during the transitional period as the Common Market was being formed.

[33] See fuller account, including a comparison of EEC and GATT safeguard clauses, in Kravis 1963.

[34] E.g. Kravis 1963: 302.

[35] Art 36 of the Treaty of Rome: "The provisions of Articles 30 to 34 shall not preclude prohibitions or restrictions on imports, exports or goods in transit justified on grounds of public morality, public policy or public security; the protection of health and life of humans, animals or plants; the protection of national treasures possessing artistic historic or archaeological value; or the protection of industrial and commercial property. Such prohibitions or restrictions shall not, however, constitute a means of arbitrary discrimination or a disguised restriction on trade between Member States."

[36] Garrett and Weingast 1993: 198–199 including ft 55; Garrett 1995: 178–180, criticized effectively in Mattli and Slaughter 1995: 186–187.

on the public policy purposes for which restrictions on the free movement of goods and services may be justified *and* vigorously emphasized that even where such national measures can be justified, these may nonetheless constitute an impermissible disguised restriction on trade between the EU member states (Gormley 1985: 220–221). It has consistently, from the 1960s, refused to permit economic considerations of the sort that usually motivate safeguard clauses in trade regimes to be used to justify national restrictions on the intra-European market.[37] In short, Article 36 does not provide national policy-makers with a general safeguard clause, and the ECJ's interpretations of Article 36 are better understood as demonstrating the EU's eager subordination of national policy-making autonomy to the demands of international integration.[38]

The growing scholarship on the use of trade remedies as escape or flexibility mechanisms therefore provides another example of the way that scholarship on international trade politics tends to forego engagement with the European Union as a trade regime. None of the leading political science publications on the vital flexibility role of anti-dumping and other trade remedies mentions, or offers an explanation for, the EU's rejection of anti-dumping, countervailing, and safeguard mechanisms. Just like states that employ anti-dumping and other escape mechanisms in other trade regimes, the EU is a trading community of democratic governments that face uncertain interest group pressures, but nevertheless the market between the EU member states does not provide EU policy-makers with these apparently essential legal safety valves.

Assessment and Conclusion

This discussion of scholarship on enforcement and escape in international trade politics has demonstrated that the literature offers little consideration of the possibility that a demanding international trade regime—like

[37] Kapteyn and VerLoren Van Themaat 1973: 234, Case 7/61 *Commission v. Italy* [1961] ECR 317.

[38] Gormley 1985: 123, 220 and throughout: "Article 36, although looking like a vehicle to drive clear pathways in important areas through the free movement of goods—and thus constitute a source of reserved powers [for the member states]—is, in fact, nothing of the sort. In the words of Harris, "according to the Bible, 'the Lord hath given and the Lord hath taken away;' so too does Article 36." Thus the various grounds provided for are subject to two overriding requirements; first of all that prohibitions or restrictions under these provisions must be justified and, secondly, that they may not "constitute a means of arbitrary discrimination or a disguised restriction on trade between Member States."... [The ECJ's] policy [of refusing to allow economic matters to be brought within Article 36] has undoubtedly contributed to the maintenance of the strict interpretation of Article 36 and has prevented the Member States from being able to interfere unilaterally with intra-Community trade at the behest of pressure groups or as a panacea for economic difficulties.... Article 36 does not establish a generic safeguard clause in the Treaty..."

the EU—could operate without the use of WTO-style inter-state sanctioning mechanisms, or without WTO-style trade remedies. It tends to assume that only one form of trigger strategy—the threat of imposing "equivalent" trade sanctions to punish any national measures that fail to comply with trade obligations—is a viable enforcement mechanism in international trade politics. While it considers variation in the length and size of inter-state retaliation punishments, there is not much consideration of variation in the *type* of events, or state behaviors, that might trigger inter-state retaliation.

In terms of the criteria for a satisfactory explanation of the EU's rejection of inter-state countermeasures and trade remedies discussed at the end of chapter 2, this literature has no difficulty in identifying explanations for state behavior rooted in the interests of, and incentives for, policy-makers in participating states. The arguments contained in this scholarship tend to be relatively straightforward adjustments to, and developments of, generalist explanations of state behavior, including the common application of Prisoners' Dilemma models to international trade organization. On the other hand, this literature does not offer an explanation for the remarkable *relative* effectiveness of the European legal order compared to dispute resolution in other international trade organizations. Painting with a broad brush, we may say that, in this scholarship, all roads appear to lead to the WTO, or to the many regional trade agreements that replicate the WTO's essential organizing principles with only relatively modest variations. The EU demonstrates, however, that other paths are possible.

This discussion does suggest one important conclusion: any explanation for a self-contained trade regime that rejects the use of trade remedy instruments must focus on the domestic political management of adversely affected organized interests. The scholarship on the enforcement of obligations in international trade regimes is in unanimous agreement that the main reason that states need these safety valves is because organized interests facing income loss press policy-makers to defy treaty obligations (e.g. Kucik and Reinhardt 2008: 480; Zimmermann 2011: 389, 405). Explaining the EU as a self-contained regime that operates without common forms of legal escape mechanisms therefore requires a focus on the domestic politics of organized interests facing demanding trade obligations in the EU member states.

4

Explaining the EU's Rejection of Inter-State Trade Sanctions and Trade Remedies

Analysis

The first chapter of this book established that the European Union's most distinctive features as an international trade organization consisted of its rejection of inter-state countermeasures and the three most common forms of trade remedies (anti-dumping, countervailing duties, and industry safeguard mechanisms). That is the outcome that this book is attempting to explain. The second chapter demonstrated that existing scholarship on the European legal order has not attempted to explain this outcome, and often focuses on material of only limited relevance to this puzzle. The third chapter demonstrated that scholarship on enforcement and escape in international trade politics had not offered an explanation for the European Union's (EU's) rejection of World Trade Organization (WTO)-style trade sanctions and trade remedies, and that this literature tended to assume that a demanding trade regime that does not employ trade sanctions or trade remedies is all but impossible.

This chapter puts forward a new explanation for the EU's particular form of legal obligation and dispute settlement mechanism. It first develops an incentive-based argument for circumstances under which state policy-makers might choose to behave in ways that would produce a demanding international trade regime that does not use inter-state countermeasures or trade remedies. It then tests whether the observable implications of this argument are consistent with empirical data for the EU case, and whether it can explain the variation in the use of inter-state countermeasures and trade remedies between the EU and other trade regimes, global and regional. Unlike the scholarship that has focused almost exclusively on the politics of courts and lawyers in creating European law rights and doctrines, this approach therefore concentrates on incentives for *state policy-makers* to behave in ways that would produce the international trading environment that those rights and doctrines imply, and thus to accept the development of the European legal order by the European Court of Justice (ECJ) and national courts.

The chapter begins by demonstrating that any transformation of WTO-style regimes into EU-style regimes involves policy-makers automatically accepting a more frequent, and less predictable, stream of intrusive trade-related policy adjustments on organized narrow interests within their states. It then builds on political economy approaches to understanding the influence of interest groups on state behavior to argue that a group of states whose domestic institutions, in conjunction with a manageable stream of adjustment costs, allow their policy-makers to better prioritize general interests would be able to form a trade regime that uses neither inter-state retaliation mechanisms nor trade remedy instruments. Trade politics scholarship suggests that trading relationships that involve intra-industry trade, as well as states endowed with inclusive and authoritative democratic decision-making institutions, together with well-developed social insurance systems, would give policy-makers within trade regimes stronger incentives to consistently prioritize trade obligations even when narrow interest groups face adjustments.

In practice, this means that a group of interdependent states could allow the use of inter-state countermeasures to be taken "off the table" in an international trade regime by making international dispute settlement outcomes applicable as law by domestic courts. States would continue to have the power to unilaterally oust this automatic application of treaty obligations by their own courts, but only at the risk of a "fall-back," or reversion, to the possible use of retaliatory trade sanctions by their trading partners. Where political and economic conditions are favorable, however, state policy-makers would be able to consistently behave in ways that would avoid prompting any such fall-back on the use of inter-state countermeasures. In such conditions, a self-contained international trade regime would be a stable equilibrium outcome.

The application of this theoretical argument to the EU case has observable implications that allow it to be tested. It could be rejected if the EU member states did not possess relatively inclusive and authoritative democratic political institutions or more extensive welfare states than, for example, the states that are members of the World Trade Organization (hereafter, WTO), or if intra-industry trade was not a distinctive feature of intra-European trade. The final section of this chapter provides empirical tests of different aspects of this argument.

State Behavior in a Self-contained International Trade Regime

We will start by restating the variation-to-be-explained as two distinct types of *state behavior* within an international trade regime. The first type is the ordinary multilateral trade regime, recognizable from so many studies of the WTO in particular. In a *WTO-style trade regime*, states agree to lower barriers to trade on a reciprocal basis. Dispute resolution mechanisms are only open to use by the governments of other state parties, not by private actors. After a dispute has been adjudicated, states may either change their domestic policy to make it consistent with the tribunal's decision, or risk the imposition of "equivalent" retaliatory trading barriers by their trading partners. States also use a wide range of unilateral mechanisms, such as anti-dumping and countervailing duties, to legally escape their trade policy obligations.

The second type consists of the essential features of the EU as a trade regime, restated in general terms. In the *EU-style trade regime*, states agree to mutually lower barriers to trade. However, further reductions in trade barriers do not necessarily require the unanimous agreement of policy-makers in all the participating states. Dispute resolution mechanisms are open to use by the governments of other states but also by private actors and international bureaucracies. After the dispute in question has been adjudicated, states automatically apply the international tribunal's decision as law in their national courts. In this regime type, states also manage the domestic adjustments required by trade openness without using temporary tariff barriers such as anti-dumping duties as unilateral legal escape mechanisms.

This comparison between WTO-style and EU-style regimes allows us to highlight the *behavioral changes* required of states participating in a WTO-style regime that would transform it into an approximation of an EU-style regime. Two differences in behavior are revealed as essential.

The *first difference* is a much greater use by states of international dispute resolution procedures. If states in a WTO-style regime were willing to pursue every possible grievance advanced by firms or citizens about other states' trade policies, a WTO-style dispute settlement system would take a large step toward becoming an EU-style dispute settlement system, open to access by non-state actors. A state could, for example, unilaterally legislate to require their trade diplomats to automatically activate the WTO's dispute settlement procedures upon the presentation of a reasoned argument by an adversely affected firm. It is clear that there are many examples of potential trade disputes which are not pursued through the WTO dispute settlement system, so there is room for the number of disputes taken up to be vastly expanded. Of 126 Japanese trade barriers identified by the US National Trade Estimate

Report between 1995 and 2004, for example, only six were addressed in formal WTO dispute settlement (Davis 2012: 9).[1]

As we have seen, however, there are, of course, important reasons why states in WTO-style trade regimes do not legally pursue every possible trade complaint whose resolution would benefit their firms and citizens. Those reasons are intimately tied to the countermeasure and "reciprocal measure" basis of enforcement systems in such regimes. The threat of imposing trade sanctions is a hostile diplomatic action and policy-makers will therefore take into account the possibility that important international political relationships would be damaged by the pursuit of trade litigation (Levy and Srinivasan 1996; Odell 2000: 25; Davis 2012). Japanese policy-makers, for example, appear to be reluctant to use the WTO's dispute settlement institutions to pursue complaints about Chinese trade policies (Davis and Shirato 2007). The threat or imposition of trade sanctions may also be disruptive of wider market exchange—or even of domestic political relationships in the state pursuing the legal claim, through a "boomerang" effect, because other states may react by activating dispute settlement claims of their own (Busch and Reinhardt 2002: 464).

It is therefore logical that the ability to activate dispute settlement processes in WTO-style trade regimes should be restricted to national policy-makers, which weigh their constituents' demands to pursue trade disputes against wider diplomatic and economic concerns (Sykes 2005). If there was open access to these dispute settlement systems, private parties would have incentives to pursue trade disputes regardless of the possibility that these might lead to trade wars or diplomatic ruptures. As we mentioned earlier, EU policy-makers appear to have decided not to immediately pursue complaints about subsidies for Chinese telecoms equipment companies, after China indicated that it would respond by initiating investigations into subsidies for various EU firms.[2] However, in a trade regime that does *not* use inter-state countermeasures and reciprocity mechanisms, the use of dispute resolution mechanisms cannot lead to disruptive inter-state trade sanctions. Thus, private-actor access to dispute resolution mechanisms in international economic regimes is highly facilitated by the non-use of inter-state countermeasures within such regimes. Rather than non-state actor access to dispute settlement *forcing* states to comply with dispute settlement outcomes, as the EU-specific literature tends to suggest, it seems more likely that it is the ability of state policy-makers to routinely accept a less predictable and more intrusive stream of trade-related policy adjustments arising from dispute settlement processes which *permits* non-state-actor access to such mechanisms.

[1] Some of the remainder were addressed in bilateral negotiations.

[2] "China raises heat in EU trade dispute," July 9, 2012, *Financial Times*.

For this reason, the *second difference* in the behavior of states required by WTO-style and EU-style international economic regimes is even more fundamental. If states in a WTO-style regime were willing to automatically and immediately change their domestic law to apply the decisions of international dispute settlement tribunals, the regime in question would take a very large step toward an EU-style regime. Recall that the threat and practice of imposing inter-state countermeasures in institutionalized international economic regimes is essentially a result of states *not* changing their policies in line with the outcomes of dispute settlement processes. In the WTO itself, for example, the possibility of countermeasures occurs only as a "last resort" *after* dispute settlement findings of fault are completed *and* the state has not changed its policies within the required "reasonable" period of time.[3] Sanctions are approved only after the mandatory dispute settlement process is completed (Brewster 2011: 109).[4] Thus states could radically reduce the use of—and threat of the use of—trade sanctions in the WTO regime if they decided, for example, to legislate to make decisions of WTO dispute settlement panels automatically enforceable as law by their domestic courts.

States do sometimes choose to make international dispute settlement outcomes enforceable as law in their domestic courts. One of the more interesting aspects of the NAFTA negotiations between the US and Canada was Canada's insistence that it preferred to make dispute settlement outcomes relating to environmental and labor obligations in the NAFTA "Side Agreements" automatically enforceable by courts within the Canadian legal system, rather than through the possibility of market-disrupting trade sanctions.[5] So while the

[3] In Art 3.7 of WTO's Dispute Settlement Understanding, suspension of concessions is described as a "last resort."

[4] This reflects a development and institutionalization of the more general international law obligation to notify and consult the target state prior to imposing countermeasures.

[5] The North American Agreement on Environmental Cooperation provides, in Annex 36A, 2(c) that "the [dispute settlement] panel determination, for purposes of enforcement, shall become an order of the [Canadian] court." For discussion, see: "The United States and Mexico agreed that in extreme cases of failure to enforce national law, an international dispute panel could authorize trade sanctions. Canada, unwilling to allow the possibility, however remote, that international trade sanctions could be used against them (a sensitive matter in Canadian politics), agreed instead to make the decisions of the international dispute panel enforceable in Canadian courts" (Mayer 1998: 166). "Canada put up an intense fight against trade sanctions.... In a breakthrough,.... the United States and Mexico agreed that Canada would be exempt from trade sanctions for the non-enforcement of standards. To get this deal, Hockin agreed to have Parliament approve a special clause giving the Canadian Federal Court powers to fine federal or provincial governments if they were found by a trinational panel to have failed to enforce their own standards" (Cameron and Tomlin 2000: 198). "In the extremely unlikely event that the subject of a complaint fails to pay its fine or still refuses to enforce its environmental law, other remedies will be available. In a dispute between Mexico and the United States, the complaining party or parties can suspend the NAFTA benefits based on the amount of the assessment. Most likely, the sanction would involve "snapping back" tariffs to their pre-NAFTA levels. In the case of Canada, the Commission [NAFTA's Commission for Environmental Cooperation]—at the request of the complainant—collects the fine and enforces an action plan in summary proceedings, without reconsidering the merits of the case, before a Canadian court of competent jurisdiction" (Grayson 1995: 143).

treaty provides that complaints by the US against Mexico relating to these particular NAFTA obligations can be enforced by "snapping back" tariffs to their pre-NAFTA levels, complaints by the US against Canada cannot be. Canada was not trying to remove the possible use of trade sanctions against it in the context of more directly trade-related NAFTA disputes, and was certainly not attempting to turn NAFTA as a whole into a regime that rejects the use of trade sanctions and trade remedies. This particular—relatively minor—provision of the NAFTA agreements, however, illustrates that the national application of treaty obligations as law by national courts is a potential *substitute* for the use of inter-state countermeasures as an enforcement mechanism. It is a way of taking trade sanctions "off the table" in international dispute resolution, even in scenarios where a state party is found to have failed to fulfill its treaty obligations.[6] The Canadian example further demonstrates that it is not impossible for state policy-makers to appreciate its advantages.[7]

Thus, national court enforcement of treaty obligations is not merely a mechanism for the protection of individual rights, or the empowerment of national judges, as current accounts of European legal integration tend to stress. It can also be an essential component in an inter-state bargain whereby states give up their right to use trade retaliation or similar inter-state countermeasures as mechanisms to enforce treaty obligations because their partner states have allowed their treaty obligations to be enforced by domestic courts. The NAFTA Side Agreement example makes this especially obvious, because this bargain was explicitly agreed by state policy-makers, because national courts would be enforcing *inter-state* complaints against Canada, and because domestic court enforcement was agreed only in relation to the obligations of one of the treaty parties, but the same underlying bargain is present in the European legal order—even though there it is complaints by private parties that are enforced in national courts, direct effect has come to be accepted by all member states, and the outcome developed over time from initially incomplete and ambiguous treaty provisions.

Allowing national court enforcement of treaty obligations—and, in particular, the decisions of treaty-based dispute settlement institutions—should therefore be understood as an instrument that states can employ to deprive *other* states of justification to threaten or employ inter-state

[6] That granting direct effect to treaty obligations is a mechanism for removing trade retaliation as an enforcement mechanism is equally apparent in debates over whether WTO obligations, or decisions produced by the WTO dispute settlement institutions, should be granted direct effect within the EU (e.g. Eeckhout 2011: 331–381).

[7] The NAFTA Side Agreements as they apply to Canada illustrate legal instruments by which application of treaty obligations by domestic courts may substitute for enforcement through inter-state retaliation, but the dispute settlement system established in these agreements has yet to be used in practice. For more detailed comparison of the legal provisions of the NAFTA Side Agreements and the European legal order, see Phelan 2013d.

countermeasures to enforce trade-related treaty obligations. By the same logic, allowing such directly effective treaty obligations to enjoy "supremacy" over conflicting national law is an instrument that states can employ to protect this tool of inter-state politics from being removed or restricted by, particularly, the stream of subsequent national legislative enactments.

Just as with the restrictions on private party access to legalized dispute settlement arrangements, however, there are of course obvious reasons why states would not want to automatically apply international dispute settlement outcomes as law in their national courts. The findings of dispute settlement panels may require alterations to domestic policies that would change relative prices to the disadvantage of organized interests. In turn, those organized narrow interests may press state policy-makers to retain the existing policy in question, even if this will result in retaliatory trade sanctions being threatened or imposed by other states. After all, the costs of retaliation may fall on other, perhaps more export-orientated interests, or impact diplomatic relationships whose benefits are not always internalized by particular narrow interests. The same logic explains why states insist on legal rights to use trade remedy instruments such as anti-dumping duties in many international trade regimes: they allow policy-makers to protect organized narrow interests from unwelcome changes in relative prices, even if they disrupt international trade or may prompt international retaliation.

By restating the variation-to-be-explained as two distinct types of state behaviors within international trade regimes, and by stating the changes in behavior that would be required by states in a WTO-style regime for a transformation into an EU-style regime, the research question has been both simplified and clarified. While the EU-specific literature talks of the legally enforceable rights of market participants, this discussion of state behaviors in the two regime types makes clear that any transformation of WTO-style regimes into EU-style regimes involves policy-makers automatically accepting a much greater stream of more intrusive and less predictable trade-related policy adjustments on narrow organized interests within the participating states. That, in turn, is the enabling condition that permits automatic access to dispute settlement procedures by non-state actors, including private parties. Explaining international economic regimes that operate without inter-state countermeasures must, therefore, centrally focus on the politics of managing income loss by narrow organized interests in the participating states.

Domestic Politics and International Trade Organization

At this point, let us revert to a more direct discussion of incentives for policy-makers to choose different types of trade politics behaviors.[8] According to political economy approaches, incentives for state behavior in the area of international trade are understood to be set by economic theory in interaction with domestic collective action problems—that is to say, the politics of lobbying. The economic theory can be simply stated: Ricardian comparative advantage, all but universally accepted among contemporary economists, argues that unilateral trade openness is the policy which maximizes a state's aggregate welfare, by promoting the most efficient use of domestic factors of production. Of course, there are caveats to that general finding—special circumstances where a state's aggregate welfare might be improved by protectionism, such as the incentives that "large" states possess to adopt an "optimal tariff"—but in the ordinary case, the economic effects of trade, considered alone, provide incentives for policy-makers to choose unilateral trade openness (Conybeare 1984).

However, this incentive for trade openness is apparently reversed when domestic collective action problems are considered. Trade openness changes relative prices and thus imposes adjustments on workers and firms in industries where the price of products is altered by foreign competition. Because the benefits of economic efficiency accrue largely to society as a whole while its costs frequently fall on narrower constituencies of firms and workers, policy-makers within states have incentives to supply more protectionism than economic theory alone would suggest. Narrow interests are more effective lobbies than broad constituencies and have little incentive to internalize aggregate welfare concerns (Olson 1965, 1982). As a result, again in the normal case, narrow economic interests have both the ability and the incentive to require policy-makers to adopt protectionist policies.[9] An open international market is therefore achievable only in the context of strategies of contingent cooperation between states within an iterated interaction, often relying on the political influence of export-orientated narrow interests to counter-act the pressure from import-competing groups (Gilligan 1997a).

This is, of course, the reason that many scholars have characterized international trade politics as a Prisoners' Dilemma, wherein states have incentives to adopt protectionist policies, but these can be restrained through repeated interactions with their trading partners, mutual monitoring, and

[8] This section draws on an earlier publication in *International Theory* by this author (Phelan 2011a).

[9] E.g. through pressure from domestic manufacturers: Keohane 1984; through campaign contributions and blocs of votes: Grossman and Helpman 1994; through domestic inequalities more generally: Moravcsik 1997.

threats of inter-state retaliation (Axelrod 1984; Keohane 1984). Repeated interactions between states provides policy-makers with incentives to value gains from a stream of future interactions. Monitoring by international institutions reduces the likelihood that state protectionism will go undetected, and allows uncertainty about whether particular behaviors are permitted or proscribed by international treaties to be authoritatively resolved. *Legalized* international institutions can provide increased precision and coherence, and greater delegation of interpretative authority to third parties, in such monitoring procedures and dispute resolution mechanisms (Goldstein et al. 2001). Threats of inter-state retaliation, or, to use the more common contemporary term, "trigger strategies," ensure that defection from prior agreements comes at a potential cost to export-orientated industries within the defecting state.

The most prominent trigger strategy is GATT-style "proportionate retaliation" by "equivalent" trade sanctions, despite the associated disruption of international markets. Trade agreements between states with diverse economic interests enforced by "suspension of equivalent concessions" mechanisms, however, tend to involve considerable market disorder. Even with *ex ante* unanimity among states, as political and economic circumstances change, narrow economic interests facing adjustment costs may successfully demand selective *ex post* protectionism even if export opportunities will be lost. This in turn may prompt trading partners to threaten to withdraw "equivalent" trading opportunities, further disturbing the international market for firms in both states. Alternatively, protectionist policies may be allowed to persist, as policy-makers in trading-partner states decline to employ retaliation-based dispute settlement mechanisms because of the additional diplomatic and trade disruption they may precipitate. In the anarchical environment of international relations, there may seem to be no exit from this situation, and of course it is in fact a common one in international trade politics.

However, understanding international trade politics as a Prisoners' Dilemma involving reciprocity-and-retaliation behaviors does not mean that *WTO-style* reciprocity-and-retaliation behaviors are the only possible outcome. The reason that international trade regimes use WTO-style trade sanctions and trade remedies is that policy-makers in the participating states can be forced by powerful domestic interests to remove the domestic application of their trade treaty obligations, regardless of the wider benefits of international cooperation or any amount of threatened retaliation from their trading partners. It is this intermittent extreme pressure to break treaty commitments by narrow interests facing costly adjustments, not the overall solution to Prisoners' Dilemma trading relationships between states, which limits the depth of possible international cooperation, and necessitates the use of WTO-style "suspension-of-equivalent-concessions" trade sanctions (Downs and Rocke 1995; Downs et al. 1996). A different sort of international market would be possible between states whose policy-makers are capable of more consistently managing the domestic politics of trade regime membership, for example where demanding trade regulations will result in lower adjustment costs, or because political institutions are less responsive to narrow-interest-group demands for defection from treaty obligations, and more capable of prioritizing a general interest in stable trading relations (Phelan 2011a). While the existing literature on this topic has tended to focus on at-the-margin effects on unilateral state behavior, such as variation in trade openness and dispute outcomes, *within* the WTO regime, the possibility that *groups of states* can produce forms of international trade organization that are *qualitatively distinct* from WTO-style regimes has not been fully appreciated.

It is, of course, necessarily a *group* of states that can create and sustain a self-contained international trade regime. Just as a single state cannot unilaterally ensure peaceful relationships (that is, excluding armed conflict) with other states, so a single state cannot unilaterally create an international trading regime that rejects the use of trade sanctions or unilaterally activated escape mechanisms such as anti-dumping duties. A self-contained trade regime results when a group of states seeking to respond to international interdependence by lowering the transaction costs of international interactions and exchanging mutual concessions are also states whose domestic institutions and international economic relationships allow them to behave in ways that will not trigger the use of inter-state countermeasures by each other. As previous scholarship has emphasized, WTO-style inter-state retaliation will be used even by states that do not intermittently face intense domestic pressures to violate trade policies as long as their partners sometimes do so (Downs and Rocke 1995: 91ff). Only when both partners to a bilateral interaction are capable of managing their domestic interest groups to avoid triggering the other party's use of inter-state retaliation is a self-contained trading regime possible. In comparative terms, therefore, one of the distinctions of international organization based on WTO-style reciprocity is that it constitutes a "come one, come all" macro-institution that facilitates international organization between states with a great variety of domestic political structures and economic interests, whereas self-contained trade regimes are only likely to be possible in a much narrower range of circumstances.

A group of interdependent states whose policy-makers were capable of sufficiently managing their domestic interests facing trade policy adjustments would have incentives to eliminate the use of "suspension of equivalent concessions" enforcement mechanisms (with all their market-disrupting disadvantages) in favor of a mutual commitment to automatic application of regime obligations as law before domestic courts. Because this regime obligation would be accepted on a *reciprocal* basis, the outcome would rest in part on a retaliation incentive: the incentive to avoid triggering trading partners' reversion to WTO-style reciprocity behaviors. This inter-state relationship is therefore still a Prisoners' Dilemma, and "something of value that can be taken away" by other states is very much part of the incentive structure (Bown 2009: 44). At the same time, this outcome would also require that domestic conditions provide incentives for national policy-makers to behave in ways compatible with this more demanding international bargain, rather than remove the application of treaty obligations by domestic courts if interest group pressure became intense. These states could enjoy the greater reliability of international trade and cooperation possible where policy-makers cannot be intermittently forced by narrow domestic interests into GATT-style limitations and interruptions of trading relations (Downs and Rocke 1995: 87–91).

To be sure, state policy-makers in such a self-contained trade regime would certainly not be wholly unresponsive to narrow interest demands. Rather, policy-makers in such regimes would oblige *narrow interests* to obtain policy advantages (even inefficient advantages) that are compatible with policy-makers' *general interest* in maintaining a self-contained trade regime between the participating states—which is to say, do not require interference with the automatic application of treaty obligations by national courts.[10]

What sort of state behavior within an EU-style trade regime could trigger a reversion to WTO-style inter-state countermeasures and trade sanctions by its trading partners? Recall the example of Canada's insistence on making dispute settlement outcomes automatically enforceable as law by a Canadian court in order to take the possibility of US trade sanctions "off the table," at least in relation to enforcing these particular NAFTA "Side Agreement" obligations. It takes little imagination to understand how policy-makers in Canada could behave in ways that would prompt the US to revert to the trade sanctions instrument. A reversion to trade sanctions would not, however, be triggered merely by Canada's policies failing to meet the standards required by the environmental or labor obligations prescribed in the NAFTA "Side Agreements." On the contrary, if Canada were found to be in violation of these NAFTA commitments, that is when this mechanism would prove its worth, because the outcome of NAFTA dispute settlement processes would be enforced as law by Canadian courts without raising the possibility of trade

[10] This argument has some similarities with Garrett's emphasis on states' general interests in accepting the European legal order (Garrett 1995), but note that there is no argument here that the particular decisions of such international tribunals must be highly responsive to the issue-specific demands of powerful member states, or—as should become clear in the following passages—that states in such a "self-contained" trade regime enforced by national courts could simply unilaterally ignore unwanted dispute settlement outcomes.

sanctions. Instead, a reversion to the use of trade sanctions would be triggered only if Canadian policy-makers unilaterally acted to disrupt the mechanism by which an adverse dispute settlement outcome of this sort would be applied as law by Canadian courts. The trigger for the use of inter-state retaliation would therefore move away from one event—policy-makers' failure to ensure that domestic policies were compatible with their treaty obligations—and toward another—policy-makers' interruption of institutional processes that would ensure the automatic application of international dispute settlement outcomes as law in national courts.[11]

Similarly, within a self-contained regime on the model of the EU, the member states commit to applying treaty obligations and international dispute resolution outcomes as law in their national legal orders. It is therefore failure to follow through on *this specific commitment* that would raise the question of a reversion to WTO-style inter-state countermeasures. State behavior that is merely contrary to treaty obligations would not—and indeed, within the EU, does not—prompt trading partners to revert to inter-state countermeasure mechanisms. Only state behavior that breaks the commitment to inter-state retaliation's substitute—the automatic application of treaty obligations and dispute settlement outcomes as law in the national legal order—would raise the question of a "fall-back" on the use of inter-state retaliation mechanisms.[12]

This account therefore recognizes the distinction between *two* different ways in which a national government could attempt to "ignore" or "refuse to comply with" a decision of the ECJ (cf. Garrett 1992, 1995).[13] If state policy-makers do not wish to remove the automatic domestic application of EU obligations, then any attempt to ignore ECJ decisions is constrained to an important degree, particularly if interests that stand to benefit from the European law right have the resources for a determined and repeated litigation strategy. Such intermittent foot-dragging and initially minimalist

[11] The possibility that Canada might unilaterally alter these enforcement procedures appears to be envisaged in the text of the NAFTA "Side Agreements." Annex 36A of the North American Agreement on Environmental Cooperation, after describing the process by which dispute settlement outcomes are to be applied as law by Canadian courts, states, in 36A 4, that "Any change by Canada to the procedures adopted and maintained by Canada under this Annex that have the effect of undermining the provisions of this Annex shall be considered a breach of this Agreement." Such a "breach of this Agreement" would raise the possibility of a reversion to the use of trade sanctions by Canada's NAFTA trade partners.

[12] One should not therefore be mislead by the relatively small number of occasions that the EU member states directly pursue legal claims against each other before the ECJ to believe that state policy-makers are little concerned by the effectiveness of the European legal order in the other member states. State policy-makers may not pursue many claims against other member states directly, but that is because many claims are pursued by the European Commission and by private parties through the national courts, and it is the enforcement role of national courts, in particular, that allows the member states to forego the inter-state countermeasure mechanisms normally employed by international trade regimes.

[13] See discussion pp. 62–63 of this volume.

compliance by national policy-makers is entirely compatible with the EU's continued rejection of inter-state sanctioning methods, but of course it does not ensure that state policy-makers will enjoy full freedom of action over policy outcomes within their states. National policy-makers do have the alternative option of more definitively "refusing to comply" with ECJ decisions by unilaterally removing or selectively restricting the automatic application of European treaty obligations by their national courts, but that decision would raise the possibility of a reversion to the use of inter-state trade sanctions by the other member states, and policy-makers in the EU member states have incentives to avoid triggering that outcome.

The understanding of the European legal order developed here also makes sense of the widely acknowledged limits to the acceptance of the supremacy of European law by the national courts. National judges, loyal to their national constitutions, have been able to claim that they apply EU obligations as law because their democratically elected parliaments, and national constitutions, require them to do so, and they have not been required to generate national legal doctrines that would prevent the domestic application of an express act of national legislation unilaterally removing the application of directly effective European law obligations (Phelan 2010).[14] However, the attenuated version of European law's "supremacy" that many national courts do acknowledge has been quite sufficient to allow the EU to obtain a remarkably effective treaty-based dispute settlement system, because national policy-makers have chosen to behave in ways that respect its constraint.

States within WTO-style and EU-style international trade organizations therefore employ different trigger strategies, within which a variety of state behaviors, both compliant and non-compliant, play themselves out. In the WTO-style international trade organization, states' inter-state retaliatory behavior is triggered when another state's measures—policies or practices—fail to provide the trading opportunities promised in previous negotiations, and the punishment strategy involves the withdrawal of roughly equivalent trading opportunities through trade sanctions as a countermeasure. Whether trade sanctions are actually being applied or not at any particular moment, in such a trade regime the possibility of inter-state trade sanctions is always "on the table" in international dispute settlement, and, more fundamentally, whenever any states' policies are inconsistent with their treaty obligations. In the EU-style international trade organization, states' inter-state retaliatory behavior would be triggered instead only by their partner's removal of the automatic application of treaty obligations as law in their domestic courts, and the punishment strategy would involve a reversion to

[14] See discussion pp. 57–62 of this volume.

a WTO-style trading relationship, complete with the ever-present possibility of inter-state countermeasures.[15] Unless a member state interferes with the domestic application of treaty obligations as law by national courts, however, inter-state trade sanctions remain "off the table," even if the participating states are repeatedly found to have failed to fulfill their treaty obligations.

The behavior required within such a self-contained regime is therefore, in a sense, similar to the "constitutional obedience" required by federal legal orders, such as the US Constitution. In federal states, many infractions of federal obligations take place in the state jurisdictions, and states and individuals are constantly litigating to dispute and shape the exact obligations derived from federal legislation, but federal obligations, including the final decision of the federal courts, are automatically applied as law in state courts. It is therefore easy to see why many scholars have come to view the EU in "constitutional" or "federal" terms. However, this "constitutional obedience" is also "self-contained regime obedience"—that is to say, the sort of behavior required to sustain a reciprocal agreement to avoid the use of inter-state countermeasures in an international trade regime, because domestic application of treaty obligations as law by national courts can act as a substitute for inter-state retaliation mechanisms.[16]

The possibility of the EU member states' reversion to the use of inter-state countermeasures was discussed by the very scholar most identified with discussions of the EU as a self-contained regime, Bruno Simma. Writing of a scenario where a member state does not change its course of action despite repeated condemnations by the ECJ, he supports the view that a "fall-back" on countermeasures as provided by general international law would be available as a last resort "after all the legal and political means within the EEC system have been exhausted to no avail":[17]

> [I]f and when the remedies provided within this regime [the EU] definitively fail to put an end to persistent violations of Community law, the situation may reach the point where further fulfillment of community obligations towards a defaulting member state would simply become an intolerable burden on the injured party or parties. *Through such a fundamental change of circumstances any treaty*

[15] The careful reader may note that, in some ways, state policy-makers in an EU-style regime lose important tools to enforce international trade obligations. Participating states give up the right to use trade sanctions merely on the justification that another state's measures fail to offer the benefits promised in the treaty negotiations. The gains are overwhelmingly gains *in process*, and, even if these processes offer considerable gains taken in the aggregate, come at the cost of foreswearing the use of a tool—trade sanctions—that could be used much more directly to lever open market access in particular industries.

[16] An earlier paper by this author used the description "constitutional obedience" to characterize the behavior that the EU member states demonstrate toward the European legal order, by contrast with more common forms of state behavior toward their treaty obligations (Phelan 2008b, a characterization taken up by Karen Alter in Alter 2013: 353—354, also ft 8).

[17] Simma 1985: 126.

> *system excluding the applicability of...countermeasures will fall back on the general regime [of countermeasures provided by international law].* At this stage [legal scholarship] may close its eyes and resort to the argument that, luckily, such a case has not yet arisen, but such a view ought not to be taken for a legal solution.
>
> (Simma 1985: 123–129, 127, emphasis added)

As Simma indicates, the possibility of a reversion to the use of inter-state countermeasures between EU member states is rarely discussed by scholars of the European legal order.[18] That discussing this possibility is somewhat "taboo," however, does not undermine—and may even underline—its real significance. In fact, the number of legal analysts who emphasize a last resort return to inter-state reprisals between EU member states is not so small (see references in e.g. Simma 1985; Dero 2006; Simma and Pulkowski 2006). The best evidence for the possibility of a reversion to the logic of inter-state countermeasures lies not in legal scholarship, however, no matter how distinguished, but in the persistent use of such mechanisms in other international trade regimes and in the history of international law.

Table 4.1 sets out the differences in trigger strategies—in the potential for trade sanctions, the event that triggers the inter-state punishment, and the type of punishment that might be triggered—between WTO-style and EU-style international trade regimes. These two trigger strategies can be understood as describing two different types of institutionalized trade cooperation between states in international anarchy, or, put more simply, two distinct forms of international organization.

Varieties of Trade and Domestic Institutions, and the possibility of a Self-contained International Trade Regime

The argument that this chapter has developed is that states can maintain a "self-contained regime" type of international market between themselves when political and economic conditions allow them to sufficiently consistently prioritize fulfilling their trade obligations. By contrast, where an international trade regime includes states whose political institutions are too responsive to narrow interests intermittently demanding the removal of the domestic application of regime obligations, then an international trade regime that uses inter-state countermeasures and trade remedies may be all

[18] See also Simma 1985: 127: "The opposition of Community lawyers against even residual application of international law to the EEC 'subsystem' seems mainly to be based on *Berührungsangst*: on the fear that the more highly integrated EEC legal order could otherwise be 'infected' by the more "primitive" international law processes of autodetermination and self-help."

Table 4.1 WTO-style and EU-style trigger strategies

	Possibility of inter-state trade sanctions	Event triggering punishment	Punishment	Suitable for which conditions?
WTO-style "suspension of equivalent concessions" trade regime	Always "on the table" in dispute settlement, even if not being applied at any point in time	Member state "measures" inconsistent with trade agreement obligations	Loss of "equivalent" trading opportunities through trade sanctions	Capable of organizing international trade in a wide range of economic conditions and between a wide variety of state regime types
EU-style "self-contained" trade regime	"Off the table" in dispute settlement, even if states found to have failed to fulfill treaty obligations	Member state unilaterally restricts the automatic application of treaty obligations as law in domestic courts	Reversion to WTO-style trading relationship, including the ever-present possibility of trade sanctions	Stable without reversion to WTO-style trade relationship only when political and economic conditions give policy-makers incentives to sufficiently consistently prioritize fulfilling their trade obligations

that is possible, even in well-institutionalized international trade organizations. We will therefore consider three different incentives—over and above high rates of interdependence, which is the essential starting point, and separate from the legal networking emphasized by previous scholarship—for state policy-makers to accept the development of a highly intrusive form of treaty-based dispute settlement.

We will focus first on variation in the type of international economic interaction, before turning to the discussion of the role of domestic institutions in trade politics.

Discussions of the role of trade retaliation and trade remedies in international politics tend to start their analysis by emphasizing that these mechanisms are needed because state policy-makers will intermittently face fierce and unmanageable resistance from interest groups opposed to trade liberalization. As Kucik and Reinhardt explain, in their analysis of the politics of anti-dumping, "governments face domestic political pressure to violate the terms of agreements. The magnitude of these pressures varies over time and may be so intense that upholding costly international commitments is temporarily impossible" (Kucik and Reinhardt 2008: 480; also e.g. Zimmermann 2011: 389, 405). Such a terse introduction to the politics of "escape" correctly captures the importance of interest group activity to trade politics, and the pervasive presence of these sorts of pressures in a great many international trading relationships.

However, not all demanding international trade relationships generate the same degree of domestic political pressure to violate the terms of international trade agreements. Ricardian approaches to explaining international trade expect states to produce very different goods (capital-intensive or labor-intensive, for example, depending on their endowments), in different industry sectors, and exchange them internationally according to comparative advantage. To take Ricardo's own famous example, state A sells wine to state B, while state B sells cloth to state A. In this type of trading relationship, states trade standardized products distinguished on the basis of cost, and there is no reason to expect that states will both import and export similar goods. This type of exchange brings overall gains to the trading states, but at the same time involves a great deal of adjustment by organized interests involved in the import-competing production of goods and services. After all, production in whole sectors of the economy is expected to be replaced by foreign goods, so the efficiency gains are associated with significant reallocation of resources within the trading states.

However, this "textbook" approach to understanding gains from trade does not describe the only sort of important international trading relationship. In contrast to the "*inter*-industry" trade described earlier, trade between nations can also be "*intra*-industry trade." Intra-industry trade consists of the exchange of relatively similar products between states, for example where state A sells cars to state B, while state B also sells cars to state A. The logic behind this sort of exchange is that consumers gain from the availability of relatively similar goods that are nonetheless differentiated by reason of quality or brand, while the larger market generated by trade openness allows firms to produce more specialized products given economies of scale in production (Balassa 1966). Trade of this sort predominantly takes place between advanced industrialized economies, because their relative factor endowments tend to be similar.

Importantly, the domestic political implications of intra-industry trade differ from those of inter-industry trade. In intra-industry trade, increased exchange can take place without substantial changes in the structure of production in the various participating states. Thus, the costs of adjustment in terms of unemployment may be less if the expanding and contracting activities take place within the same industry (that is, different product lines in the same sector) than if they take place in different industries. Labor may be more mobile within industries than between them, for example, because skills acquired in a contracting firm may be more easily applied in an expanding firm of the same industry.[19] In discussions of intra-industry trade, this political economy effect is referred to as the "smooth adjustment hypothesis."[20]

[19] Brülhart and Elliott 1998: 229.

[20] Balassa 1966: 472. But see Gilligan 1997b and Kono 2009 for doubts that the reduced adjustment costs of intra-industry trade necessarily facilitate trade liberalization.

Furthermore, in the presence of intra-industry trade, industry sectors are no longer so clearly "import-competing" or "export-orientated," but rather a bit of both, so that lobbying for or against trade openness no longer takes place at the sector level, but instead by different firms with diverse interests within the same sector, potentially giving national policy-makers more room for maneuver.[21]

The role of intra-industry trade in facilitating adjustment has certainly been recognized in the study of trade politics. It has been employed as an explanation for contemporary global trade integration and for the sometimes limited effect of political tensions on trade relations (Milner 1999; Davis and Meunier 2011).[22] Variation in intra-industry trade has been used to explain the success of the postwar GATT system, as well as the difficulties of trade liberalization in the late nineteenth century (Ruggie 1982; Verdier 1998). A higher level of intra-industry trade has also been used to explain the relatively easier trading relationship between the US and the EU, on the one hand, and the US and Japan on the other, where intra-industry trade is less important (Gawande and Hansen 1999). Prominent accounts of European integration by Milward and Moravcsik have emphasized the special role of intra-industry trade in postwar Europe (Milward et al. 1992: 124; Moravcsik 1998: 88, 235, 495).[23] Finally, recent work on variation in obligations and escape mechanisms in preferential trade agreements has argued that increases in intra-industry trade may incentivize states to accept more rigid forms of agreement (Baccini et al. 2012; Kucik 2012). Accordingly, we can expect that policy-makers in an international trade regime will face less unmanageable resistance from interest groups (of the sort that necessitates common forms of enforcement and escape mechanisms) as intra-industry trade becomes more important.

We will now turn to the relative responsiveness of domestic institutions to narrow interests that may demand defection from treaty obligations.[24] Of course, the political institution that is most obviously responsive to the interests of a narrow group is an undemocratic form of government—but here we are particularly interested in variation in *democratic* political institutions' responsiveness to narrow economic interests.

Political institutions in democracies vary in the degree to which they orientate policy-makers toward responding to the interests of small or large groups. To be sure, the debate about the impact of diverse political institutions on policy-makers' behaviors is one of the oldest in political science, reflecting very different conceptions of how the general interest can be made to prevail

[21] I am grateful to Marius Brülhart for a discussion on the topic of intra-industry trade.

[22] Even outside trade politics: Peterson and Thies 2013.

[23] See also Busch and Milner 1993 on demand for regionalism driven by demand for scale economies associated with intra-industry trade.

[24] An earlier version of the argument developed in this section appeared in Phelan 2011a.

in democratic political action, and addressing a huge variety of political institutions—diverse electoral and legislative systems, and non-majoritarian institutions such as courts, bureaucracies, and central banks—in many possible permutations.

Recent scholarship by Gerring and Thacker, however, has convincingly built on old debates on constitutional design to group diverse aspects of democratic decision-making procedures together to the degree that they contribute to producing democratic political institutions that combine "inclusiveness" with "authority."[25] Inclusiveness refers to the degree to which policy-makers have incentives to broadly reach out to ideas, interests, and identities in their society (Gerring and Thacker 2008: 15). Authority refers to centralized mechanisms for effectively reaching (and implementing) agreement on common policies (Gerring and Thacker 2008: 15). These two properties of certain forms of democratic governance may appear to be contradictory, but they can be reconciled by understanding that inclusiveness and authority can be combined in political institutions that draw *diverse* strands of society toward a *single* locus of authoritative decision-making (Gerring and Thacker 2008: 20). Such institutions attempt, in Gerring and Thacker's account, to accommodate both John Stuart Mill's argument for the true representativeness of proportional representation electoral systems and Walter Bagehot's admiration for the "English Constitution" as one where "ultimate power upon all questions is in the hands of the same persons."[26]

Gerring and Thacker describe democratic institutions that combine inclusiveness and authority as "centripetal" (Gerring and Thacker 2008: 9, following James Bryce).[27] They argue that such institutions tend to produce generally better policy outcomes through the incentives they create for "strong" party organizations, the mediation of conflicts by bringing elite actors together, and better policy coordination across issues. By contrast, more decentralized forms of inclusiveness that focus on diffusing power tend to fragment political parties, exacerbate conflicts by providing incentives for political actors to defect on agreements, and reduce the degree of cross-issue policy coordination, with adverse consequences on policy outcomes.

By this logic, three important features of constitutional design may contribute, separately and jointly, to the production of inclusive and centralized democratic authority. These are parliamentary rather than separation-of-powers

[25] Gerring and Thacker 2008, acknowledging, of course, a *very* wide range of scholarship contributing to this question.

[26] Mill 1993 [1865]; Bagehot 2001 [1867]: 154; Gerring and Thacker 2008: 10, 13.

[27] The logic of the argument is similar to that of the "encompassing group" in collective action theory, where, for example, "encompassing" labor federations, both inclusive of a wide range of diverse groups of workers and possessing the ability to authoritatively coordinate policy across issues, are understood to have incentives to accept costs on particular constituents where this

("presidential") legislative institutions, proportional representation rather than first-past-the-post electoral systems, and unitary rather than federal state structures (Gerring and Thacker 2008). Parliamentary legislative arrangements encourage the production of national public goods, because separation-of-powers systems offer more opportunities for powerful narrow interests to influence issue-specific policy outcomes than cohesive cabinet government (e.g. Cox 1987; Bagehot 2001 [1867]). Proportional representation electoral systems, particularly closed-list PR systems, encourage the production of national public goods because single-member districts and candidate-centered systems tend to privilege localist tendencies in general and a relatively small group of constituencies and their interests in particular (e.g. Mill 1993 [1865]; Carey and Shugart 1995; Heitshusen et al. 2005). Finally, unitary state structures encourage the production of national public goods, because federal structures tend to provide incentives for territorially fragmented policy-making and outcomes (e.g. Pressman and Wildavsky 1973; Wibbels 2000). By this logic, policy-makers in states that possess parliamentary legislative systems, proportional electoral rules, and unitary state structures are more likely to pursue relatively coherent, broadly targeted general-interest policies than policy-makers in states that possess separation-of-powers legislative systems, first-past-the-post electoral systems, and federal state structures.[28]

These institutional arrangements have been associated with relatively greater policy-maker responsiveness to broad constituencies over a wide range of outcomes in human and economic development (Gerring and Thacker 2008: esp. 101–142). Recent research also supports the claim that variation in trade policy behavior, in particular, can be explained by variation in such political institutions. For example: democratic GATT/WTO members whose politicians are elected by majoritarian rules and/or in single-member districts are more likely to violate GATT/WTO agreements than those elected via proportional electoral rules or multi-member districts (Rickard 2010; Davis 2012); centralized political parties with stable linkages to large groups of the electorate are more likely to choose freer trade policies (Hankla 2006); and delegation of trade policy authority to presidents—that is, politicians with a national constituency—in Latin America is significantly related to trade liberalization (Nielson 2003). These examples are but the latest contributions to a scholarship relating trade policy to the design of domestic political

will provide benefits for the labor movement as a whole (Olson 1982; Jankowski 1988; see also Phelan 2011a).

[28] A great deal of trade-related public policy, including the creation of both tariff and non-tariff barriers, is, of course, delegated to specialized ministries and administrative agencies, rather than the national political institutions whose features are measured by these variables. However, the national political structure provides powerful incentives for the behavior of such subordinate political institutions.

institutions that has been developing for some time (e.g. Katzenstein 1985; Bailey et al. 1987; Rogowski 1987; Bueno de Mesquita et al. 2003).

The other domestic institution widely associated with international trade openness is social insurance. Unemployment insurance and similar policies may reduce interest-group opposition to trade openness by weakening the link between imports and income loss. As Cameron explained, "[G]overnments in nations with open economies have sought to counter the effects of external dependence by expanding their control over the domestic economy through the "nationalization" of a large portion of consumption" (Cameron 1978: 1253; see also e.g. Bates et al. 1991; Rodrik 1998; Adserà and Boix 2002; Huberman 2012). Even governments dominated by right-wing parties have increased public spending, measured by government revenues as a proportion of GDP, as trade openness has increased. The expansion of the public sector is therefore an alternative to employing mercantilist or protectionist trading strategies, particularly for small, open economies (Cameron 1978: 1260).

On a similar logic, the US-led open international economy after 1945 has been influentially characterized as "embedded liberalism," because a liberalizing international market coexisted with national demands for "social protection," encompassing both national welfare states and GATT "safeguards, exemptions, exceptions, and restrictions" that protected domestic social policies (Ruggie 1982: 388, 396). Its adjustment costs were acceptable because of its many authorized exemptions, because of the growth of intra-industry trade, and because of the looseness of international legal obligations (Ruggie 1982: 412). The GATT was therefore a system of multilateral obligations compatible with domestic stability (Ruggie 1982: 397, 399, 411).

This scholarship on the role of domestic institutions in trade politics rarely focuses on understanding the politics or law of European integration.[29] The scholarship on parliamentarism, electoral systems, and so on, tends to concentrate on explaining variation in trade policy behavior within the global trading system. Discussions of trade liberalization and social insurance are overwhelmingly linked to the GATT and WTO.[30] The literature on international trade and the varieties of domestic political and social insurance institutions has therefore yet to engage fully with the distinctive legal institutionalization of the market between the EU member states.

[29] See, however, Gillingham 2003 for an emphasis on embedded liberalism in the early years of European integration, and Kleine "Making Cooperation Work: Informal Governance in the EU and Beyond" (forthcoming from Cornell University Press), for an emphasis on embedded responsiveness to domestic pressures in the member states within the EU's policy-making process.

[30] Certainly, Ruggie's discussion of the necessarily limited role of international law, and the need for safeguards and escape clauses, does not address trade between the European member states. Rodrik mentions Spain's increasing spending on social transfers as it opened its economy in joining the EU, and Adserà and Boix emphasize that the Spanish case also involved a move away from autocracy to democracy (Rodrik 1998: 1028–1029; Adserà and Boix 2002: 252–253).

Building on this literature on domestic political institutions and on social insurance mechanisms, we can expect that policy-makers in an international trade regime will face less uncontrollable resistance from interest groups, of the sort that necessitates common forms of enforcement and escape mechanisms, as their domestic political institutions combine greater inclusiveness and centralized authority, and as domestic social insurance systems reduce the income loss associated with trade liberalization. Together with the manageable adjustment costs associated with intra-industry trade, we can expect that these two domestic institutional arrangements will allow state policy-makers to routinely accept a wider range of more intrusive and less predictable policy adjustments derived from international dispute settlement outcomes, and, therefore, to permit open access by non-state actors such as firms and citizens to binding international dispute settlement mechanisms.

Testing the Argument for the EU Case

So far, this chapter has developed a theoretical explanation for the existence of an international trade regime that does not use inter-state countermeasures and trade remedy instruments, but instead relies on the automatic application of treaty obligations and dispute settlement outcomes as law in the domestic courts of the participating states. Before we test this explanation for the EU as a self-contained regime, however, two preliminary issues should be acknowledged.

First, the EU member states share characteristics that existing scholarship suggests should make them more likely to make active use of legalized dispute settlement. Within the WTO, democratic states are more likely to be complainants as well as targets of complaints in dispute settlement (Busch 2000; Davis and Bermeo 2009; Sattler and Bernauer 2011). Furthermore, states that share alliances with other states are more likely to activate the WTO's legal dispute settlement process against each other ("friends can fight with friends") (Davis 2012: 92–100, 93). Just as democratic allies, therefore, the EU member states already have a relatively strong propensity for legalized international dispute adjudication in trade politics.

Second, right from the beginnings of the European Economic Community in 1958, the inter-state bargain underlying the Treaty of Rome, and its subsequent development over the 1960s, involved the establishment and common financing of a Common Agricultural Policy (CAP) designed to increase farmers' incomes through high prices, subsidies, and protection from global markets.[31] The CAP nonetheless authorized considerable national autonomy

[31] On the role of the CAP in inter-state bargains, see Milward et al. 1992 and Moravcsik 1998;

within the context of a European agricultural system, allowing policy-makers in the individual member states to politically manage their agricultural markets.[32] The CAP therefore greatly alleviated the political pressures of agricultural trade liberalization within the EU. By contrast, there is no equivalent to the CAP's common financing and price management of agriculture in the global trade regime. Certainly, agricultural products are frequent beneficiaries of GATT trade remedies such as anti-dumping, and some of the best-known trade disputes involve agricultural trade restrictions and subsidies, including the WTO dispute on beef produced with hormones, and the NAFTA/WTO dispute on Mexican taxes on soft drinks sweetened by anything other than cane sugar (Reynolds and Su 2005; Devereaux et al. 2006: 31–96; Kuijper 2008: 703ff). By coordinating their agricultural subsidies with each other, but still authorizing a significant degree of national policy-making autonomy in that issue-area, the EU has significantly reduced one form of pressure for the use of inter-state retaliation and trade remedies between the EU member states.

The CAP by itself, however, does not fully explain the EU's ability to reject the use of inter-state trade retaliation mechanisms and trade remedies. While trade in agricultural products is well represented in international trade disputes and among beneficiaries of trade remedy instruments, it is far from the only industry associated with trade disputes or the use of trade remedy instruments. Furthermore, even if the CAP largely protects EU farmers from global markets, and authorizes many national measures of protection, farmers in particular nations nonetheless remain subject to competition from intra-EU trade, with olive oil producers in France, for example, competing with producers in Italy, Spain, and Portugal. Indeed, many important European court cases on trade barriers have involved disputes over intra-EU agricultural trade.[33] Therefore, even after acknowledging the importance of the CAP, the EU's rejection of inter-state countermeasures, and trade remedies, very much remains to be explained.

The argument developed here is that the variety of economic exchange, intra-industry trade, and the type of domestic institutions within a group of trading states—particularly inclusive and authoritative political

on the agreements to set common, and high, prices for agricultural commodities that launched the CAP in the 1960s, see Knudsen 2009.

[32] On national policy-making autonomy within the CAP in various forms, including "monetary compensatory amounts" that many saw as similar in effect to intra-EU customs duties, see e.g. Kravis 1963: 331; Rieger 2000: 189; Knudsen 2009: 259–260, 280–282, 316.

[33] E.g. Cases 42/82 *Commission v. France* [1983] ECR 1013, C-265/95 *Commission v. France* [1997] ECR I-6959.

decision-making structures and generous social insurance systems—give national policy-makers incentives to behave in ways compatible with their membership of a trade regime that rejects the use of inter-state countermeasures and trade remedy instruments. This argument has observable implications for the sort of international economic exchange and domestic institutions we should expect to find in states participating in such a self-contained trade regime. Applied to the EU case, the argument could be rejected if comparative analysis demonstrated that the EU member states have not been distinctively involved in intra-industry trade or lack the sort of domestic institutions that allow policy-makers to better prioritize a general interest in binding trade commitments even when these impose a stream of market and policy adjustments on organized narrow interests.

Intra-industry trade can be measured in various different ways. A common approach is to measure the degree to which industry sectors overlap between imports and exports, with more "overlap" indicating more intra-industry trade. Such measures are, of course, sensitive to the levels of sectoral aggregation chosen—that is, whether particular industries are narrowly or broadly defined. Some scholarship also separates out "horizontal" intra-industry trade ("HIIT"), where truly "like products" are exchanged, from "vertical" intra-industry trade ("VIIT"), where component parts are exchanged for finished products within the same industry, as international specialization across forms of production according to comparative advantage may be taking place more intensively in the latter case, with relatively increased adjustment costs and different forms of political lobbying.[34]

Given the various ways in which intra-industry trade has been measured, the best approach to testing the argument presented may be to report a variety of measures of intra-industry trade in the EU, demonstrating both its growth over time and its distinction by comparison with the composition of trade in other prominent international trade regimes or regions (Ecochard et al. 2006; Brülhart 2009; Kang 2011). Even where the measures used by different authors are not directly comparable with each other, the broad picture is clear. Table 4.2 shows both the increase in intra-industry trade, particularly horizontal intra-industry trade, in Europe over time from the 1960s to the 1990s, and the divergence in the composition of trade within (Western) Europe compared to trade within many other regions of the world.[35] EU trade with the rest of the world, by contrast, is much more likely to be inter-industry trade: Ecochard et al.'s analysis found that while only 38 percent of

[34] "Vertical" intra-industry trade is indicated where the export and import unit values diverge substantially (e.g. Ecochard et al. 2006: 37–38).

[35] Only the NAFTANorth American region can match or exceed the level of intra-industry trade found between the EU member states.

Table 4.2 Intra-industry trade

	Brülhart 2009	Ecochard et al. 2006	Kang 2011
European Union/ Western Europe	1962: 17% 1975: 29% 1990: 43% 2006: 45%	2002: HIIT: 27% VIIT: 35%	1970: 60% 1990: 70% 2005: 73% 2004: HIIT: 44% VIIT: 45%
NAFTA/ North America	1962: 11% 1975: 33% 1990: 52% 2006: 55%	2002: HIIT: 19% VIIT: 34%	
Mercosur/Andean Community/ South America	1962: 0% 1975: 3% 1990: 8% 2006: 18%	2002: HIIT: 13% VIIT: 14%	
ASEAN/ Northeast Asia/ East Asia	1962: 1% 1975: 6% 1990: 22% 2006: 27%	2002: HIIT: 5% VIIT: 19%	1970: 22% 1990: 40% 2005: 51% 2004: HIIT: 10% VIIT: 61%

HIIT: Horizontal intra-industry trade; VIIT: Vertical intra-industry trade.

Sources: Brülhart 2009: 432 for intra-industry trade within World Bank-defined regions, "Western Europe," "North America," "South America," and "Northeast Asia," 1962–2006, 5-digit level of industry aggregation. Ecochard et al. 2006: 43, 46, 49, 52 for share of "two-way horizontal" and "two-way vertical" trade in intra-zone trade of the EU25, NAFTA, "East Asia" of ten states, and Mercosur in 2002, 6-digit level of industry aggregation. Note that Ecochard et al. 2006 find a considerable amount of intra-industry trade in the NAFTA region that cannot be classified as either HIIT or VIIT for lack of data. Kang 2011: 143 for regional average intra-industry trade within Europe and East Asia 1970–2005, 118 manufacturing industries, "Europe" made up of 15 countries, "East Asia" of 13, 4-digit level of industry aggregation. Kang 2011: 151, 153 for share of VIIT and HIIT in intra-regional trade in Europe and East Asia in 2004, "Europe" made up of 15 countries, "East Asia" of 10, 28 manufacturing industries, 3-digit level of industry aggregation. See also Moravcsik 1998: 495.

intra-EU trade was "one way" inter-industry trade in 2002, over 75 percent of EU trade with the rest of the world was "one way" inter-industry trade (Ecochard et al. 2006: 43).

This cross-temporal and cross-regional data is supported by a large literature on the role of intra-industry trade in European economic integration. Indeed, early discussions of the intra-industry trade phenomenon appear to have been inspired by observations of the relatively smooth adjustment of European industries to the creation of the Common Market in the 1960s (Balassa 1966). Repeated analyses over differing time periods—the 1970s, the 1980s, after the "1992 single market" program—have shown how intra-industry trade as a whole has continued to grow within the EU, as well as how intra-industry trade within the EU has expanded even in narrowly defined industries (Greenaway and Hine 1991; Brülhart and Elliott 1998; Brülhart and Hine 1998; Brülhart 2009; including trade in services, e.g. Nowak et al. 2012). To be sure, the member states vary significantly in how much they engage in intra-industry or inter-industry trade, and the level of intra-industry trade varies by industry as well. But Pelkmans' succinct assessment—that "the bulk of intra-EU trade" has become intra-industry trade—captures this essential and distinctive feature of economic exchange between the EU member states (Pelkmans 2006: 111). The argument that the EU's ability to reject the use of inter-state countermeasures and trade remedies is facilitated by the high level of intra-industry trade between the EU member states has therefore not been falsified by this empirical analysis.

We will now turn to the discussion of domestic institutions, which requires measures of institutions across states, both inside and outside the EU. The domestic institutions of states will be measured here using three different criteria. First, the degree to which states possess inclusive and authoritative democratic political institutions will be measured by scoring states' institutions on the criteria of parliamentary or separation-of-powers legislative systems, unitary or federal state structures, and closed-list proportional representation or first-past-the-post electoral systems. For cross-national data on these institutions, we rely on Gerring and Thacker's dataset, which scores more than 100 states on these three criteria, producing an aggregate score for the inclusiveness and authority of their democratic political systems over a period of many decades.[36] This score ranges from zero to two for each component, for a total score that ranges from zero to six. A presidential, federal, first-past-the-post electoral system state such as the United States in 2000 is scored at the minimum of score of zero, while a state with parliamentary, unitary, and closed-list PR political institutions such as Denmark is scored at the maximum six. Malaysia, with a federalized state structure, a parliamentary legislature, and first-past-the-post electoral system, possesses political institutions that score at 2.5. Of course, some important trading states, including China, remain under non-democratic forms of government, and are scored distinctly as such.

Second, we will measure the size of states' public sectors by government revenues as a percentage of GDP. As previous scholarship has discussed, there are a variety of different datasets that make this information available, each with their particular limitations. The World Bank's World Development Indicators (WDI) covers the greatest number of countries, but only from the mid-1970s onwards, and only provides data on revenues of the central government (that is, excluding revenues raised by state and local governments).[37] The OECD provides data on a smaller number of countries, but the OECD's measure of revenue as a percentage of GDP has the benefit of including *all*

[36] These data are available at the "Macrodata Guide," run by the Norwegian Social Science Data Services, <http://www.nsd.uib.no/macrodataguide/set.html?id=2&sub=1>.

[37] The World Development Indicators provide two measures of government revenue as a proportion of GDP. We will use the measure "revenue as % of GDP," which includes social insurance contributions, rather than "tax as % of GDP," which excludes social insurance contributions.

government revenues (central, state, and local), and runs from 1965 in the case of OECD countries (or from 1991 in the case of selected non-OECD Latin American countries).[38] Government revenue as a percentage of GDP varies widely across states and time, with Mexico's revenues amounting to 20.9 percent of its 2008 GDP on the OECD measures, while the Belgian government's revenues on the same measure were 44.1 percent of GDP in the same year.

Government revenue as a percentage of GDP is the best single measure of the size of the public sector, and the measure that best connects this study with previous discussions of the relationship of trade and the size of government. Because variation in social insurance systems is so relevant to the argument being developed here, we will also include a measure of variation in unemployment compensation. Here we will rely on Vroman and Brusentsev's data on the relative generosity of national unemployment compensation systems in the 2000s (Vroman and Brusentsev 2009).[39] Unemployment compensation here refers to unemployment insurance or (means-tested) unemployment assistance programs that offer periodic payments to qualifying workers who are unemployed but able and available for work. It does not include general welfare programs, "workfare" schemes, or rights accrued from past employment, such as severance payments.

The relative generosity of such unemployment compensation systems varies in two important ways: the "recipiency rate" and the "replacement rate." The "recipiency rate" refers to the number of people in receipt of unemployment compensation payments as a proportion of the number of those unemployed and looking for work, as estimated by labor force surveys.[40] Unemployment compensation programs vary considerably in the degree to which those unemployed and looking for work in fact receive payments. In 2007 in Argentina, for example, the recipiency rate was 0.07, so that the number of those receiving unemployment compensation was only 7 percent of the number of those unemployed and looking for work, while in Germany in 2005 the equivalent recipiency rate was 0.93. The "wage replacement rate" measures the proportion of the economy-wide average weekly wage that is paid as unemployment compensation, and this too varies considerably from state to state (Vroman

[38] Cameron 1978 uses OECD data on revenues as a percentage of GDP for a limited number of developed countries. Rodrik 1998 uses Penn World Tables and World Bank data on government consumption as a percentage of GDP for a much larger group of developed and developing countries. Adserà and Boix 2002 use revenue as a percentage of GDP using UN and OECD data for 65 countries, of which 22 are OECD countries.

[39] Dr Vroman generously provided the detailed country data underlying this chapter. Vroman and Brusentsev's approach to measuring variation in unemployment compensation systems in comparative context was first set out in Vroman and Brusentsev 2005.

[40] More strictly, the criteria relate to people unemployed, available for work, able to work, and actively looking for work (Vroman and Brusentsev 2009: 3). Note that some countries only conduct labor force surveys for limited populations, e.g. the urban workforce.

and Brusentsev 2005: 59–60).[41] In Portugal in 2005, the replacement rate for unemployment compensation was 0.44, or 44 percent of the average weekly wage, while in Estonia in 2007, it was only 0.06, or 6 percent of the average weekly wage.

It is important to note that levels of coverage and the replacement rates do not always increase in tandem: Argentina's low recipiency rate of 0.07, for example, goes with a relatively high replacement rate of 0.41, while the United Kingdom's unemployment compensation program in 2007 had a relatively low replacement rate of 0.10 but a high recipiency rate of 0.45. Vroman and Brusentsev also report an aggregated measure of the "generosity" of unemployment compensation systems, multiplying the recipiency rate by the replacement rate. In 2007, for example, in Uruguay, the unemployment compensation recipiency rate was 0.13 and the replacement rate was 0.12, producing an overall generosity score of 0.02.

To be sure, there are limitations to this measure. Vroman and Brusentsev's measures of unemployment insurance cover a period from the 2000s onwards when the European legal order was already well established.[42] Focusing on unemployment compensation systems may also neglect other important aspects of welfare state systems. Some countries may offer limited unemployment insurance but generous universal healthcare and pension benefits, for example. Even in relation to protecting workers from the risks of unemployment, policies other than unemployment compensation, such as severance payment requirements or temporary jobs programs, can also be important.[43] Nonetheless, measures of the relative generosity of unemployment compensation schemes offer an unrivalled cross-national measure of a vitally important aspect of national welfare states.

We will start by looking at the scores of the domestic institutions in the EU member states, before comparing these to scores for members of the WTO.

As far as their political institutions are concerned, all twenty-seven member states of the EU are democratic regimes. Furthermore, their political decision-making is based on institutions that encourage both inclusiveness and authoritative central decision-making. Twenty-two EU member states obtain the maximum score of 2 (full parliamentarism) on the "parliamentarism—presidentialism" measure. Seventeen EU member states obtain the maximum score of 2 (full closed-list PR) on the "closed-list PR—first-past-the-post" measure.

[41] Because low-skilled workers frequently disproportionately face unemployment, unemployment compensation programs may replace a relatively higher proportion of their previous wage income, depending on program design.

[42] Their work on unemployment compensation in the 1990s demonstrates similar distinctiveness of policies in the EU member states compared to non-EU members, albeit for a smaller sample of countries (Vroman and Brusentsev 2005).

[43] Furthermore, agricultural workers, self-employed workers, and workers in informal sectors are frequently excluded from participation in unemployment compensation programs.

Seventeen EU member states obtain the maximum score of 2 (unitary states) on the "unitary—federal" measure. The mean score for overall inclusiveness and authority for the current twenty-seven member states is 4.8 out of a possible 6. The lowest score for an EU member state is recorded for France, at 2.5. All the other EU member states score at 4 or higher. The EU's membership is largely made up of parliamentary regimes governing unitary states where politicians are selected by proportional representation electoral systems, and thus by states whose political institutions tend to combine both relative inclusiveness and centralized authority.

As for the size of the public sectors in the EU member states, we have OECD data on revenues as a percentage of GDP for twenty-one of these states in 2008. The proportion of government revenue as a percentage of GDP varied from 29.1 percent in Ireland to 48.1 percent in Denmark, with a mean of 37.7 percent. OECD historical data shows that the original six members of the then European Economic Community obtained a mean of 30.5 percent of GDP in revenues in 1965, around the time of the ECJ's landmark decisions *Van Gend en Loos* and *Commission v. Luxembourg and Belgium*. The lowest government revenue take of an EEC country in 1965 was Italy's, at 25.5 percent of GDP. All twenty-seven EU member states except Luxembourg, Malta, and Cyprus (Greek) have WDI scores for government revenue as a percentage of GDP, and, using 2000 data, the twenty-four then members and members-to-be (that is, including the states of Central and Eastern Europe then in the process of accession to the EU) together had a mean government revenue of 35.2 percent of GDP. The country with the lowest proportion of revenue to GDP in 2000 on the WDI measure was then member-to-be Romania at 25.8 percent, while the lowest score of any then EU member state in 2000 was Germany at 30.6 percent.

As for unemployment insurance, Vroman and Brusentsev provide data on unemployment compensation schemes for twenty-four of these twenty-seven states in the early 2000s.[44] All have unemployment compensation systems. Of those twenty-four programs, the mean recipiency rate is 0.66, the mean replacement rate is 0.34, and the mean overall generosity score is 0.25. To be sure, there is considerable diversity between one state's unemployment compensation program and the next. The Netherlands provides unemployment compensation to more than 100 percent of the number of those unemployed and looking for work according to labor force surveys,

[44] Vroman and Brusentsev do not include data for Cyprus (Greek), Malta, or Luxembourg. According to the OECD's Benefits Directory, the unemployment benefit net replacement rate (single person, earning the average wage) for the initial phase of unemployment was 30% in Malta and 84% in Luxembourg during 2010. The equivalent figure for Cyprus is only available for 2007, when it was 58%: data downloaded from <http://www.oecd.org/els/benefitsandwagesstatistics.htm> on (August 2012). The OECD's estimates of unemployment compensation replacement rates may not be calculated on the same basis as Vroman and Brusentsev 2009, but are suggestive of relatively generous welfare states.

and Dutch unemployment compensation replaces 45 percent of the average weekly wage. At the other end, Slovakia's unemployment compensation scheme extends only to 9 percent of the number unemployed and looking for work, and provides a replacement rate of 31 percent of the average weekly wage. Data on domestic political and social institutions in the EU member states is set out in Table 4.3.

Now, for comparative purposes we will look at the domestic institutions of the states that make up the global trading regime, the WTO, as the archetypal trade regime based on the logic of inter-state retaliation and countermeasures, as well as whose members also make extensive use of trade remedies. There are currently (as of 2012) 155 members of the WTO, which of course includes the 27 EU member states as well as the EU itself.[45] We will focus our analysis on the political institutions of WTO members that are *not* also EU member states. Even excluding these, there of course remain a great many more members of the WTO than there are member states of the EU. In order to present information about WTO members in an accessible manner, we will focus on the leading participants in the WTO's dispute settlement system—that is, the twenty-one WTO members (other than EU member states) who have been "respondents"—we might say, targets—in complaints using the WTO's dispute settlement system at least three times since that system was established in 1995.[46] We will refer to these states as the "WTO-21," and data on these states' domestic political and social institutions is set out in Table 4.4.

The WTO is comprised of a mix of democratic and non-democratic states. Among non-democracies in today's WTO, we can include China, Hong Kong (a distinct member of the WTO), Egypt, Saudi Arabia, Oman, Kuwait, Jordan, and Vietnam.[47] The domestic institutions of three significant democratic members of the WTO—Brazil, Nigeria, and the United States—each have an *overall* score for inclusiveness and authority of *zero*. Even among the WTO-21, the diversity is considerable: the group includes two non-democracies, as well as democratic states with both highly inclusive and authoritative (Turkey) and highly fragmented (United States, India) political institutions. The mean level of aggregate inclusiveness and authority of the political institutions of the democratic members of the WTO-21 is 2.5. The WTO is obviously an international regime that organizes trade relations between states with a great variety of domestic institutions.

[45] Russia is in the process of becoming the 156th member in July 2012.

[46] World Trade Organization, Annual Report 2012, pages 86–87, Table 1: WTO members involved in disputes, 1995 to 2011. The WTO-21 states are listed in Table 4.4.

[47] This is not an exhaustive list. Some of these non-democratic members of the WTO joined very recently, and indeed after 2000: China joined the WTO in 2001, Saudi Arabia in 2005, Vietnam in 2007.

Table 4.3 Domestic institutions in EU member states

	POLITICAL INSTITUTIONS				PUBLIC SPENDING						UNEMPLOYMENT COMPENSATION			
	Unitary or federal?	Parl. or president?	Closed list PR?	Aggregate inclusiv-eness?	OECD revenue % GDP			WDI revenue % GDP			Year of data	Recipiency rate	Replacement rate	Generosity index
	0–2	0–2	0–2	0–6	1965	1995	2008	1980	2000	2010				
Austria	1.5	2.0	2.0	5.5	33.9	41.4	42.8	34.6	37.7	36.6	2005	1.09	0.30	0.33
Belgium	0.5	2.0	2.0	4.5	31.1	43.5	44.1	43.7	42.8	40.7	2005	1.28	0.56	0.72
Bulgaria	2.0	2.0	2.0	6.0					32.9	32.4	2005	0.23	0.30	0.07
Cyprus (Greek)	2.0	0.0	2.0	4.0						39.7				
Czech Republic	1.5	2.0	2.0	5.5		37.6	36.0		30.5	29.6	2005	0.34	0.24	0.08
Denmark	2.0	2.0	2.0	6.0	30.0	48.8	48.1	35.5	36.2	39.8	2007	0.76	0.50	0.38
Estonia	2.0	2.0	2.0	6.0		36.3	31.7		31.0	36.8	2007	0.19	0.06	0.01
Finland	2.0	2.0	0.0	4.0	30.4	45.7	42.9	27.2	40.9	38.8	2006	1.23	0.29	0.36
France	1.5	1.0	0.0	2.5	34.2	42.9	43.5	39.6	42.9	40.9	2007	0.97	0.49	0.47
Germany	0.0	2.0	2.0	4.0	31.6	37.2	36.4		30.6	29.7	2005	0.93	0.35	0.33
Greece	2.0	2.0	0.0	4.0	17.8	28.9	31.5	30.7	41.9	37.1	2004	0.28	0.26	0.07
Hungary	2.0	2.0	1.0	5.0		41.5	40.1	[53.4]	38.6	41.3	2005	0.37	0.36	0.13
Ireland	2.0	2.0	0.0	4.0	24.9	32.5	29.1	34.7	33.0	31.0	2005	1.50	0.28	0.42
Italy	1.0	2.0	1.0	4.0	25.5	40.1	43.3	31.2	36.9	38.4	2005	0.63	0.21	0.13

Latvia	2.0	2.0	2.0	6.0					26.1	25.0	2005	0.38	0.25	0.10
Lithuania	2.0	1.0	1.0	4.0					25.9	27.4	2005	0.12	0.25	0.03
Luxembourg	2.0	2.0	0.0	4.0	27.7	37.1	35.5							
Malta	2.0	2.0	0.0	4.0										
Netherlands	1.5	2.0	2.0	5.5	32.8	41.5	39.1	49.4	40.7	40.9	2005	1.67	0.45	0.75
Poland	1.5	1.0	2.0	4.5		36.2	34.2		31.5	30.0	2005	0.13	0.28	0.04
Portugal	2.0	2.0	2.0	6.0	15.9	29.3	32.5	26.2	34.6	34.5	2005	1.09	0.44	0.49
Romania	1.5	1.0	2.0	4.5				[45.3]	25.8	30.9	2004	0.42	0.37	0.16
Slovakia	2.0	2.0	2.0	6.0		40.3	29.4		35.3	28.6	2005	0.09	0.31	0.03
Slovenia	2.0	2.0	2.0	6.0		39.0	37.0		38.9	36.9	2005	0.25	0.50	0.12
Spain	1.0	2.0	2.0	5.0	14.7	32.1	33.3	24.2	31.1	24.9	2005	0.65	0.43	0.28
Sweden	2.0	2.0	2.0	6.0	33.3	47.5	46.4	35.0	42.2	34.8	2005	0.81	0.64	0.52
United Kingdom	2.0	2.0	0.0	4.0	30.4	34.0	35.7	35.2	37.1	36.0	2007	0.45	0.10	0.05

Table 4.4 Domestic institutions in 21 members of the World Trade Organization

	POLITICAL INSTITUTIONS				PUBLIC SPENDING						UNEMPLOYMENT COMPENSATION			
	Unitary or federal?	Parl. or president?	Closed list PR?	Aggregate inclusiv-eness?	OECD revenue % GDP			WDI revenue % GDP			Year of data	Recipiency rate	Replacement rate	Generosity index
	0–2	0–2	0–2	0–6	1965	1995	2008	1980	2000	2010				
Argentina	0.5	0.0	2.0	2.5		20.3	30.7	15.6	14.1		2007	0.07	0.41	0.03
Australia	0.0	2.0	0.0	2.0	20.4	28.1	27.0	21.7	25.8	24.6	2006	0.83	0.24	0.20
Brazil	0.0	0.0	0.0	0.0		26.8	33.6	22.6	19.9	23.1	2007	0.24	0.50	0.12
Canada	1.0	2.0	0.0	3.0	25.7	35.6	32.2	18.7	20.9	17.2	2007	0.47	0.41	0.19
Chile	1.0	0.0	0.0	1.0		19.0	22.5	32.0	21.6	22.0	2007	0.22	0.28	0.06
China				Non-dem					7.1	11.9	2003	0.52	0.14	0.07
Colombia	0.5	0.0	0.0	0.5		13.2	17.9	12.0	15.1	18.2	No UC	0.00	0.00	0.00
Dominican Republic	1.0	0.0	1.0	2.0		10.6	15.0	14.2		14.5	No UC	0.00	0.00	0.00
Ecuador	1.5	0.0	0.0	1.5				12.8			No data	-	-	-
Egypt				Non-dem				45.5	24.3	24.8	2001	0.00	0.02	0.00
India	0.0	2.0	0.0	2.0				11.7	11.9	11.4	No UC	0.00	0.00	0.00
Indonesia	2.0	1.0	2.0	5.0				21.3	18.3	15.1	No UC	0.00	0.00	0.00

Japan	1.5	2.0	1.0	4.5	18.0	26.8	28.3	11.6			2007	0.22	0.37	0.08
Korea, South	2.0	1.0	1.0	4.0		20.0	26.5	17.4	22.3	22.7	2006	0.28	0.30	0.08
Mexico	0.0	0.0	1.0	1.0		15.2	20.9	15.1	14.7		No UC	0.00	0.00	0.00
Peru	1.5	0.0	2.0	3.5		15.4	17.8	17.1	17.4	18.5	No UC	0.00	0.00	0.00
Philippines	0.5	0.0	0.0	0.5				14.0	14.2	13.4	No UC	0.00	0.00	0.00
South Africa	0.5	2.0	2.0	4.5				23.5	26.3	28.4	2006	0.02	0.23	0.01
Thailand	1.5	2.0	1.0	4.5				14.3	19.5	20.3	2007	0.10	0.36	0.03
Turkey	2.0	2.0	2.0	6.0	10.6	16.8	24.2	18.1		24.4	2003	0.02	0.21	0.00
United States	0.0	0.0	0.0	0.0	24.7	27.8	26.3	20.2	20.1	16.9	2007	0.31	0.33	0.10

Data sources for Tables 4.3 and 4.4: *Political Institutions*: Gerring and Thacker 2008, country scores for year 2000. The "Aggregate Inclusiveness" column refers to political institutions' score aggregating both inclusiveness and authority: see discussion in text *Public Spending:* OECD, Revenue Statistics 1965–2010, page 19, Table A. OECD, Revenue Statistics in Latin America, 1990–2009, page 18, Table A. World Development Indicators, World Bank. Figures for 2010 and 2000 drawn from 2012 World Development Indicators, Table 4.12. Figures for 1980 drawn from 1997 World Development Indicators, Table 4.16. Hungary and Romania were both "communist" economies in 1980. *Unemployment Compensation:* data generously provided by Dr Wayne Vroman of the Urban Institute, Vroman and Brusentsev 2005, 2009. Note that in the case of China, the estimate of unemployment compensation recipiency and replacement rates relates only to urban areas, a workforce of some 200 millions.

As for the size of the public sectors in these WTO members, the WDI provides scores for government revenue as a percentage of GDP for a large number of these states in 2000. The mean level of government revenue as a percentage of GDP ranges widely across WTO-21 members—from 7.1 percent in China to 11.9 percent in India to 18.3 percent in Indonesia to 20.9 percent in Canada to 26.3 percent in South Africa. The mean government revenue in 2000 as a percentage of GDP for the WTO-21 states on the WDI measures (where data is available) was 18.4 percent. The mean government revenue on the OECD measure for 2008, covering a more limited group of thirteen of the WTO-21 states, was 24.8 percent.

These states also vary widely in their unemployment compensation mechanisms. Indeed, many WTO members do not offer unemployment compensation for their citizens. Among the WTO-21, seven members do not provide their citizens with compensation for unemployment, while the mean recipiency rate for unemployment compensation is 0.17, the mean replacement rate is 0.19, and the mean overall generosity of unemployment compensation is 0.05.[48] As can be seen, therefore, the WTO organizes international trade between states which often do not provide much financial compensation to their citizens who are unemployed and looking for work.

This comparison of the domestic institutions of the EU member states and those of WTO members (that are not member states of the EU) clearly reveals what is often overlooked in discussions of the European legal order: the diversity of domestic institutional structures in the EU member states is comparatively restricted. These states overwhelmingly possess relatively inclusive and authoritative forms of democratic governance: parliamentary structures, unitary rather than federal forms of governance, and closed-list proportional electoral systems. A high proportion of their GDP goes to government revenues and has done so consistently since the 1960s.

While comparisons of the level of welfare benefits *within* the EU reveal real and important differences between one member state and another, comparison of the EU member states with the *non-EU* member states of the WTO demonstrates that liberal unemployment compensation is a distinguishing characteristic of the EU member states. Not only do all the EU member states possess unemployment compensation programs, their programs are relatively

[48] The calculation of these means exclude Ecuador, which Vroman and Brusentsev characterize as providing an unemployment compensation program but where data on recipiency and replacement rates are not available. An alternative cross-national categorization of unemployment compensation systems produces similar results. Vodopivec's 2004 World Bank study indicates that, of the WTO-21, the Dominican Republic, India, Indonesia, Mexico, the Philippines, and Thailand did not provide unemployment compensation. Three other members of the WTO-21—Ecuador, Peru, and Colombia—provided unemployment compensation not in the form of periodic unemployment insurance or (means-tested) unemployment assistance, but unemployment insurance savings accounts that produce a lump-sum payment (Vodopivec 2004: 53–58).

generous, and they tend to cover a larger proportion of those unemployed and looking for work than unemployment compensation systems outside the EU. The differences between the EU-27 and the WTO-21 states on the inclusiveness and authority of their political decision-making institutions and the generosity of their unemployment compensation is summarized in Figure 4.1, which demonstrates the distinctive domestic institutions of the EU member states (clustered in the top and, often, toward the right of the chart) compared to the much greater variety in domestic institutions among WTO members.

The argument developed in this book—that the EU's ability to reject the use of inter-state countermeasures and trade remedy instruments relies on the domestic institutions of the EU member states—has therefore not been falsified by this empirical analysis. The EU member states possess distinctive domestic institutions that wider scholarship suggests allow policy-makers to prioritize their general interest in binding trade commitments, even when these impose a stream of market and policy adjustments on organized narrow interests.

The WTO is revealed, by contrast, as a "come one, come all" trade regime that manages global trade despite the massive diversity of the domestic political and social institutions among its participating members. Its membership includes important trading states such as China, the United States, Mexico, Brazil, and India that possess either undemocratic, or democratic but highly fragmented, policy-making institutions. As for unemployment compensation, a great many WTO member states do not provide their citizens with unemployment compensation systems, let alone generous ones (Vroman and Brusentsev 2005; Vroman and Brusentsev 2009).[49] On the logic of the argument developed here, it therefore seems unlikely that the WTO will soon be able to forego relying on the logic of trade sanctions and trade remedies, no matter how beneficial this might be for global trade.

The EU has often been compared to other regional trade agreements, so it may also help to compare the EU member states with states participating in highly institutionalized trade agreements among three groups of relatively democratic states outside Europe. Perhaps the three most prominent are the North American Free Trade Area (NAFTA), a free trade agreement between the United States, Canada, and Mexico that came into force in 1994; the Common Market of the South, better known as "Mercosur," a free trade agreement, described as a customs union with ambitions to form a common external tariff, between Argentina, Brazil, Paraguay, and Uruguay founded in 1991; and, newly prominent in the light of recent comparisons with the

[49] More than two billion people live in state jurisdictions that fail to provide unemployment compensation mechanisms (Vroman and Brusentsev 2006, Table 2).

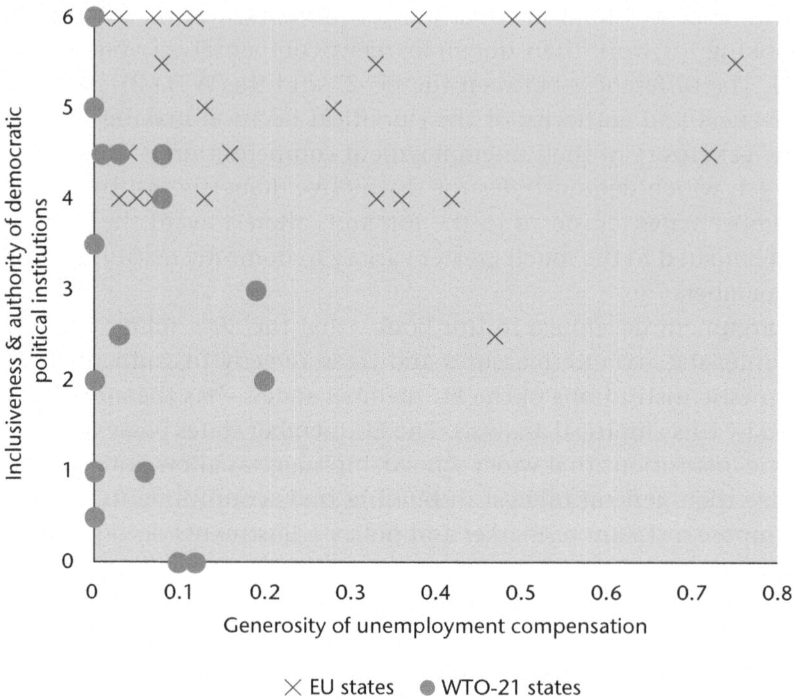

Figure 4.1 EU-27 and WTO-21 member state comparison, political institutions *c.* 2000, and unemployment compensation, *c.* 2007

The Y-axis measures the combination of inclusiveness and authority of national democratic political institutions, *c.* 2000, on a scale from zero to six. A unitary state with a parliamentary form of government and a closed-list proportional electoral system is scored at six, while a federal state with a separation-of-powers government and a "first-past-the-post" electoral system is scored at zero.

The X-axis measures the overall generosity of national unemployment compensation systems, *c.* 2007, on a scale from zero to one. A state where the number of people in receipt of unemployment compensation payments was equal to the number of those unemployed and looking for work according to labor force surveys, and where unemployment compensation payments were set at 100% of the economy-wide average weekly wage, would obtain a score of "one." See further discussion in text.

Data sources: *Political Institutions*: Gerring and Thacker 2008. *Unemployment Compensation:* data generously provided by Dr Wayne Vroman of the Urban Institute, Vroman and Brusentsev 2005, 2009. EU-27 excludes Cyprus (Greek), Luxembourg, Malta, for lack of data. WTO-21 excludes Ecuador (unemployment compensation exists but no data on generosity), as well as China and Egypt as non-democratic states.

India and the Dominican Republic share a political institutions' score of 2.0, with an unemployment compensation generosity score of zero. Colombia and the Philippines share a political institutions score of 0.5, with an unemployment compensation generosity score of zero.

EU, the Andean Community of Nations (Andean Community), described as a customs union with ambitions to form a common external tariff, between Bolivia, Colombia, Ecuador, and Peru, that was originally created in 1969 as the Andean Pact, but was renamed and reorganized as the Andean Community in 1996. Unlike the EU, each of these regional trade regimes uses inter-state retaliation mechanisms, and provides its member states with common forms of trade remedy to manage intra-regional trade, albeit sometimes subject to greater restrictions than trade remedies within the WTO.[50]

Table 4.5 summarizes the essential features of these three regional trade and integration agreements together with measures for the domestic institutions of their members, adding measures of domestic institutions in the EU member states, in 1965 and 2008, as well as, for wider comparative purposes, the institutions of the WTO-21 states. Each of these regional trade agreements includes states with highly fragmented forms of democratic institutions. Each also includes states with a relatively low rate of government revenue as a percentage of GDP by European standards. Finally, each includes states that provide their citizens with no compensation for spells of unemployment.[51] The domestic institutions of each of these regimes are therefore clearly distinct from the domestic institutions of today's EU—and even from the domestic institutions of the six founding members of the Treaty of Rome in 1965.

This outcome is consistent with conditions elaborated here for a demanding international trade regime to reject the use of inter-state countermeasures and trade remedies. To be sure, there may be other reasons why these integration regimes have limited their legalization of obligations to retaliation-based dispute settlement systems—in the NAFTA case, the relative size of the US economy in the North American region may be so large that US policy-makers have few incentives to accept a more intrusive regional treaty regime, while it has been argued that the lack of a "jurist advocacy

[50] NAFTA: Enforcement by Retaliation: Hufbauer et al. 2003: 29; Jensen 2011: 46–47. Trade Remedies: Hufbauer et al. 2003: 44 and ft 107; Vega-Canovas 1997; Blonigen 2005. Mercosur: Enforcement by Retaliation: Art 31 of the Protocol of Olivos; Vinuesa 2005: 440. Trade Remedies: Inter-American Development Bank 2011: 115–116. Note that Mercosur does not permit the use of safeguards between its member states (Teh et al. 2007: 22, 72; Voon 2010: 646). Andean Community: Enforcement by Retaliation: Art 27 of the Treaty Creating the Court of Justice of the Cartagena Agreement(Amended by the Cochabamba Protocol), Secretaría General 2006: 26. Trade Remedies: Inter-American Development Bank 2002 16–17, 103–105; Inter-American Development Bank 2005 62–63.

[51] Again, an alternative cross-national categorization of unemployment compensation systems produces similar results. Vodopivec's 2004 World Bank study indicates that Mexico (in NAFTA), Paraguay (in Mercosur), and Bolivia (in the Andean Community) did not provide unemployment compensation. The other three members of the Andean Community—Ecuador, Peru, and Colombia—provided unemployment compensation not in the form of periodic unemployment insurance or (means-tested) unemployment assistance, but unemployment insurance savings accounts that produce a lump-sum payment (Vodopivec 2004: 53–58).

Table 4.5 Regional integration agreements compared, *c.* 2008

	Domestic institutions of participating states					Rules of RIA/escape mechanisms			
	Aggregate inclusiveness and authority 2000		Rev'ue as % of GDP, OECD, 2008		Members without unemployment compensation *c.* 2007	AD	CVD	SG	Trade sanctions enforcement
	Mean	*Range*	Mean	*Range*	?	?	?	?	?
EU-27	4.8	2.5–6.0	37.7	29.1–48.1	None	No	No	No	No
EU-6 (in 1965)	4.2	2.5–5.5	30.5	25.5–34.2	None	No*	No*	No*	No
NAFTA	1.3	0–3.0	26.5	20.9–32.2	1 of 3	**Yes**	**Yes**	**Yes**	**Yes**
Mercosur	2.0	0–3.5	28.8	22.0–33.6	1 of 4	**Yes**	**Yes**	No	**Yes**
Andean Comm'ty	2.3	0.5–3.5	17.9	17.8–17.9	3 of 4	**Yes**	**Yes**	**Yes**	**Yes**
WTO-21	2.5, excluding Non-dems	0–6, excluding Non-dems	24.8	15.0–33.6	7 of 21	**Yes**	**Yes**	**Yes**	**Yes**

Escape mechanisms included are anti-dumping (AD), countervailing duties (CVD), and industry safeguards (SGs).

* The then EEC in 1965 did not provide anti-dumping, countervailing duties, or industry safeguard mechanisms in the manner of the GATT system, but it did provide a variety of safeguard and other escape mechanisms particularly for the transitional period, including in Art 226 a variant of an industry safeguard mechanism under the supervision of the European Commission. See discussion in Chapter 3.

Data sources: *Political Institutions*: Gerring and Thacker 2008. *Public Spending:* OECD, Revenue Statistics 1965–2010, page 19, Table A. OECD, Revenue Statistics in Latin America, 1990–2009, page 18, Table A. Revenue as % of GDP on OECD measure, 2008, only includes states for which data are available. For the EU-27, it includes 21 states per Table 4.3. For the WTO-21, it includes 13 states per Table 4.4. For Mercosur, it includes Argentina, Brazil, Uruguay, and excludes Paraguay. For the Andean Community, it includes Peru and Colombia, and excludes Ecuador and Bolivia. *Unemployment Compensation:* data generously provided by Dr Wayne Vroman of the Urban Institute, Vroman and Brusentsev 2005, 2009. Unemployment compensation in the EU-6 in 1965: see Vroman and Brusentsev 2005: 53. States that do not provide unemployment compensation systems—NAFTA: Mexico, Mercosur: Paraguay, Andean Community: Bolivia, Colombia, Peru. *Rules of RIA/ Escape Mechanisms*: Teh et al. 2007, Voon 2010 for trade remedies. See also ft 50 in this chapter.

network" was important in preventing the successful "constitutionalization" of the Andean Community (Helfer and Alter 2008–2009: 927). At the same time, however, it is clear that national policy-makers in these regional trade agreements do not have the same incentives and tools as policy-makers in the EU member states to manage the domestic politics of demanding and intrusive forms of international trade integration. The incentive-based argument for circumstances under which state policy-makers might choose to behave in ways that would produce a demanding international trade regime that does not use inter-state countermeasures or trade remedies is therefore consistent with the observations for the EU case, in comparison with both the global trading regime and other regional integration agreements between democratic states.

Assessment and Conclusion

This chapter has built on, and responded to, the criticisms of previous scholarship emphasized in earlier chapters. It has argued that states can substitute the application of treaty obligations as law in domestic courts for the use of inter-state countermeasures, and that such substitution, combined with open access by private parties to dispute settlement processes and the foregoing of common forms of *ex post* escape mechanisms, is possible where interdependent state policy-makers are able to accept a more frequent, more intrusive, less predictable, and more binding stream of trade-related policy adjustments. Inclusive and authoritative democratic political institutions, generous social insurance systems, and a high level of intra-industry trade give policy-makers incentives to do so. This argument was then tested by examining the characteristic features of intra-European trade and of domestic institutions of the EU member states in comparative context, and demonstrating that the same combination of economic relationships and national social and political institutions are not present among the members of other institutionalized trade agreements, both global and regional. The exceptional legalization of intra-European trade therefore takes place within the context of a regional grouping of states whose trading relationships and domestic institutions also occupy extreme positions on several dimensions—economic interdependence, the exchange of similar products, democratic constitutional design, and social welfare institutions—from which we should expect a distinctive willingness to accept binding forms of trade-related dispute settlement on the part of any group of state policy-makers.

The multicausal argument advanced here involves a much larger "cast of characters" than many previous explanations of development of the European legal order. Instead of a close concentration on, for example, judicial dialogues between the ECJ and national courts on the role of human rights protections, here the transnational network of lawyers and courts is joined by other actors, institutions, and altered interactions, including interest groups and compensation mechanisms, state policy-makers and parliamentary systems, the adjustments associated with trade—particularly intra-industry trade—and, above all, the change in states' relationships *with each other* enabled by the use of domestic courts to enforce treaty obligations. By including these previously neglected aspects of politics and economics in postwar Europe, this chapter has provided a description of incentives for policy-makers in the member states to behave in ways that would produce the international trading environment required by the rights and doctrines created by the development of the European legal order.

Chapter 5 builds on this analysis to offer an alternative narrative of the development of the European legal order from the Treaty of Rome onwards.

5

Explaining the EU's Rejection of Inter-State Trade Sanctions and Trade Remedies

Narrative

The preceding chapter offered an explanation of the EU's rejection of inter-state trade sanctions and trade remedies in the social science tradition: identifying a "variation to be explained" defined in generalizable, "no-proper-names" terms, developing an incentive-based explanation for variation in the behavior of important actors across cases, and testing the observable implications of the explanation offered against empirical data. Such an approach is the dominant one in contemporary political science.

Existing explanations of the development of the European legal order have, however, often been put forward as *narratives*. Weiler's account of *The Transformation of Europe*, published in the Yale Law Journal in 1991, is perhaps the most influential of these (Weiler 1991). Not only is it a leading interpretation in its own right, it has also provided a foundation for prominent political science scholarship in the "neofunctionalist" and "historical institutionalist" traditions (Burley [Slaughter] and Mattli 1993; Alter 2001). Weiler's narrative of the creation of the European legal order emphasizes (as do those works of political science) the interactions between national and European judges, the limited controls that national governments possess over their domestic courts, and the vital role of the protection of fundamental rights in inducing the national courts to cooperate with the development of European law.

The explanation advanced here may therefore benefit from being communicated in a similar narrative form. Accordingly, this chapter sets out to describe the development of the European legal order from the Treaty of Rome through the mid-1990s, the same time period addressed by Weiler,

Burley and Mattli, and others. This narrative supplements the analysis of legal doctrines and court behaviors with a fresh weight on the variables, outcomes, and causal mechanisms emphasized by the argument developed in chapter 4. To be sure, like any concise overarching account, it does not attempt to describe or explain every aspect of the European legal order's development, or every moment where the European legal order failed to live up to its promise, particularly in its early decades. Rather, it seeks to identify the European legal order's essential features in comparative context, as well as the political and economic environment that facilitated its distinctive evolution.

The European Legal Order Rejects Inter-State Retaliation

In 1947, more than twenty nations in Geneva signed the General Agreement on Tariffs and Trade, seeking "substantial reduction of tariffs and other trade barriers...on a reciprocal and mutually advantageous basis."[1] Thus was born the GATT, the treaty that still provides the central element of today's global trade regime known since 1995 as the World Trade Organization (WTO). Its founding members were highly diverse, including Brazil, Ceylon (now Sri Lanka), India, South Africa, and the United States, as well as many European countries, and that diversity continues to the present day, as the WTO's current membership of more than one hundred and fifty nations includes dictatorships as well as democracies of all varieties. The GATT provided a set of rules and institutions that facilitated bargaining between its members to reduce barriers to trade as well as dispute settlement procedures (which became much more developed over time) by which a GATT member could complain that another member's policies were inconsistent with their GATT obligations.

One persistent feature of the GATT (now WTO) trade system is the extensive range of "trade remedies," "safety valves," "flexibility provisions," or "escape clauses" built into the institution.[2] So policy-makers in GATT member nations can (and often do) impose anti-dumping duties, countervailing duties, and "safeguard" tariffs to protect particular industries facing severe adjustments. They have the right to permanently and unilaterally withdraw from previously assumed GATT obligations. Above all, and in line with the use of inter-state countermeasures as an age-old enforcement mechanism in general international law, GATT members may selectively default on their

[1] Preamble to the General Agreement on Tariffs and Trade.
[2] See discussion pp. 85–87 in this volume.

GATT obligations at the risk of other GATT members imposing retaliatory trade restrictions in response.

Thus, GATT members have a wide range of *ex post* instruments provided by the treaty by which they may unilaterally choose to impose new trade barriers to protect firms and workers facing the adjustment costs of trade openness. To be sure, decisions by policy-makers to use escape mechanisms such as anti-dumping duties, or to behave in ways that may prompt other states to threaten the use of trade retaliation, are highly disruptive to firms and individuals engaged in international economic exchange between GATT members. An EU–US dispute in the WTO over trade distortions arising from US tax law, for example, eventually led to retaliatory trade sanctions being imposed by the EU in 2004 on imports of fork-lift trucks, fish-hooks, refrigerators, toilet paper, and jewelry from the US, and this sort of outcome is always a possibility in such dispute settlement systems (Ahearn 2005; Bown 2009: 131). Because of such disruptions, almost nobody has a good word to say about the use of inter-state countermeasures such as trade retaliation to enforce trade regime obligations, except to emphasize that a mechanism is needed to restrain states' incentives to defect on demanding international obligations, and that retaliatory actions by other states can—unlike fines or decisions of international tribunals—be imposed on defaulting states even if the latter do not cooperate in accepting them (e.g. Lawrence 2003: 81; Brewster 2011: 147). However, such escape-and-retaliation mechanisms are widely understood to be vital if state policy-makers are to accept the risks and uncertainties of greater trade openness, particularly in democratic states where future economic and political developments cannot be clearly foreseen, because policy-makers cannot be expected to sufficiently consistently prioritize compliance with their trade obligations (Downs and Rocke 1995; Rosendorff and Milner 2001). The GATT treaty therefore set out a range of enforcement and escape mechanisms that were subsequently incorporated, with various modifications, into many subsequent bilateral and multilateral trade agreements (Teh et al. 2007; Chase et al. 2013).[3]

In 1958, by contrast, an ambitious international trade and integration regime—the European Economic Community—was established by treaty between six states—France, the Federal Republic of Germany, Italy, Belgium, the Netherlands, and Luxembourg, whose trade interdependence was rapidly increasing (Mongelli et al. 2005).[4] It lowered barriers to trade between its member states and established a customs union vis-à-vis the outside world.

[3] Retaliation in NAFTA: MacDonald 2009; Alexander and Soukup 2010. Retaliation in the Andean Community: Secretaría General 2006: 26.

[4] The European Economic Community built on, and developed, the institutions established by the European Coal and Steel Community, established in 1952.

The legal provisions of this treaty regime were unusual: it provided that "Regulations" agreed by the member states were required to be automatically applied in the national legal orders without any need for national legislation to ratify or transpose these obligations; it provided for a tribunal—the European Court of Justice (ECJ)—with compulsory and exclusive competence to adjudicate on disputes under the Treaty; it provided for an international bureaucracy, the European Commission, which, as well as being involved in making policy proposals, could take legal action against member states before the ECJ; and it provided a process—likely of limited original purpose—by which national courts, faced with a question about the validity or interpretation of a treaty obligation or European regulation, could make a "preliminary reference" to the ECJ to obtain an answer.[5] Among its other notable features, the Treaty provided that new obligations could be imposed on the member states through the Council of Ministers (representing the governments of the participating states) without unanimous agreement, while it failed to provide the member states with the most common forms of "escape mechanisms" or "trade remedies" (anti-dumping, countervailing, and industry safeguard provisions) so prevalent in other trade regimes.[6]

From these founding elements the European Economic Community—renamed the European Union in 1994—created a remarkable treaty-based legal system, breaking with several longstanding features of general international law. National courts came to play a vital role in the enforcement of European law, allowing private parties to use domestic litigation to vindicate rights granted to them by the European treaties or rules agreed by the European institutions. Furthermore, the national courts came to see their role as enforcing European law obligations as these were interpreted (and re-interpreted) by the ECJ itself, not least through the use of the "preliminary reference" procedure that served as a link between national and European courts. European law therefore benefited from a decentralized enforcement mechanism involving a multitude of private parties, whereas the dispute settlement arrangements of the GATT/WTO, and many other international trade regimes, even as these became more institutionalized over the years, persisted in reserving rights to initiate dispute resolution procedures to state

[5] Art 189 of the Treaty of Rome provided that "Regulations shall have a general application. They shall be binding in every respect and directly applicable in each Member State." Art 177 of the Treaty of Rome provided for the "preliminary ruling" procedure, including the national courts' role in requesting rulings.

[6] Art 148 of the Treaty of Rome set out a weighted voting procedure for the member states to agree new policy outputs, however unanimity agreement was the de facto rule until the mid-1980s. Various escape mechanisms, such as the safeguard mechanism contained in Art 226 of the Treaty of Rome, were provided for by the Treaty of Rome, but their use required authorization by the European institutions, and their availability was substantially restricted after the early transitional period. For the distinction between the EU and more common forms of international trade regime as regards trade remedies, see Voon 2010.

policy-makers (who tend to be cautious about making use of them) and continued to back their international legal obligations with the threat of inter-state retaliation through trade sanctions. The impact of European law on the member states, and on organized groups inside them, is therefore much more frequent, more intrusive, less predictable, and more binding than the legal obligations deriving from other trade and integration treaties.

What can explain these profound differences between the European legal order, as it came to be called, and the enforcement mechanisms of other well-institutionalized international trade regimes? One place to start is with the ECJ's willingness—often at the urging of the European Commission—to make a series of bold decisions affecting both European law's enforcement mechanisms and its substantive obligations. The ECJ expanded the role of national courts in the enforcement of European obligations, and refused to allow the development of unilateral "escape mechanisms" within the Common Market, creating a highly binding system of treaty obligation (Gormley 1985; Weiler 1991). On substance, the Court developed a demanding, and relatively consistently applied, approach to scrutinizing national policies so as to remove barriers to trade.[7] These decisions were encouraged, and propagandized, by elite networks of pro-integrationist lawyers, both transnational and in the various member states, even as national courts were sometimes reluctant to accept them (Burley [Slaughter] and Mattli 1993; Alter 2001; Alter 2009b; Vauchez 2010; Davies 2012). However, as we will see, the wider economic and political environment in postwar Europe also provided important reasons for state policy-makers to acquiesce in the path-breaking decisions of the ECJ (Garrett and Weingast 1993: 196). We will begin by discussing some of the ECJ's most important judgments, before turning to the wider context.

Three decisions of the ECJ in the early 1960s—*Van Gend en Loos, Costa v. ENEL*, and *Commission v. Luxembourg and Belgium*—can be seen as creating the potential for dispute resolution under the Treaty of Rome to develop in a qualitatively different manner from general international law, what many refer to as the "constitutionalization" of the European treaties. *Van Gend en Loos* claimed that certain provisions of the Treaty of Rome could be automatically enforced as law by private parties through national courts even in the absence of any national law granting them that right.[8] This became known as the "direct effect" of European law. *Costa* claimed that where national and

[7] E.g. Case 8/74 *Procureur du Roi v. Dassonville* [1974] ECR 837; Gormley 1985. Certainly, the ECJ was willing to make judgments that conflicted with positions advanced by even the most powerful member states (as argued in Mattli and Slaughter 1995). That does not rule out the possibility that certain variations in ECJ decision-making might be explained in part by variations in positions taken by member states on cases before the ECJ (e.g. Larsson and Naurin 2013).

[8] Case 26/62 *Van Gend en Loos v. Nederlandse Administratie der Belastingen* [1963] ECR 1.

European legal obligations unavoidably conflicted, national courts were to apply the European, not the national, legal obligation, even when the national obligation was more recently enacted.[9] This became known as the "supremacy" of European law. The third decision, often unjustifiably neglected, *Commission v. Luxembourg and Belgium*, claimed that it was impermissible for the member states to make use of their widely acknowledged international law right to employ "self-help" reprisals or countermeasures—that is, to withhold their performance of treaty obligations because they had been injured by the failure of another party to perform its own obligations.[10] *Luxembourg and Belgium* is the rock on which the EU's rejection of inter-state retaliation is founded, pointing the EU's development toward what Simma would later describe as a "self-contained regime" (Simma 1985).[11] The importance of this decision cannot be overemphasized, because "self-help" countermeasures of this sort are a vital enforcement mechanism in general international law, and in many international trade regimes, but *not* in the European legal order (Simma 1981: 29–30; Weiler 1985: 294; Weiler 1991: 2422, ft 42; Gradoni and Tanzi 2008).[12] "Nothing is more alien to Community law," the ECJ's Advocate General Léger would later claim, "than the idea of a measure of retaliation or *reciprocity* proper to classical public international law."[13]

These ECJ decisions were important, but also built in part on pre-existing features of the Treaty of Rome and national law. The direct effect of provisions of the Treaty of Rome granted these treaty provisions a somewhat similar status to that already granted to directly applicable Regulations enacted by the Treaty institutions: it was an extension and development of a novelty, not the complete novelty it would have been if European Regulations had not already enjoyed direct applicability. The supremacy of treaty obligations required by the ECJ involved an obligation to apply European obligations when they conflicted with subsequent, "later-in-time" domestic legislation. That obligation could in practice be met by national courts, without too much disturbance to national constitutional

[9] Case 6/64 *Costa v. ENEL* [1964] ECR 585.

[10] Cases 90 and 91/63 *Commission v. Luxembourg and Belgium* [1964] ECR 625.

[11] Simma defines a self-contained regime as a treaty regime that rejects the use of inter-state countermeasures as a mechanism to enforce its obligations.

[12] An arbitral tribunal addressing a dispute between the United States and France in 1978 described the role of inter-state countermeasures in public international law as follows: "If a situation arises which, in one State's view, results in the violation of an international legal obligation by another State, the first State is entitled... to affirm its rights through 'countermeasures'," *France v. United States*, 18 RIAA 417. On the importance of such tit-for-tat retaliation strategies between states in organizing cooperation under anarchy in international relations, see Axelrod 1984; Keohane 1984; and, more recently, Bown 2009. On the significance of the ECJ's break with such enforcement mechanisms, see Phelan 2013b.

[13] Advocate General's Opinion in Case C-5/94 *The Queen v. Ministry of Agriculture ex parte Hedley Lomas* [1996] ECR I-2553. Emphasis in the original.

rules, by adopting the assumption that, unless the national legislature clearly and explicitly revealed its contrary intention, their national parliaments wished to fulfill their European obligations, and resolving conflicts with subsequent national law in favor of European law obligations on that basis.[14] Even the remarkable decision in *Luxembourg and Belgium* can be normalized in part by recognizing that other international legal regimes reject the use of inter-state countermeasures *before a certain point* (before consultations have occurred, before dispute resolution has completed, before the end of a reasonable period of time within which states can alter their policies, and so on).[15]

The three decisions were profoundly inter-connected. The rejection of inter-state countermeasures in *Luxembourg and Belgium* should be understood as premised on the acceptance by the member states of the automatic application of European obligations as law in national courts as required by *Van Gend en Loos* and the Treaty of Rome itself.[16] The supremacy doctrine protects that application of European obligations by domestic courts by ensuring that it is not disrupted by conflicts between European and national legal obligations. The direct effect and supremacy doctrines together, therefore, together with the link to treaty-based dispute settlement through the preliminary reference procedure, create the environment for the secure domestic application of treaty obligations that, as the Canadian decision to make the dispute settlement outcomes of the NAFTA "Side Agreements" enforceable by Canadian courts demonstrates, allows states to give up the right to use inter-state trade retaliation to enforce treaty obligations (Government of Canada 1993: 5; Grayson 1995: 143; Mayer 1998: 166; Cameron and Tomlin 2000: 198; Phelan 2013d).[17] That is to say, inter-state countermeasures are "off the table," so long as EU obligations benefitting from the European law doctrines of direct effect/direct applicability are applied as law in the national legal orders, while any deliberate action by a member state's policy-makers to oust the enforcement of European obligations by its domestic courts would raise the possibility of a "fall back," or reversion, to the use of common forms of

[14] Such methods of resolving conflicts between treaty obligations and subsequently enacted national legislation were already practiced, to varying degrees, in some of the member states' national legal orders (Phelan 2010).

[15] In Art 3.7 of WTO's Dispute Settlement Understanding, suspension of concessions is described as a "last resort."

[16] Legal scholarship on the *Van Gend* and *Costa* decisions does not address their relationship with *Commission v. Luxembourg and Belgium*, and vice versa. From follow-up research as the book goes to press, however, we can see that the logical connection between these three ECJ judgments was acknowledged in a little-known short paper published in 1965 by influential ECJ Judge Robert Lecourt (Lecourt 1965).

[17] For a discussion on how granting direct effect to WTO obligations, or to decisions resulting from the WTO's dispute settlement process, in the EU might remove the possible application of trade retaliation against the EU by other WTO members, see e.g. Eeckhout 2011: 331–381.

trade retaliation as enforcement mechanisms between the European states (Simma 1985). And so, under the influence of these three foundational decisions, the stream of ambitious obligations that flowed from membership of the European Economic Community, now European Union, came to be enforced by national courts, rather than the reprisals or countermeasures employed by general international law, as well as by prominent trade regimes, above all the GATT/WTO.

Of course, these three ECJ decisions did not immediately create the highly binding European legal order as we know it today.[18] It was quietly built by iterated interactions between state policy-makers and the European and national courts (Weiler 1994). Politically, the growing use of the European institutions by the member states to manage joint policy-making in an ever-wider range of policy-areas was of course vital, as state policy-makers created, and then—particularly in the 1980s—intensified, the intra-European market.[19] On the legal side, the development of the European legal order was marked by the readier use of European law rights and obligations, and the increasing use of the preliminary reference procedure, in the resolution of disputes involving private parties, as well as by the partial accommodation of the ECJ's "constitutional" doctrines by the national courts (Stone Sweet and Brunell 1998b; European Court of Justice 2012: 115–118).

Two of those doctrinal claims have always been recognized as the most salient. The first is the obligation on national courts to apply European obligations even when they conflict with a subsequent, "later-in-time," national statute. Without such a "supremacy" rule, the application of European obligations by national courts, and thus the ability of the EU to break with enforcement through threats of inter-state retaliation, would constantly be put at risk by the stream of new legislative enactments in the various member states. The ECJ consistently emphasized that the national courts had a direct European law obligation to apply the European obligation under these circumstances. However, national courts in several, at least, of the member states have by contrast insisted on deriving their recognition of the supremacy and

[18] Indeed, the scope and meaning of these decisions only became clear as they were supplemented and reinforced by later ECJ judgments. Even a short list must include Case 11/70 *Internationale Handelsgesellschaft v. Einfuhr- und Vorratsstelle für Getreide* [1970] ECR 1125, Case 34/73 *Variola v. Amministrazione Italiana delle Finanze* [1973] ECR 981, Case 41/74 *Van Duyn v. Home Office* [1974] ECR 1337, Case 106/77 *Amministrazione delle Finanze dello Stato v. Simmenthal* [1978] ECR 629, Cases 142 and 143/80 *Amministrazione delle Finanze dello Stato v. Essevi* [1980] ECR 1413, Case C-38/89 *Ministère Public v. Guy Blanguernon* [1990] ECR I-83, and Case C-6 and 9/90 *Francovich v. Italy* [1991] ECR I-5357.

[19] The use of the European institutions by the member states encompassed both treaty revisions and the use of the procedure contained in Art 235 of the Treaty of Rome, allowing the Community to take action to further the objectives of the Community through unanimous agreement by the member states even if the Treaty has not provided the necessary powers (Weiler 1991).

direct effect of European law from *national* legal sources.[20] So, the German Constitutional Court claimed that European law was applied in Germany because the *Bundestag* so requires, while the Court of Appeals in England and Wales justified its application of European law because the House of Commons continued to require it to do so.[21] That is to say, national courts have resolved conflicts in favor of European law not on the basis of the latter's inherent supremacy, but rather on the basis that they could claim that their national parliaments, or national constitutions, supported this approach to resolving these conflicts.[22] In important ways, therefore, national courts' acknowledgment of the supremacy of European law over national legislation often remained ambiguous and incomplete (Phelan 2010).

The second salient doctrinal claim is the obligation on national courts to apply European obligations even where they conflicted with protections of fundamental rights specified by national constitutions. Applying the European obligation in such circumstances might appear to involve a violation of constitutionally protected human rights, and possibly create a grave difficulty for national judges (Alter 2001: 72, and throughout the German case study; Weiler 1991: 2417–2418; Davies 2012). This scenario certainly generated considerable scholarly debate, eventually connecting with both the ECJ's claim that it would *itself* protect against the possibility that European law violated fundamental rights, and with the 1977 joint declaration by the European institutions of their respect for the European Convention of Human Rights.[23]

[20] Hogan and Whelan's description of the way in which the Irish and British legal orders accommodate the claims of European law is relevant to many member states: "[A]dherents [to the EEC] such as Ireland... acknowledge expressly or by implication... many of the incidents of the constitutional claims of the Communities as expressed by the European Court of Justice... They do not really accept the basis of these claims, however, in so far as these [national] constitutional provisions and other acts of reception are still considered, as a matter of national law, to be necessary for Community constitutional law to have force in the national legal order and legal "space."... From the national constitutional perspective, Community law can be superior, directly applicable, and so on, only if the national constitution permits this in some *nationally effective* fashion.... While Community law is operative in the United Kingdom legal order, as in that of Ireland, only by virtue of relevant incorporating provisions of the European Communities Acts (section 2(1) in the Irish case, as supplemented by the terms of Article 29.4.3–5 of the Constitution), it is sought by that act of incorporation to grant to Community law the effect in the national legal order which it itself requires" (Hogan and Whelan 1995: 8–9, 11–12, emphasis in the original). On this distinction more generally, see Hogan and Whelan 1995; Phelan 1997; Phelan 2010; and the many other writings on the limited accommodation of the constitutional claims of European law by the national legal orders.

[21] *Maastricht-Urteil*: 89 BVerfGE 155, Oppenheimer 1994: 526–575, *Thoburn*: [2003] QB 151, [2002] 4 All ER 156.

[22] See discussion pp. 57–63 of this volume, demonstrating that for several member states, at least, possibilities remain for national parliaments unilaterally and selectively to legislate to remove the application of EU obligations from the national legal order, most obviously by explicitly amending or restricting the national statutes or constitutional provisions that introduce European obligations into the national legal order.

[23] Case 29/69 *Stauder v. City of Ulm* [1969] ECR 419, Case 11/70 *Internationale Handelsgesellschaft v. Einfuhr- und Vorratsstelle für Getreide* [1970] ECR 1125. For the scholarly debate in Germany

In member states such as Italy and Germany, where individual rights enjoyed constitutional protection, however, the problem was less intense than it might first appear. Their constitutional courts, while insisting on their right to review treaty obligations on national constitutional rights grounds, and on the inviolability of a limited set of fundamental constitutional principles, have repeatedly demonstrated a willingness to limit the application of national constitutional rights in practice where vital matters of foreign policy so required.[24] This mixture of flexibility and principle was adapted to accommodate the particular circumstances of the obligations produced by the European Economic Community, helping to make a compromise outcome possible. So, while national constitutional courts often discussed the possibility that European law obligations might not be applied in their national legal orders if they came into conflict with the most fundamental principles protected by national constitutional rights, the same national constitutional courts refrained from actually unilaterally declaring directly effective European obligations to be unconstitutional on these grounds.

Thus, in relation to the most salient conflicts between European law and national law, national courts were able to accommodate the most demanding obligations required by European law in ways that respected the autonomy of their national legal orders, as well as building on pre-existing approaches to managing potential conflicts between national law and treaty obligations.

The development of the European legal order was not, however, a matter of legal politics alone. Effective international dispute settlement systems must be compatible with incentives for the behavior of policy-makers in the participating states. For policy-makers in a group of highly interdependent trading states, the possibility that the market between the European member states would be uncluttered by the constant possibility of trade retaliation and trade remedies, even if the associated economic regulations were demanding and dispute settlement processes were to be actively employed, was potentially a great prize. A mutual arrangement to forego the use of these inefficient dispute settlement and trade remedy instruments would produce a much more reliable market between the participating states. Private interests, in particular, would gain. Such a result would be good for "litigants"—business interests pressing for the use of international dispute resolution mechanisms to secure the fulfillment of demanding treaty obligations. Just as important, such a result would also be good for "non-litigants"—the wider range of interests *not* directly involved in the litigation of any particular

about the relationship between European law and national constitutional rights, see Alter 2001, and especially Davies 2012.

[24] See Münch 1957: 290–291, commenting on the flexible approach shown by the German Constitutional Court in relation to the constitutionality of the Saar Agreement, BverfGE 4, 157. For a more extensive discussion, see Phelan 2013c.

dispute but nonetheless facing the possibility of finding themselves the victim of the retaliatory trade sanctions employed in many international dispute settlement systems. This is the advantageous international outcome that policy-makers in the European member states, and their firms and citizens, could, perhaps, obtain.

The benefits of a trading regime that rejects the use of inter-state countermeasures and trade remedy instruments are, however, all too obvious. Every international trade regime would provide a more reliable trading environment for firms and individuals if states foreswore the use of these instruments. The common stumbling block is that policy-makers in the participating states lack incentives to behave in ways compatible with such an outcome. Well-organized narrow interests press policy-makers to violate trade regime obligations, regardless of the disruption of markets or the possibility of retaliation. The escape clause provisions, and state-to-state dispute settlement procedures, of many trade treaty regimes merely recognize, and attempt to partially regulate, this apparently inescapable political relationship between policy-makers and the lobbying power of organized narrow interests.[25] Unilateral escape clauses and defect-at-the-risk-of-retaliation mechanisms provide the necessary political insurance for policy-makers responsive to narrow interests, who would be unable to cope with a more frequent, less predictable, and more binding form of international dispute settlement. In Europe's postwar trade and integration regime, however, these difficulties were mitigated for a variety of reasons.

In one important sector—agriculture—the EU member states established a treaty-based regulatory regime that allowed market integration to be combined with ambitious, internationally agreed, welfare objectives. [26] Combining high prices and common, European-level, financing with considerable policy-making autonomy at the national level, Europe's Common Agricultural Policy (CAP) reduced many of the tensions of intra-European liberalization in agricultural trade to a manageable level.[27] The CAP must have played a role in allowing the European legal order its distinctive divergence from more ordinary forms of international dispute resolution. After all, the use of both retaliation mechanisms and escape mechanisms to manage the politics of agricultural trade is common in other international trade regimes. The development of the European legal order, however, was also

[25] Roitinger 2004: 205 stresses the need for such escape mechanisms because lobby group pressure may be "irresistible anyway."

[26] On international negotiations to establish the CAP, see Milward et al. 1992; Moravcsik 1998; Knudsen 2009. On the CAP as part of the postwar welfare state, see e.g. Rieger 2000; Knudsen 2009.

[27] Reduced but did not eliminate: many ECJ decisions on non-tariff barriers to trade relate to disputes over intra-EU trade in agricultural goods.

the beneficiary of three more general features of postwar trade and political development.

First, trade between the European member states has tended to be "*intra*-industry trade" (Pelkmans 2006: 111). *Inter*-industry trade between countries with different economic endowments involves the exchange of very different products—say capital-intensive for labor-intensive goods—and is the basic form of international economic exchange described by classical trade theory. By contrast, in Milward's vivid image, the expanding trade between European states in the 1950s and beyond "increasingly took the form of train loads of manufactures destined for one national market passing train loads of exports of almost identical products going in the reverse direction" (Milward et al. 1992: 124; similarly Brülhart and Hine 1998: esp 98–117; Moravcsik 1998: 88, 235, 495). Trade of this sort is based on quality and brand differences between similar goods, as well as the economy-of-scale advantages of production for a larger international market. Intra-industry trade has long been a distinctive feature of European trade integration in comparison with other trading regions (Brülhart 2009: 438–440).

Importantly, the expansion of intra-industry trade appears to involve smaller adjustment costs than inter-industry trade.[28] In an inter-industry trade scenario, trade based on comparative advantage may lead countries to considerably reduce production in whole sectors of the economy, leading to substantial income losses for firms and workers employed there. By contrast, in an intra-industry trade scenario, the same industry sectors continue to trade and co-exist within the various trading partners. As a result, workers displaced by trade competition are more likely to find employment in their existing domestic industrial sectors, suffering less income loss (Brülhart and Elliott 1998: 229). In other words, in the context of intra-industry trade, domestic actors are not harmed so much by the removal of trade barriers. For this reason, state policy-makers have incentives to accept a more intrusive, less predictable, and more binding form of dispute settlement in international trade politics where a trade relationship has a substantial and growing intra-industry trade component (Baccini et al. 2012; Kucik 2012).

Second, compared to other regions of the world, the integrating nation states of postwar Europe had distinctive democratic political institutions. As part of a long process of European political development that ended in the rejection of *both* undemocratic state structures *and* fragmented ("separation-of-powers") democratic regimes, political decision-making authority tended

[28] E.g. Balassa 1966; Greenaway and Hine 1991; Brülhart 2009—the latter with an emphasis on "marginal" intra-industry trade as the better measure of reduced adjustment pressures. Intra-industry trade also reduces the degree to which national industry sectors become clearly defined lobbies for or against trade liberalization, as particular sectors will contain both export-orientated and import-competing firms.

to be concentrated among cabinet ministers, selected by and responsible to parliamentary assemblies largely under cabinet influence. Thus the reinvention of German democracy after 1945 as an executive-led "Chancellor democracy" (*"Kanzlerdemokratie"*), the marginalization of the national assembly in De Gaulle's Fifth Republic France, and the stripping away of the "checks and balances" in Ireland's 1922 constitution by the Cosgrave and De Valera governments in the 1920s and 1930s, all led their countries toward a partial convergence with a model of democratic cabinet government, and associated forms of delegated and administrative governance, which had already been well under way in the United Kingdom before 1914.[29] Separation-of-powers concepts continued as constitutional and legal norms—but rarely as significant political realities—in postwar Europe.

The constitutional stabilization of postwar Europe was a stabilization built on rationalized and regulated parliamentarism, as well as, in many cases, list-based proportional electoral systems that encourage policy-makers to be more responsive to the interests of broader constituencies. Policy-making in the EU member states therefore tends to combine incentives to be responsive to a wide range of interests with relatively centralized authoritative decision-making (Gerring and Thacker 2008). The prevalence of national policy-making institutions of this sort is distinctive to postwar Europe, especially in comparison with the very varied political institutions characteristic of the membership of other trade regimes, both regional and global.

Policy-makers selected by such institutions have stronger incentives to prioritize their countries' general interest in maintaining their trade commitments even when these impose adjustments on important narrow interests (Rickard 2010; Davis 2012).[30] They therefore have incentives to accept a more intrusive, less predictable, and more binding form of dispute settlement in international trade politics.[31]

[29] Lindseth 2010 is the outstanding work on the connection of national forms of governance with European legal integration, with particular reference to the UK, France, and Germany. For a compatible account of Irish political development, see Ward 1994. For an earlier discussion by this author of interactions between national policy-making institutions and European integration, see Phelan 2002.

[30] On the more general connection between these institutions and the orientation of policy-makers toward broadly based public goods, see Gerring and Thacker 2008.

[31] By allowing national court enforcement of treaty obligations, state policy-makers not only accepted intrusive forms of treaty enforcement in their own domestic arenas but also gave up their right to use trade sanctions and other inter-state countermeasures as an enforcement mechanism against *other* member states. Here again, aspects of the democratic political and legal systems of the EU's member states may have been important. As the NAFTA "Side Agreements" example again demonstrates, policy-makers are more willing to give up their right to enforce international obligations through trade retaliation in favor of application of treaty obligations by national courts where courts in *other* states appear to be sufficiently independent from national political influence in a "rule of law" environment (Grayson 1995: 143; Cameron and Tomlin 2000: 199).

A third and final distinctive characteristic of post-1945 Europe was the growth of the public sector, as states took on a greater role in protecting their citizens from the risks of poverty, ill-health, and old age. In the integrating nation states of the Treaty of Rome, the government was involved, as never before, in providing housing, family benefits, pensions, and unemployment insurance, in widening access to education, and in expanding the number of state employees. Each country's history contains occasions and incidents that demonstrate the new, collectivist role of the state, many of which long pre-date the ECJ's landmark decisions of the early 1960s. In West Germany, the 1949 Constitution declared that Germany was not just a democratic and federal, but also a "social," state, and, in the spring of 1957, Konrad Adenauer's center-right government awarded a 60-percent increase in pensions benefits.[32] In France, 1945 saw the founding of France's social security structure—today's *la Sécu*—in Pierre Laroque's package of decrees establishing family allowances and social insurance systems run by employer-worker boards (Nord 2010). In Britain, which joined the European Communities in 1972, the famous moments were the publication of the Beveridge Report in 1942, the creation of the National Health Service in 1948, and perhaps the 1950s electioneering slogan of centrist Conservative Harold Macmillan that "most of our people have never had it so good." To be sure, the exact manner in which the public sector was expanded differed a great deal from one European state to another, and of course particular benefits were altered, or removed, over time.[33] Everywhere, however, public spending, and various forms of social insurance, grew and grew.

Here again, these forms of social insurance systems mark a significant difference between the EU member states and states elsewhere in the global trading system. Even fifty years later, many members of the GATT/WTO trading system do not provide their citizens with an unemployment compensation system, whereas all the member states of the then European Economic Community had unemployment compensation systems at the time that the ECJ made its landmark decisions in *Van Gend en Loos* and *Commission v. Luxembourg and Belgium* (Vroman and Brusentsev 2005, 2009; Sjöberg et al. 2010).

In this environment, policy-makers in the integrating member states could more easily forego the anti-dumping duties and other unilateral legal escape mechanisms so common to international trade regimes. Instead of the industry-specific "political insurance" offered by such trade remedies, policy-makers could rely on the social insurance instruments of their

[32] Art 20(1) of the German Constitution, Hinrichs and Kangas 2003: 575–576.

[33] Esping-Andersen 1990 is the canonical citation for the diversity of European welfare states, but of course the literature is large.

developing welfare states and on the size of the public sector more generally. Trade-related risks were reduced, particularly after the initial transitional period, not by safeguard mechanisms or the looseness of international treaty controls, but by unemployment assistance, state employment, and pension rights. A more generalized system of compensation (to be sure, with many industry- and geography-specific elements, and far from all of it "efficient") could take the place of a highly trade-disruptive system of industry-specific insurance through intermittent tariff and non-tariff barriers. Again, policy-makers drawn from states with such institutions have incentives to accept a more intrusive, less predictable, and more binding form of dispute settlement in international trade politics.[34]

Of course, scholarship has long recognized the vital importance of understanding why state policy-makers, and not just courts and lawyers, came to behave in ways compatible with the development of today's European legal order. How, so the question goes, did the "constitutionalization" of the treaties occur with such a minimal level of political opposition by the member states (Weiler 1991: 2428)? What could explain the "rarity and softness of tone" of member state resistance to the ECJ (Goldstein 2001: 15)?[35] Previous accounts have answered such questions by focusing on the legal constraints that the European legal order imposed on national policy-makers, and on "politics of law" mechanisms such as law's apparent ability to mask political power and conflict (Burley [Slaughter] and Mattli 1993: 72–73), or "the mythical neutrality and religious-like authority with which we invest our supreme courts" (Weiler 1991: 2428).

Here instead, and in line with more common approaches to explaining important outcomes in international politics, the EU member states came to adopt a particular form of behavior, and to accept the doctrines put forward by the ECJ, because it allowed them, in conjunction with reciprocal behavior from other states, to obtain a better international outcome than the available alternatives.

On the one hand, the most straightforward answer to the above questions is that state policy-makers accepted the constitutionalization of the treaties because they came to prefer a trading regime based on enforcement by domestic courts, however much they disagreed with some of the ECJ's individual decisions, to one based on enforcement by constant threats of inter-state retaliation, with all the associated disruption of economic exchange. After all, the member states were increasingly highly dependent on each other as export markets for large proportions of their economic activity, and that

[34] This argument is a development of Cameron 1978 and Ruggie 1982.

[35] Similarly, Alter writes that "national politicians apparently lacked the will" to oppose national court cooperation with European legal integration (Alter 2001: 194).

created demand for organized and reliable European trading opportunities (Mongelli et al. 2005; Teh et al. 2007: 81). Those trading opportunities would be more reliable and certain with a system of legal obligation and dispute settlement that was more ambitious and effective than common forms of international trade law.

On the other hand, resistance by national policy-makers to such intrusive legal scrutiny was minimal and rare, not only due to the considerable and growing interdependence of their national economies, but also because their constituents were so well protected from any adverse consequences arising from the intensification of the European legal order. Distributional conflicts arising from international integration, for example, were much softened by the role of intra-industry trade as well as by the tax and spending priorities of generous national welfare states.

The elite interactions between courts and lawyers that created European law as a highly binding form of treaty obligation therefore found their counterpart in the mass politics and trading relationships that characterized post-1945 Europe. The incomplete supremacy of European law over national legislation was compensated, so to speak, by the domestic political and social institutions of the participating member states, and by the limited adjustment costs associated with intra-industry trade. The European legal order was an international dispute resolution institution well suited to an international trade and integration regime made up of a group of highly interdependent parliamentary welfare states facing a manageable stream of trade-related adjustment costs.[36]

To be sure, the legal arrangements of the full-blown European legal order as we now know it were only partly set out in the Treaty of Rome, and were subsequently elaborated by ECJ judges, lawyers, and legal propagandists, at times contrary to the arguments advanced by legal representatives of the member states (Stein 1981; Mancini 1989; Alter 2001).[37] The ECJ produced

[36] It may also be that some rough degree of equality of size and influence between the member states is required for such an outcome. If the most powerful European state was large enough that interdependence was extremely asymmetric, then policy-makers in the state with the best unilateral alternatives to forming a trade regime might not have incentives to accept such a constraining and intrusive treaty system.

[37] In the German case, however, objections by a state's legal representatives did not always imply that state policy-makers were opposed to the ECJ's decisions (Davies 2012). While there were always state policy-makers, and lawyers, concerned about the constitutional issues raised by the impact of European law on national legal orders, there were also always other national policy-makers, and lawyers, ready to draw attention back to the bigger, international picture. Davies's new history of Germany's reception of European law provides a nice example: at an August 1964 meeting of German government lawyers to discuss the ECJ's *Costa* decision, Foreign Ministry lawyers focusing on German constitutional problems were confronted with lawyers from the Interior Ministry who "had to make it clear that rejection of primacy [that is, European law supremacy] would fundamentally undermine the functioning of the Community, which in turn would seriously damage the West German economy. The Legal Section of the Foreign

a stream of decisions that expanded the scope of European obligations and reinforced the role of national judges in the domestic enforcement of European law. But this is only one element in the story, because the legal entrepreneurship that built the European legal order took place in a setting where national policy-makers had strong incentives to accept ambitious interpretations of international commitments, even if not clearly included in the original bargain.[38] The price of a "self-contained" international trade regime was national court enforcement of European treaty obligations, and policy-makers in the member states were willing, and able, to pay it.[39]

The acceptance by sovereign states, with only relatively modest hesitations, of such momentous interpretations of treaty commitments may appear to be a rather startling outcome for much scholarship in international law and international relations, which frequently emphasizes that states' egoist behavior is responsible for the fragility of treaty agreements (Carr 1940; Mearsheimer 1994/1995). "Over-obedience" to treaty obligations, however, just as much as "under-obedience," can be the result of rational decision-making by self-interested state policy-makers. Incentives for states to demonstrate such over-obedience require only that this behavior produces better outcomes for the constituents to which policy-makers are responsible.

So, in these particular conditions, the European Union's dispute settlement system came to impose a continuous stream of binding policy adjustments on its member states, and their firms and citizens, without requiring either the use of international law's usual retaliation and escape mechanisms, or the creation of a common coercive structure in the form of a European federal state. Europe's union of parliaments and welfare states has needed neither to create a system of binding treaty obligation and economic exchange so far unparalleled in world history.

Ministry was forced to admit that it had never seen the question from this viewpoint before." (Davies 2012: 161–162).

[38] This and the following passage draw on an earlier discussion of over-obedience to treaty obligations in a publication in *International Theory* by this author: see Phelan 2011a: 299.

[39] Thus, in place of the oft-repeated statement that the ECJ operated in a permissive environment because the individual member states could only overturn judgments against them by obtaining unanimous agreement on new policies from the other member states (e.g. Pierson 1996: 143; Alter 1998: 136–140; Stone Sweet and Brunell 1998a: 74; Stone Sweet 2004: 25), instead—or, rather, more fundamentally—the ECJ operated in a permissive environment because policy-makers in the member states benefitted from the development of a trade regime that rejected the disruptions caused by WTO-style trade retaliation by making treaty obligations enforceable by national courts, and *that* encouraged them to forego unilateral behaviors that would put at risk this distinctive feature of the developing European trade regime.

6

Conclusion

This book has advanced a new explanation of the European Union's distinctive form of international dispute settlement. Building on the arguments of Simma and Weiler, it first identified the European Union's special distinction as an international trade regime imposing a stream of demanding trade-related policy adjustments on organized interests but rejecting the use of inter-state countermeasures as well as unilateral *ex post* escape mechanisms such as trade remedies. It then put forward an explanation for this outcome by arguing that trade regimes between interdependent states whose policy-makers are sufficiently able to manage the political costs of trade openness can function without inter-state retaliation systems and trade remedies. It looked for the observable implications of this argument and demonstrated that, in comparative context, the EU member states possess political institutions that combine inclusiveness and centralized democratic authority, that their social policies are characterized by high tax revenues and generous welfare provision, and that trade between them has unusually high intra-industry content.

The argument of this book is therefore made up of a variety of building blocks: identification of the EU's rejection of inter-state countermeasures and the three most prominent forms of trade remedies as an important qualitative distinction between the EU and other international trade regimes, and therefore the outcome to be explained; the identification of the application of treaty obligations as law in domestic courts as an instrument to deprive other states of occasion to threaten or employ inter-state countermeasures to enforce trade obligations, and therefore the link between the ECJ's *Van Gend en Loos* and *Commission v. Luxembourg and Belgium* decisions; an emphasis on the need for an explanation of why *policy-makers*, and not just courts and lawyers, would benefit from the construction of the European legal order; recognition that the essential challenge for state policy-makers participating in an EU-style, rather than WTO-style, regime is the more frequent, less predictable, and more binding trade policy adjustments that treaty obligations will impose on organized narrow interests; the argument that social insurance institutions and a sizeable public sector can substitute for the "political insurance" provided by escape clauses in trade regimes; and the application to the case of European integration of the domestic institutional and international economic variables used to explain policy-makers' propensity toward trade openness and demanding dispute settlement arrangements in other international trade regimes. These building blocks combine to offer a new explanation for the EU's dispute settlement arrangements.

This explanation meets the challenges set by contributors to a earlier celebrated debate on the development of the European legal order. It directly responds to Garrett's assertion that an explanation for the EU's dispute settlement institutions must be rooted in the interests of policy-makers in the EU member states and their incentives to address credible commitment and incomplete contracting problems (Garrett 1992: 556–557; Garrett and Weingast 1993: 197ff). However, it also addresses Burley and Mattli's riposte to Garrett by providing a reason—indeed, several mutually reinforcing reasons—for the remarkable *relative* effectiveness of the European legal order in comparison with more common forms of international dispute settlement in trade politics (Mattli and Slaughter 1995: 184–185).

While this account—in line with the particular puzzle being addressed by this book—has emphasized the role that the distinctive political and social insurance institutions of the EU member states, as well as their distinctive form of trade interdependence, play in allowing the EU to reject the use of WTO-style trade sanctions and trade remedies, it should be stressed that these institutions, and distinctive trade interactions, no doubt have an impact *throughout* the law and politics of European integration. The existence of these institutions and transactions likely encourages the ECJ to build ambitious legal doctrines, encourages national courts to support the automatic application of EU obligations in the national legal orders, encourages the European Commission to propose ambitious schemes for market unification and regulatory harmonization, and, above all, allows and encourages national policy-makers, negotiating in Brussels, to agree on a continuous stream of demanding market-building EU obligations—and even to allow less than unanimous decision-making rules to create such policies—all because the adjustments required are relatively manageable for both policy-makers and wider society.

Nothing in this book's analysis is meant to suggest that the EU member states are not part of a specifically legal form of international organization that requires them to fulfill binding obligations as a matter of law. However, the quality and effectiveness of legal obligation cannot be understood in isolation from wider social and political conditions. Indeed, the very dichotomy of law and politics is questionable, as others have argued in previous efforts to move explanations of the European legal order away from treating the European treaties as "sacred texts" embodying "legal truth" (Barav 1980; Shapiro 1980; Weiler 1991: 2409). The difference between this and earlier attempts to discuss European law "in context," however, is that this book places the construction of the European legal order within the distinctive context of mass politics, international economics, and inter-state relations in post-1945 Europe, and not just the elite activities of the ECJ, national courts, Euro-law advocacy networks, and the like.

Furthermore, nothing in this discussion should be taken to mean that all directly effective/directly applicable EU obligations are perfectly effective all of the time, or that there are *no* escape opportunities (or protectionist possibilities) left to the member states within the European legal order. There are, no doubt, still significant limits on both the effectiveness of European law and on intra-European trade liberalization, and these limits may vary across industries and across member states. The argument is rather that variation in the effectiveness of these EU obligations plays out within the context of the automatic application of treaty obligations as law in the courts of the member states, open to the use of private parties, rather than within the context of the logic of inter-state trade sanctions, and that this, together with the rejection of ordinary forms of trade remedy instrument, removes a great many of the legally provided-for, unilateral *ex post* escape mechanisms most commonly used by policy-makers in other international trade regimes.[1] When combined with the demanding substance of many EU trade obligations, this makes for a highly reliable international trading environment.

Of previous scholarship on the European legal order, and European integration, the work of three scholars—Geoffrey Garrett, Peter Lindseth, and Alan Milward—stands out as providing the intellectual foundations for this book's approach. Much more than his neofunctionalist rivals in the debates of the 1990s, Garrett claimed that any account of the impact of the ECJ's path-breaking legal judgments needed to be matched with a description of the benefits that states obtained from acquiescing in them, and distinguished between states' general interests in an effective dispute settlement system and their particular interests in the outcomes of individual disputes. Whatever criticisms might be advanced of its particular claims about the roles

[1] It may be worth repeating here the comment made in footnote 32 in Chapter 1 of this volume that by focusing on the EU's directly effective/directly applicable obligations, this book focuses on providing an explanation for EU obligations that leave the least "escape" options available to policy-makers in the member states. EU obligations contained in "Directives," which require transposition/implementation by a national legislative or regulatory act, may perhaps provide national policy-makers with options to transpose these EU obligations late, or incorrectly, in ways that are not available in relation to automatically applied EU obligations benefitting from direct effect/direct application.

of the ECJ and national courts—and we have put forward several in these pages—Garrett's scholarship demonstrated that it was possible to attempt an explanation of the European legal order as a development of relatively "ordinary" themes in international relations theory, and that influence can be seen throughout this book.[2]

Lindseth's influence is somewhat different. His work stands out for its claim that the European legal order was created in a Europe that was "already institutionalized" by structures of domestic governance and public law that permitted considerable delegation of administrative authority while maintaining the central legitimizing role of national parliaments (Lindseth 2010: 57). Thus, the ECJ was the beneficiary of a domestic political environment that very much favored the delegation of decision-making authority outside national parliamentary control. Lindseth's emphasis on the relationship between the ECJ and domestic political and administrative arrangements *other than courts* in the member states has been an important influence here.[3]

(At this point it may be worth emphasizing, as is also relevant to Lindseth's scholarship, that underscoring important commonalities in the domestic institutions of the various member states does not amount to a claim that the domestic institutions of the EU member states are "all the same" (Lindseth 2010: 44). There is, of course, a lot of variation between the European states in, for example, their forms of parliamentary organization and electoral systems, and, not least, in the purposes and generosity of their social insurance institutions. The argument is rather that this variation, while significant, is nonetheless significantly *bounded* compared to the domestic institutions within states and regions outside Europe, not to mention earlier periods of European history.)

Alan Milward provides a third notable influence on this book's argument. The great economic historian of European integration in the 1950s and beyond always insisted that the European Economic Community was the creation not just of European states, but of European *welfare states*, seeking to maintain their citizens' loyalty after the catastrophes of the 1930s and the Second World War (Milward et al. 1992: 4, 31–33). To be sure, the exact connection between international integration and domestic social insurance was not always particularly well defined in Milward's writings, and Milward was little interested in the European legal order. Milward's connection between

[2] Andrew Moravcsik's *Choice for Europe* (1998), with its stress on state policy-makers in explanations of the "grand bargains" between states that underlie the European treaties, has been influential for similar reasons, as well as for its emphasis on the role of intra-industry trade in European integration.

[3] For an earlier discussion of this issue by this author, see Phelan 2002.

European integration and the expansion of social insurance systems in postwar Europe was, however, a valuable insight.[4]

Milward and Lindseth both emphasized the links between long-term trends in European political development and European integration (Milward et al. 1992: x; Lindseth 2010: 41–44; see also Poggi 1978). Here we have shown how a connection can be drawn between these features of the postwar European state and the European legal order's break with inter-state countermeasures as a mechanism to enforce demanding treaty obligations.

We will now turn to the discussion of the limits and advantages of this approach to explaining the EU's dispute settlement system. We will start with the limits.

One limit of this account of the EU as a self-contained regime is that it has not described in full depth the complete range of legal sanctions that European treaties claim to impose on the EU member states.[5] The essential features of supremacy and direct effect/direct application have, as the European legal order has been developed and further treaties have been ratified, been supplemented by additional obligations and regulations, to ensure the better application of European legal obligations by national courts and administrations. To mention just a few examples, since the Maastricht Treaty came into force in 1993, the ECJ has the power to impose fines on the member states for non-compliance with their obligation.[6] The ECJ has also (in 1991) declared that the member states are liable to pay damages to private parties harmed by the non-implementation of European obligations.[7] In the Amsterdam treaty, which entered into force in 1999, a process was established under which an EU member state's rights to vote in the Council of Ministers could be suspended if it seriously and persistently breaches the principles of democracy, liberty, and the rule of law.[8]

Such additional regulatory mechanisms provided by the European treaties or developed by the ECJ do not, however, displace the fundamental

[4] Other influences to mention: Rosendorff and Milner's observation that certain domestic institutions might reduce incentives for policy-makers to use escape mechanisms in treaty regimes (Rosendorff and Milner 2001: 842); Fischer and Prusa's comment that the use of anti-dumping mechanisms is driven by the political economy problem of raising tax revenues (Fischer and Prusa 2003: 747); Jensen and Slapin's application of concepts from the "escape" literature to the politics of multi-speed integration in the EU (Jensen and Slapin 2012); Davies' renewed focus on the role of the German government, rather than German lawyers, in understanding Germany's acceptance of European law (Davies 2012); and, of course, Gerring and Thacker's approach to the analysis of democratic constitutional design (Gerring and Thacker 2008).

[5] Nor has it considered any complications to the argument developed here by the European Monetary Union.

[6] The first fine was imposed in 2000, on Greece in Case C-387/97, *Kouroupitos* [2000] ECR I-5047.

[7] Case C-6 and 9/90 *Francovich v. Italy* [1991] ECR I-5357.

[8] This is contained in Art 7 of the current EU Treaty. The Lisbon treaty added the possibility of preventative action where there was clear risk of a serious breach of these principles.

importance of the supremacy and direct effect/direct application of European law, and the rejection of inter-state countermeasures, in the construction of the EU as a distinctive form of international trade organization. Current scholarship on the development of the European legal order correctly identifies the supremacy and direct-effect doctrines, rather than these subsidiary mechanisms, as the essential differences between the EU and other treaty regimes. These additional regulatory mechanisms developed subsequent to, and their effectiveness is derivative on, the EU's prior stabilization as a self-contained international trade regime that rejects self-help enforcement activities by its member states.

This book has developed an explanation of the EU as a distinctive form of international organization, connecting its persistent rejection of inter-state countermeasures and trade remedy instruments with the member states' distinctive political institutions, high tax revenues, and generous social insurance systems, as well as the high level of intra-industry trade. It has thus offered a general explanation of the EU's most distinctive features as an international trade regime, from its founding moments to the current day. However, the substantive trade obligations that the European treaties have imposed on the member states have changed considerably over time, particularly as the regulation of non-tariff barriers has been expanded, notably as part of the intensification of intra-European trade competition through the "Single European Act" of 1986, and correspondingly the room for unilateral protectionism through national regulation has been further reduced. These changes in the European market have no doubt interacted with developments in both national regulatory policy-making and the generosity and design of national social insurance systems, which have themselves changed in many ways, as enterprises have been privatized and as policy-makers have recognized new forms of risk (Gillingham 2003). Further investigation of these important interactions must, however, be left to future research.

One real limit to this book's explanation is inherent in the difficulties of explaining an international political outcome that is both qualitatively distinct and highly unusual, even after that distinctive outcome has been translated into a political economy puzzle stated in generalizable terms. If there were many contemporary examples of international trade regimes with highly active dispute settlement systems that nevertheless rejected inter-state countermeasure and trade remedy mechanisms, it might be possible to generate a much more fine-grained set of conditions for these outcomes. While the explanation advanced here offers good reasons why we should expect self-contained international trade regimes to be rare in both the contemporary world and, even more so, in past history, it remains the case that an explanation for a single remarkable outcome can only be tested in relatively broad terms, and the full set of scope conditions underlying the creation of an EU-style international organization cannot be very precisely specified. To be sure, this criticism applies just as strongly to many previous explanations of the European legal order, but it remains an important limitation of the approach developed here.[9] For example, if it is accepted that a group of highly interdependent democratic states whose political institutions combine *more* inclusiveness and centralized authority are *more* capable of participating in a self-contained international trade regime, it is hard to say very precisely at which point—how inclusive and authoritative, how many states, how interdependent, in the presence of how much legal networking, etc.—the qualitative shift from a retaliation-based regime to a self-contained regime can occur. It is certainly easier to say that the mechanisms introduced here have been unjustifiably neglected in previous explanations of the European legal order than to make exact calculations of their possible impact upon the creation of self-contained trade regimes in other scenarios.

Furthermore, the *relative* importance of the various factors emphasized here—international interdependence, legal networks, intra-industry trade, inclusive and authoritative political institutions, social insurance mechanisms, and common financing of agriculture—remains hard to distinguish, since each of them have been distinctive features of integration and democracy in postwar Europe. It is quite possible that the presence of all these factors was necessary for such a profound, but quiet, qualitative shift in inter-state relations (Weiler 1994). On the other hand, future developments in international politics may reveal if some of these variables have a much greater influence than others, and whether a self-contained trade regime with demanding obligations is possible in different conditions than those present in postwar Europe. Finally on this aspect, while we believe that the variables discussed here have been—as suggested by wider research on international politics and dispute resolution—the most relevant to facilitating the development of the European legal order, we do not rule out that there may be further, additional features of international interactions between, and domestic institutions within, the EU member states that may also have facilitated the EU's break with inter-state retaliation mechanisms. Other relevant variables might include the administrative and infrastructural capacities of the EU member states and the rise of intra-firm trade.

A further set of limitations is more specific to this book's discussion of the EU. The EU is essentially treated here as a liberalizing international trade regime, and it is true that the market between the member states has been, and

[9] Like other explanations of the European legal order, we have also assumed as a background condition the generally benign geopolitical relationship between the participating states. We have also focused on the development of the European legal order through the 1990s, without giving special attention to its extension to the new member states of Central and Eastern Europe after 2000.

remains, the fundamental aspect of EU governance. But the EU has always been more than a trade regime, and is certainly far more than a trade regime today. Even restricting our view to EU obligations that are automatically applied and compulsory, the EU is also—among other things—a migration regime, an environmental regime, and a human rights regime. Furthermore, right from the start, the EU has contained less liberal elements, including the price-raising and subsidy cartel known as the Common Agricultural Policy, while, on the other hand, many EU obligations may help address "coordination issues" where there are few incentives for narrow interests to demand defection (Stein 1982).

At the start of this book, it was argued that any explanation of the EU as an international organization must *at least* entail an explanation for an international trade regime that rejects the use of inter-state countermeasures and trade remedies, and that has been the focus here. The explanation developed here for the EU's distinctive trade regime may also go a long way toward explaining the EU's ability to authoritatively regulate many issues outside the core issue-area of trade. The social insurance mechanisms in the EU member states, for example, provide a favorable institutional environment that can support not only the free movement of goods and services, but also the free movement of workers and capital between the EU member states. Moreover, they provide a conducive setting for joint policy-making in issue-areas such as environmental regulation, where European policies would change relative prices in ways that adversely affect organized interests in the member states. Given the international interdependence of policy-making on many issues, and given that domestic institutions in the EU member states tend to combine both inclusiveness and centralized authority, joint policy-making at the European level in a wide range of issue-areas beyond trade—issue-areas that require significant adjustments as well as "coordination" issue-areas—is a logical outcome.

A further acknowledged limit to this argument is that the explanatory variables emphasized here are not entirely exogenous either from each other—"inclusive" democratic institutions such as proportional representation are associated with higher taxation, for example—or from states' trade policies—as constitutional architects in small open economies may have incentives to design political institutions that favor trade openness, policy-makers may have incentives to increase social welfare spending to compensate the losers from trade openness, and regional agreements may increase intra-industry trade (Cameron 1978; Katzenstein 1985; Iversen and Soskice 2006; Persson et al. 2007; Foster and Stehrer 2011). Furthermore, the spread of intra-industry trade and the development of social security institutions may in turn be derived from the relatively high levels of economic development in many European states, as higher per capita incomes tend to produce certain characteristic interactions between, and within, domestic politics and economies.

This book by itself cannot, of course, attempt to disentangle every possible interaction between trade regimes, dispute settlement systems, regionalism, constitutional structures, social insurance mechanisms, democracy, economic development, levels of interdependence, and varieties of economic exchange. It aims to contribute to debates on these important topics by demonstrating how a particular form of legalization in a regional trade and integration regime is made possible by distinctive types of domestic institutions and international economic interactions. In the case of many early EU member states including France, Germany, and the United Kingdom, however, it is worth noting that the creation of the most important of these domestic institutions—disciplined forms of parliamentary government, state responsibility for the poor, the sick, and the old—antedate the ECJ's "constitutionalizing" decisions of 1963 and 1964. The political choices that created these domestic institutions are often attributed to a variety of causes, including the functional needs of mass democracy, the imperatives of class and religious compromise and constitutional stabilization after the conflicts of the 1930s, and the transnational attractions of British-style "disciplined" parliamentarism, as well as to the influences of trade politics (Poggi 1978; Katzenstein 1985; Rogowski 1987; Ward 1994; Lindseth 2010). Even the beginnings of the rise of intra-industry trade and greater economic interdependence between the European member states pre-date the creation of the Common Market, although of course they have continued to expand since then (Milward et al. 1992; Moravcsik 1998).

Finally, some might be tempted to argue that this approach to explaining the EU's system of dispute settlement is also limited in that it does not attempt to explain variations in dispute settlement outcomes *within* the EU's self-contained regime. After all, there is considerable variety: some member states, more than others, are found in litigation to have failed to fulfill their EU obligations, particular issue-areas sometimes have distinctive outcomes, individual national courts cooperate with the ECJ to a greater or lesser degree and describe the relationship between national and European law in diverse ways, and so on. These are all topics that have rightly attracted considerable scholarly attention. Properly understood, however, a failure to address these topics is not a limitation of the argument developed here. Rather, these are different research questions.[10] This book has attempted to explain why the EU is a self-contained regime when so many international trade regimes require inter-state retaliation mechanisms and trade remedies. It therefore

[10] For the same reason, a failure to explain intra-EU variation of this sort was not a weakness in the explanations of the European legal order put forward by Burley and Mattli, Alter, and others.

explains why the full range of legal outcomes within the EU regime, including outcomes where the member states are found to have failed to fulfill their obligations, take place within the context of the automatic application of treaty obligations as law by domestic courts, rather than within the much more common context of the logic of inter-state countermeasures.

Keeping these limits fresh in mind, the main advantage of this book's approach over existing explanations of the development of the European legal order may lie in its better integration with wider international relations scholarship. The outcome to be explained has been described in generalizable terms as a trade regime that uses domestic court enforcement in place of inter-state retaliation and rejects the use of trade remedy instruments such as anti-dumping. That description is intuitively comprehensible to generalist international relations scholars and, at the same time, directly connected to understandings of the essential features of the European legal order identified by both leading legal theorists and the ECJ itself. The explanation for this outcome is also relatively straightforwardly developed from causal mechanisms that enjoy widespread currency in contemporary trade politics research, as well as from a detailed comparison with more common forms of international dispute settlement. This book will therefore have lasting value, we hope, if it helps to normalize analysis of the European legal order by situating that remarkable development more transparently in wider scholarly debates.

European Integration and the European Legal Order

The argument about the European legal order advanced here may have implications for a variety of research questions on particular aspects or issue-areas within the EU institutions, of the sort that contemporary studies of EU politics so often address.

This section will consider the relevance of the argument advanced here for two prominent debates in EU scholarship: the politics of decision-making by the member states when agreeing to new EU policies, and the interaction between European integration and national welfare states. Each of these topics has produced a large and growing scholarly literature, which cannot possibly be adequately summarized here. It may be sufficient to sketch the contribution that this book can make to these debates.

It is widely agreed that the most influential institution in the production of the EU's stream of new regulations is the Council of Ministers, where the political representatives (politicians and bureaucratic officials) of the twenty-seven EU member states meet to discuss and amend policy proposals advanced by the Commission, often under unanimity or high supermajority rules. According to one theoretical approach, the dominance of so many national policy-makers in EU decision-making, operating under high consensus requirements, makes the EU an "extreme variant of a multiple-veto player system," producing suboptimal policy outcomes. This is known as the EU's "joint decision-trap" (Scharpf 1988, 2006: 847–848).

Interestingly, however, as empirical studies of decision-making in the Council have proliferated, veto-players models have often been found to have little explanatory power. Scholars instead tend to emphasize deliberative processes and the importance of informal and consensus norms, rather than rational, self-interested decision-making within systems of decision-making rules (see, among others, Schimmelfennig 2001; Heisenberg 2005; Lewis 2005; Hayes-Renshaw et al. 2006; Steunenberg and Selck 2006; Thomson et al. 2006; Naurin and Wallace 2008; König and Junge 2008, the latter with extensive references). In a powerful recent contribution to this scholarship, Mareike Kleine shows that the Council decision-making process has developed *ex ante* mechanisms of "informal governance" that allow the member states to collectively assess claims by one of their number that an issue under discussion is of such particular domestic political sensitivity that their policy demands must be accommodated—even if the objector is in a minority of one.[11] Thus, the EU decision-making process has incorporated flexibility procedures whereby states (not unilaterally, but where their EU partners will so allow) can avoid being forced to accept the most politically difficult types of EU policy outputs.

The EU policy process's combination of veto-laden decision-making rules, consensus norms for agreement on new policies, and ambitious regulatory outputs (even after *ex ante* flexibility mechanisms are taken into account) may appear hard to reconcile. To be sure, policy exchanges and log-rolling across issues may well be relevant here (König and Proksch 2006). The argument of this book, however, may supply another part of the answer. After all, the apparently constraining effect of (for example) unanimity-rule decision-making in international institutions is derivative of a certain understanding of the relationship between state policy-makers and domestic interests. Consider an international organization made up of a number of states contemplating a collective decision in a "sensitive" issue-area, such as trade, that would generate benefits for broad constituencies but impose costs on organized narrow interests within each of the states. If state policy-makers in each of the member states are uniformly responsive to these narrow interests, no

[11] Kleine, *Making Cooperation Work: Informal Governance in the EU and Beyond*, forthcoming from Cornell University Press. I have been fortunate to read parts of this manuscript in draft. Another form of *ex ante* flexibility in EU policy-making consists of setting member states differentiated obligations in secondary EU legislation (Duttle et al. 2013).

decision-making rule allowing participation by *even one* of the states will allow the international organization to adopt such a policy. If, however, political institutions in the member states make policy-makers in *each of the states* responsive to broader constituencies, then even a unanimity-rule decision-making procedure would allow the international organization to adopt a constant stream of such policies. Holding the international decision-rule constant, even in a "difficult" issue-area such as trade, but changing the responsiveness of policy-makers to various domestic interests, can therefore completely change the expected outputs of international institutions' decision-making procedures.

Of course, these are extreme cases used only to illustrate the argument's logic, and, no doubt, in practice we are talking about variation of a more limited variety. Within that context, however, the EU member states are, as we have seen, distinguished among states in contemporary world politics by the inclusive and authoritative nature of their political institutions, the large shares of GDP they take as government revenue, and their generous social security systems. States with such domestic institutions, in the context of considerable interdependence and the relatively modest adjustment costs of intra-industry trade, have incentives to consensually agree ambitious policy outputs even under a unanimity decision-rule. To be sure, this general context does not explain why decisions on some EU policy-issues are more often blocked than others, and it does not deny that less-than-unanimous procedures may, in general, improve the efficiency of decision-making. It does, however, offer an explanation for why ambitious EU decision-making was—and is—often far from stalled even in the context of unanimity or "high-consensus" decision-rules.

Another important area of debate concerns the relationship between European integration, the ECJ, and national welfare states. It has become common to suggest that the EU is structurally biased against the production of a European-wide social policy because the ECJ, as an autonomous court, can unilaterally produce trade liberalizing decisions ("negative integration"), while social policy-building decisions ("positive integration") need the unanimous agreement of all the member states, with all their conflicting interests (Scharpf 1999). This perspective was reinforced by controversies over relatively recent ECJ decisions in the *Viking* and *Laval* cases, which appeared to restrict the ability of labor unions to effectively protest the use of non-union labor posted from other member states.[12] In the latest iteration of this debate, Caporaso and Tarrow noted that the ECJ's decisions have sometimes

[12] Case 438/05 *International Transport Workers' Federation v. Viking* [2007] ECR I-10779 and Case 341/05 *Laval v. Svenska Byggnadsarbetareforbundet* [2007] ECR I-11767. For analysis, see e.g. Höpner and Schäfer 2012.

led to *increased* access to welfare benefits for migrant workers and their families, while Höpner and Schäfer responded by pointing to ECJ decisions that have increased intra-EU corporate tax competition, and arguing that some of the ECJ's expansions of welfare entitlements have reduced the solidarity connection between benefit recipiency and contributions to national social insurance schemes (Caporaso and Tarrow 2009; Höpner and Schäfer 2012). The independent role of the ECJ, therefore, looms large in discussions about whether the EU can be a social market economy (Scharpf 2009). This is an important topic, and one that is likely to remain salient in discussions of the future of European integration.

Again, the argument of this book offers a different perspective on these debates. In this literature, it is common to avoid providing generalizable political economy explanations for the ECJ's distinctive independence from national governments. Instead, authors refer to "politics of lawyers" explanations for European legal integration, including power-seeking behavior by the ECJ and activism by transnational judicial communities (Scharpf 2009: 8–10, esp ft 5; Höpner and Schäfer 2012: 449 ft 82). As has been argued here, however, the ECJ would therefore be better understood not as an interloper "parachuted" into the world of European states by legal networking alone, but as an international legal institution whose special distinction (that is, its break with inter-state countermeasures) may in part be derived from common cross-national features of post-1945 European social democracy. Without the healthcare benefits, pensions, and unemployment insurance provided by European welfare states, Europe might well have a more WTO- or NAFTA-like form of international integration, where common policy-making would co-exist with the unilateral use of legal escape mechanisms and inter-state retaliation mechanisms. The EU, and the ECJ, can be understood as creations of postwar Europe's particular variant of Ruggie's *embedded liberalism*, where less national policy-making autonomy in terms of unilateral safeguards and exceptions has been compensated by more extensive, and at least significantly generalized, social welfare systems. None of these observations make the debate about the relationship between European legal integration and national welfare states any less important. These discussions may be most productive, however, if they recognize the contribution of social insurance systems, as well as other non-legal factors, to the role of the ECJ in Europe's distinctive form of international trade integration.

Indeed, the understanding of the EU developed here may be relevant to a wider range of topics and debates. To touch on a couple of possible examples, the EU's limited involvement in cross-border redistribution, through "structural funds," may appear more consistent with the logic of a self-contained trade regime than with the logic of WTO-style alternatives, while this discussion of how domestic redistributional institutions within the member states have facilitated the quiet success of the EU's distinctive legal style of trade integration may highlight, by contrast, the lack of cross-border redistributional institutions sufficient to ensure a similar success for the European common currency, the "Euro," for those member states that have adopted it. A fuller elaboration of such themes, however, must wait for subsequent research.

Enforcement and Escape in International Trade Politics

Research on enforcement and escape in international trade regimes is one of the most active research agendas in contemporary political science (Kucik and Reinhardt 2008: 498–499). This scholarship covers a wide range of topics in the law and politics of the global trading regime, including decisions to pursue litigation, the role of power in inter-state retaliation, the uses of anti-dumping duties and other escape mechanisms, and the interaction of trade litigation with other forms of diplomatic relationships. There are, in fact, few international institutions about which political scientists know as much as they do about the WTO, its Dispute Settlement Understanding, and its various safeguard mechanisms. In many ways, such scholarship on the WTO and similarly organized trade regimes serves as an admirable example to be emulated by scholarship focused on other international organizations.

If, despite this, one were to advance a broad criticism of this scholarship, it would be that the claims it makes are over-universalized. This literature tends to assume that WTO-type behaviors, with only relatively minor variations, are the only feasible type of state behaviors in an international trade regime. Time and again, scholars write in ways that suggest that demanding international trade regimes must employ "suspension of concession" retaliation systems, or must contain legal escape mechanisms such as anti-dumping, countervailing duties, or safeguard trade remedies (Downs and Rocke 1995; Rosendorff and Milner 2001; Kucik and Reinhardt 2008; Bown 2009; see also earlier discussions in Chapter 3 of this book). The use of GATT/WTO-style "self-help" enforcement systems and trade remedies may therefore appear to be a permanent instrument of trade politics statecraft—much as realist scholars expected *realpolitik* balance of power behaviors to be a permanent feature of military statecraft (Waltz 1979). This perspective is buttressed, to be sure, by centuries of examples of decentralized sanctioning and reprisals in international law and trade relations, of which the GATT and WTO regimes provide only the latest incarnations. Nevertheless, it is incorrect, as the European legal order illustrates. For scholars working on the problem of trade sanctions and trade remedies as enforcement and escape mechanisms in international trade politics, studying the politics of intra-EU trade should therefore be just as intellectually stimulating as the study of "security communities"—groups of states that settle their disputes without even considering the use of military force—should be to scholars working on the problem of war in international politics (Deutsch et al. 1957; Adler and Barnett 1998).

This book's argument inspires two further comments relating to scholarship on enforcement and escape in the WTO and other international trade regimes. First, in reviewing the empirical literature on outcomes in WTO dispute settlement, discussions of domestic institutions as independent variables tend to focus on political institutions such as presidentialism and electoral systems (e.g. Rickard 2010; Davis 2012). WTO scholarship does not yet appear to have attempted to explain at-the-margin variations in use of dispute settlement or anti-dumping mechanisms by means of variation in domestic welfare state generosity. Second, the more theoretical discussions of enforcement and escape mechanisms in international trade politics tend to focus on various retaliatory or "safety-valve" strategies without fully incorporating variations in social insurance institutions in their modeling of commitment problems in international politics (but see McGillivray and Smith 2008; Phelan 2011a on the interaction of domestic institutions and inter-state punishments). Thus, we have Downs, Rocke, and Barsoom's influential models to support the claim that, as international regulatory rules tighten, the magnitude of the inter-state punishment needed to deter state defection would have to increase (Downs et al. 1996: 391). We do not have similarly well-developed models focused on the equally valid alternative that, as international regulatory rules tighten, national compensation systems would have to be enhanced. The welfare state, however, appears to be a plausible substitute for the escape mechanisms available to policy-makers in many trade regimes: it is an instrument available for *ex post* unilateral use by state policy-makers to manage the unpredictable economic and political developments of institutionalized trade integration (Downs and Rocke 1995; Rosendorff and Milner 2001). Better yet would be models of international interactions that combined varied inter-state punishment systems with diverse domestic compensation systems. For both empirical and theoretical scholarship on enforcement and escape in international trade politics, therefore, a renewed engagement with the politics of social insurance may prove fruitful.[13]

[13] The book also tends to support approaches to the study of international trade institutions that analyze inter-state enforcement mechanisms alongside the availability of *ex post* escape mechanisms such as anti-dumping.

International Relations Scholarship: After the GATT

This book set out to pose, and answer, a particular question about European integration, and the implications of its argument are obviously most significant for research on the European legal order and on enforcement and escape in international trade politics. This final section will tie these discussions into broader themes in international relations scholarship.

One area of international relations scholarship that is assuming an ever more prominent role is the study of international human rights regimes and, perhaps unexpectedly, the argument developed in this book may be relevant to this topic. By focusing on explaining the EU as a "self-contained regime," rejecting the use of inter-state countermeasures, this book has demonstrated that the puzzle of the EU turns out to have considerable similarities with the puzzle of international human rights regimes. After all, it is a widely recognized distinction of this issue-area of international politics that the obligations of international human rights regimes are not enforced *ex post* through inter-state countermeasure or reciprocity incentives (Moravcsik 2000: 217; von Stein 2006: 24; Hathaway 2007: 592).

As this book's discussion has illustrated, however, human rights regimes are not the only international regimes that do not use inter-state countermeasures. Indeed, because of their mutual rejection of inter-state reciprocity mechanisms, international human rights regimes and the EU are sometimes grouped together by international lawyers as posing similar conceptual challenges (e.g. Simma 1985; Sicilianos 1990: 339–365; see also Phelan 2012). This book's approach to the EU thus serves to advance the integration of international relations scholarship in different issue-areas, and to raise the possibility that the national policy-making and social insurance institutions discussed here may also be relevant to explaining outcomes in international human rights politics.

Nonetheless, the similarity should not be overstated. While the EU's rejection of inter-state countermeasures as an enforcement mechanism does indeed recall similar features of international human rights regimes, the welfare and incomes of organized groups in a state within a trade regime remain contingent on policies of trade openness in other participating states much more (so it is commonly accepted) than the welfare and incomes of organized groups in a state within a human rights regime are contingent on "high" standards of human rights in other participating states. That is the reason, of course, that WTO-style inter-state reciprocity-and-retaliation mechanisms are more readily employed in trade politics than in human rights politics. For the same reason, however, a bargain to mutually substitute the use of domestic courts for the use of inter-state countermeasures in the area of trade politics may still rest powerfully on contingent behaviors by the other states within a trade regime, such as the EU, whereas the logic of such an inter-state bargain is less compelling in the case of a human rights regime.

On a different note—and perhaps to the relief of some—the reader may have noticed that this book did not begin with a rehearsal of the incentives for state behavior and international outcomes emphasized by "grand theories" of international relations, such as realism, liberalism, institutionalism, and constructivism (Waltz 1979; Keohane 1984; Wendt 1992; Moravcsik 1997). Instead, it proceeded by imitating much recent scholarship on international trade organization that straightforwardly incorporates rational state policy-makers, diverse domestic institutions, various interest groups, international tribunals and bureaucracies, and varied inter-state punishment mechanisms into explanations of international outcomes. At the same time, however, by its emphasis on the limited adjustment costs of intra-industry trade, on inclusive and authoritative democratic institutions, on domestic welfare states, and on the role of domestic courts in changing inter-state relations, it should be clear that the argument advanced here owes a great deal to the "liberal" (or, perhaps better, "state-society") approach to international relations. The argument of this book may therefore contribute to "intra-liberal" debates, particularly as they apply to international law, by suggesting that explanations of unusually binding norms in international dispute settlement can be derived not only from a close focus on lawyers and litigants, but also from incentives for state policy-makers, interest groups facing adjustments, and even non-litigating businesses to accept qualitatively changed inter-state relationships.

A final way in which this book's argument may relate to broader themes in the study of international relations concerns the centrality of the GATT/WTO model to modern understandings of international organization. As every student knows, the seminal contribution of Robert Keohane's *After Hegemony* was to challenge the argument that a hegemonic state was necessary to organize an open international market. Instead, he emphasized that a reliable open international market could be maintained if restraints on national policy-making autonomy were supported by reciprocity, reputation, and tit-for-tat retaliation incentives between a group of between more-or-less equally powerful states. As Keohane admitted, this theoretical argument generalized the experience of the GATT world trade regime in the 1970s and 1980s (Keohane 2005: xi). For Keohane, therefore, "the GATT" is what came "after hegemony." The GATT as an institution, as an alternative to power-based international regimes or disorganized international markets, and as a facilitator and organizer of reciprocity and retaliation, is thus the foundation of today's rationalist approach to the study of international organization.

If the GATT served as the qualitative counterpoint to hegemony in Keohane's work, in this book's discussions the GATT (or today's WTO) serves as a qualitative counterpoint to the EU. But here the GATT is, compared to the EU, the more disorganized and power-based form of international market because of the market disruptions and power inequalities associated with the use of trade retaliation rather than domestic courts as an enforcement mechanism. GATT-style international institutions are also revealed as "all-purpose" instruments capable of organizing international relationships in a very wide range of scenarios, while fully developed EU-style interactions have, so far, only proved possible in a narrower range of circumstances, where high levels of interdependence have combined with policy-makers' capacities to manage demanding policy adjustments. Understanding the European legal order through its rejection of inter-state retaliation mechanisms and trade remedies—understanding the EU as "after the GATT"—can therefore position our understanding of the EU, and the role of national courts and private actors in its dispute settlement system, in an intellectual tradition on the sources of stability in international markets and cooperation under anarchy that has been highly significant in the development of contemporary international relations scholarship.

Simple Glossary of Key Terms

Anti-dumping Duties involve the imposition of trade barriers by a state where policy-makers believe that an established industry is being damaged by imported goods being sold ("dumped") at less than the normal price of the products in their home market.

Countermeasures, also referred to as "reprisals" or "reciprocal measures," refer to "self-help" measures adopted by states to enforce international legal obligations and which would otherwise be contrary to international law. In the context of a trade treaty, for example, a state that claims that another state has adopted policies inconsistent with its treaty obligations might impose restrictions on goods imported from that state, restrictions which would themselves be contrary to its own treaty obligations, but are justified as a matter of international law in that they are adopted as measures to enforce the other state's treaty obligations.

Countervailing Duties are trade barriers imposed by state policy-makers to offset the effects of any subsidies inconsistent with their treaty obligations that policy-makers in other states have provided their industries.

Direct Effect refers to the obligation that European law places on national courts to automatically apply European obligations, independently of the legislation of the member states, in litigation involving private parties. In European legal integration, the ECJ's 1963 decision *Van Gend en Loos* provided for the direct effect of obligations in the European treaties.

Embedded Liberalism refers to the argument, pioneered by John Ruggie, that post-1945, global trade liberalization was made possible by the compatibility between international trade rules and national policy-makers' ability to meet demands for social protection through welfare provision, and by the extensive range of exceptions and exemptions from intrusive trade obligations.

Escape Mechanisms refer to legal instruments available to policy-makers in an international regime to temporarily or permanently "escape" demanding obligations when (especially) domestic political pressures are intense. Also referred to as "flexibility" instruments or "safety valves." In trade politics, the most common forms of escape mechanisms are anti-dumping duties, countervailing duties, and industry safeguards. The ability to defect on trade obligations at the risk of other states imposing retaliatory trade sanctions is also understood as an escape mechanism within trade regimes.

"Later-in-Time" Legislation refers to a common way of resolving conflicts between provisions between laws of equivalent rank. If two such laws conflict with each other, then the obligations of the "later-in-time" legislation will prevail. So, for example, where the provisions of a tax law enacted in 2007 disagree with provisions of a tax law enacted in 2009, following the principle that "later-in-time" legislation should prevail, the provisions of the 2009 act would be applied as law. This concept is relevant to the politics of European law because the supremacy doctrine of

European law requires that European law obligations prevail even over "later-in-time" national legislation.

Mutual Recognition is a European law obligation designed to reduce non-tariff barriers to trade. It requires that the EU member states cannot use national regulation to prevent the marketing and sale of goods where these meet the standards of regulation and marketing in the home market of another EU member state. Mutual recognition was a principle announced in the ECJ's 1979 decision, *Cassis de Dijon*.

Preliminary Reference Procedure refers to the arrangement, originally set out in Article 177 of the Treaty of Rome, whereby national courts facing a question about the interpretation of the European treaties or a European law obligation can request the ECJ to provide an interpretative ruling. This is one of the mechanisms by which the national courts communicate with the ECJ, and incorporate the ECJ's interpretation of European law obligations into their decisions.

Safeguard Measures are trade barriers imposed by state policy-makers on imports of particular products where these are causing or threatening serious injury to domestic producers.

Self-contained Regime refers to an international legal regime that rules out the use of "self-help" countermeasures between states as a mechanism to enforce its obligations. In European legal integration, the ECJ's 1964 decision *Commission v. Luxembourg and Belgium* provided that the European member states were not permitted to use such "self-help" mechanisms in the European Economic Community, providing the basis for later definitions of the EU as a "self-contained regime."

Supremacy refers to the obligation that European law places on national courts to resolve conflicts between European law obligations and national law obligations by the application of the European law obligations. According to European law's supremacy doctrine, national courts must apply European law obligations even where these are in conflict with "later-in-time" national legislation, or national constitutional provisions protecting fundamental rights. In European legal integration, the ECJ's 1964 decision *Costa v. ENEL* provided for the supremacy of European obligations over conflicting national law.

Trigger Strategy is a way of describing an actor's response to behaviors by other actors. A trigger strategy is comprised of two elements: the "triggering" event, and the "punishment" that is triggered by that event. A firm in a commodity cartel, for example, could respond to a fall in the price of the commodity (likely caused by other firms not respecting cartel "discipline") by offering goods for sale at an even lower price for a specified period of time, to punish the other cartel firms in retaliation. Similarly, a state that fails to fulfill its obligations to allow imports of goods and services in a trade regime may trigger another state to impose some sort of punishment, such as retaliatory trade sanctions.

References

Abreu, Dilip (1988). "On the Theory of Infinitely Repeated Games with Discounting." *Econometrica* 56: 383–396.

Abreu, Dilip, David Pearce, and Ennio Stacchetti (1986). "Optimal Cartel Equilibria with Imperfect Monitoring." *Journal of Economic Theory* 39: 51–69.

Abreu, Dilip, David Pearce, and Ennio Stacchetti (1989). "Renegotiation and Symmetry in Repeated Games." Discussion paper. Yale, Cowles Foundation for Research in Economics.

Adler, Emanuel and Michael Barnett (1998). *Security Communities*. Cambridge, Cambridge University Press.

Adserà, Alícia and Carles Boix (2002). "Trade, Democracy, and the Size of the Public Sector: The Political Underpinnings of Openness." *International Organization* 56(2): 229–262.

Ahearn, Raymond J. (2005). European Trade Retaliation: The FSC–ETI Case. *CRS Report for Congress*. Ahearn. Washington, DC, Congressional Research Service.

Alexander, Klint W. and Bryan J. Soukup (2010). "Obama's First Trade War: The US–Mexico Cross-Border Trucking Dispute and the Implications of Strategic Cross-Border Retaliation on US Compliance Under NAFTA." *Berkeley Journal of International Law* 28(2): 313–342.

Allee, Todd (2004). "Legal Incentives and Domestic Rewards: The Selection of Trade Disputes for GATT/WTO Dispute Resolution." Unpublished paper.

Allee, Todd (2008). "Developing Countries and the Initiation of GATT/WTO Disputes." 1st Conference on the Political Economy of International Organizations. Monte Verità, Switzerland.

Alter, Karen (1998). "Who are the "Masters of the Treaty"? European Governments and the European Court of Justice." *International Organization* 52: 121–148.

Alter, Karen (2001). *Establishing the Supremacy of European Law: The Making of an International Rule of Law in Europe*. Oxford, Oxford University Press.

Alter, Karen (2009a). *The European Court's Political Power: Selected Essays*. Oxford, Oxford University Press.

Alter, Karen (2009b). "Jurist Advocacy Movements in Europe: The Role of Euro-Law Associations in European Integration (1953–1975)." In Karen Alter (ed.) *The European Court's Political Power: Selected Essays*. Oxford, Oxford University Press: 63–91.

Alter, Karen (2013). "The Multiple Roles of International Courts and Tribunals: Enforcement, Dispute Settlement, Constitutional and Administrative Review." In Jeffrey L. Dunoff and Mark A. Pollack (eds), *Interdisciplinary Perspectives on*

International Law and International Relations: The State of the Art. Cambridge, Cambridge University Press: 345–370.

Alter, Karen and Laurence Helfer (2010). "Nature or Nurture? Judicial Law Making in the European Court of Justice and the Andean Tribunal of Justice." *International Organization* 64(4): 563–592.

Alter, Karen and Laurence Helfer (2011). "Legal Integration in the Andes: Law-Making by the Andean Tribunal of Justice." *European Law Journal* 17(5): 701–715.

Alter, Karen, Laurence Helfer, and Osvaldo Saldías (2012). "Transplanting the European Court of Justice: The Experience of the Andean Tribunal of Justice." *American Journal of Comparative Law* 60: 629–664.

Anthony, Gordon (2002). *UK Public Law and European Law*. Oxford and Portland, OR, Hart.

Axelrod, Robert M. (1984). *The Evolution of Cooperation*. New York, Basic Books.

Baccini, Leonardo, Andreas Duer, and Manfred Elsig (2012). "The Politics of Trade Agreement Design: The Obligation–Flexibility Trade-Off." *ECPR Joint Sessions*, Antwerp.

Baccini, Leonardo, Andreas Duer, Manfred Elsig, and Karolina Milewicz (2011). "The Design of Preferential Trade Agreements: A New Dataset in the Making." *World Trade Organization Economic Research and Statistics Division ERSD-2011-10*, Geneva.

Baccini, Leonardo, Andreas Duer, and Yoram Z. Haftel (2013). "Imitation and Innovation in International Governance: The Diffusion of Trade Agreement Design." Unpublished paper, presented at *EPSA Annual Meeting*, Barcelona.

Bagehot, Walter (2001 [1867]). *The English Constitution*. Cambridge, Cambridge University Press.

Bailey, Michael, Judith L. Goldstein, and Barry Weingast (1997). "The Institutional Roots of American Trade Policy: Politics, Coalitions and International Trade." *World Politics* 49(3): 309–338.

Balassa, Bela (1966). "Tariff Reductions and Trade in Manufacturers Among the Industrial Countries." *American Economic Review* 56(3): 466–473.

Barav, Ami (1980). "The Judicial Power of the European Economic Community." *Southern Californian Law Review* 53: 461–525.

Barton, John, Judith Goldstein, Timothy Josling, and Richard Steinberg (2006). *The Evolution of the Trade Regime: Politics, Law, and Economics of the GATT and the WTO*. Princeton, NJ, Princeton University Press.

Bates, Robert H., Philip Brock, and Jill Tiefenthaler (1991). "Risk and Trade Regimes: Another Exploration." *International Organization* 45(1): 1–18.

Bayard, Thomas O. and Kimberley Elliot (1994). *Reciprocity and Retaliation in US Trade Policy*. Washington, DC, Institute of International Economics.

Bechtel, Michael M. and Thomas Sattler (2012). "What Is Litigation in the World Trade Organization Worth?" Unpublished paper.

Blonigen, Bruce A. (2005). "The Effects of NAFTA on Antidumping and Countervailing Duty Activity." *The World Bank Economic Review* 19(3): 407–424.

Blonigen, Bruce A. and Thomas J. Prusa (2001). "Antidumping." NBER Working Paper Series 8398.

Boerger-De Smedt, Anne (2012). "Negotiating the Foundations of European Law, 1950–57: The Legal History of the Treaties of Paris and Rome." *Contemporary European History* 21(3): 339–356.

Bown, Chad P. (2004). "On the Economic Success of GATT/WTO Dispute Settlement." *The Review of Economics and Statistics* 86(3): 811–823.

Bown, Chad P. (2005a). "Participation in WTO Dispute Settlement: Complainants, Interested Parties and Free Riders." *World Bank Economic Review* 19(2): 287–310.

Bown, Chad P. (2005b). "Trade Remedies and World Trade Organization Dispute Settlement: Why Are So Few Challenged?" *Journal of Legal Studies* 34(2): 515–555.

Bown, Chad P. (2009). *Self-Enforcing Trade: Developing Countries and WTO Dispute Settlement*. Washington, DC, Brookings.

Bown, Chad P. and Bruce Blonigen (2003). "Antidumping and Retaliation Threats." *Journal of International Economics* 60: 249–273.

Brewster, Rachel (2011). "The Remedy Gap: Institutional Design, Retaliation, and Trade Law Enforcement." *George Washington Law Review* 80(1): 102–158.

Brülhart, Marius (2009). "An Account of Global Intraindustry Trade, 1962–2006." *The World Economy* 32(3): 401–459.

Brülhart, Marius and Robert J.R. Elliott (1998). "Adjustment to the European Single Market: Inferences from Intra-industry Trade Patterns." *Journal of Economic Studies* 25(3): 225–247.

Brülhart, Marius and Robert C. Hine (1998). *Intra-Industry Trade and Adjustment: The European Experience*. Basingstoke, Macmillan.

Bueno de Mesquita, Bruce, Alaistair Smith, Randolph Siverson and James Morrow (2003). *The Logic of Political Survival*. Cambridge, MA, MIT Press.

Burley [Slaughter], Anne-Marie and Walter Mattli (1993). "Europe Before the Court: A Political Theory of Legal Integration." *International Organization* 47(1): 41–76.

Busch, Marc (2000). "Democracy, Consultation, and the Paneling of Disputes under GATT." *Journal of Conflict Resolution* 44: 425–446.

Busch, Marc and Helen V. Milner (1993). "International Firms, Regionalism and Domestic Politics." In Richard Stubbs and Geoffrey Underhill (eds), *Political Economy and the Changing Global Order*. New York, NY, St Martin's Press: 259–276.

Busch, Marc and E. Reinhardt (2002). "Testing International Trade Law: Empirical Studies of GATTWTO Dispute Settlement." In Daniel Kennedy and James Southwick (eds), *The Political Economy of International Trade Law: Essays in Honor of Robert E. Hudec*. Cambridge, Cambridge University Press: 457–481.

Cameron, David (1978). "The Expansion of the Public Economy." *American Political Science Review* 72: 1243–61.

Cameron, Maxwell A. and Brian W. Tomlin (2000). *The Making of NAFTA: How the Deal was Done*. Ithaca, NY, Cornell University Press.

Caporaso, James A. and Sidney Tarrow (2009). "Polanyi in Brussels: Supranational Institutions and the Transnational Embedding of Markets. International Organization." *International Organization* 63(4): 593–620.

Carey, John M. and Matthew S. Shugart (1995). "Incentives to Cultivate a Personal Vote: a Rank Ordering of Electoral Formulas." *Electoral Studies* 14(4): 417–439.

Carr, Edward H. (1940). *The Twenty Years' Crisis 1919–1939: An Introduction to the Study of International Relations*. London, Macmillan.

Carrubba, Clifford J. (2005). "Courts and Compliance in International Regulatory Regimes." *Journal of Politics* 67(3): 669–689.

Carrubba, Clifford J., Matthew Gabel, and Charles Hankla (2008). "Judicial Behavior Under Political Constraints: Evidence from the European Court of Justice." *American Political Science Review* 102(4): 435–452.

Charnovitz, Steve (2001). "Rethinking WTO Trade Sanctions." *American Journal of International Law* 95(4): 792–832.

Chase, Claude, Alan Yanovich, Jo-Ann Crawford, and Pamela Ugaz (2013). "Mapping of Dispute Settlement Mechanisms in Regional Trade Agreements—Innovative or Variations on a Theme." *WTO Working Paper ERSD-2013-07*. Geneva, World Trade Organization.

Chayes, Abram and Antonia Handler Chayes (1993). "On Compliance." *International Organization* 47(2): 175–205.

Cichowski, Rachel A. (2007). *The European Court and Civil Society: Litigation, Mobilization and Governance*. Cambridge, Cambridge University Press.

Cohen, Antonin and Antoine Vauchez (2011). "The Social Construction of Law: The European Court of Justice and its Legal Revolution Revisited." *Annual Review of Law and Social Science* 7: 417–431.

Conant, Lisa J. (2002). *Justice Contained: Law and Politics in the European Union*. Ithaca, NY, Cornell University Press.

Conybeare, John A. C. (1984). "Public Goods, Prisoners' Dilemmas and the International Political Economy." *International Studies Quarterly* 28: 5–22.

Cottier, Thomas and Matthias Oesch (2012). "Direct and Indirect Discrimination in WTO and EU Law." In Sanford E. Gaines, Birgitte Elelund Olsen, and Karsten Engsig Sorensen (eds), *Liberalising Trade in the EU and the WTO: A Legal Comparison*. Cambridge, Cambridge University Press: 141–175.

Cox, Gary (1987). *The Efficient Secret: The Cabinet and the Development of Political Parties in Victorian England*. Cambridge, Cambridge University Press.

Craig, Paul and Gráinne de Búrca (2008). *EU Law: Text, Cases and Materials*. Oxford, Oxford University Press.

Crombez, Christopher and Simon Hix (2011). "Treaty Reform and the Commission's Appointment and Policy-making Role in the European Union." *European Union Politics* 12(3): 291–314.

Croome, John (1995). *Reshaping the World Trading System: A History of the Uruguay Round*. Geneva, World Trade Organization.

Dai, Xinyuan (2002). "Information Systems in Treaty Regimes." *World Politics* 54: 405–36.

Dam, Kevin (1970). *The GATT: Law and International Economic Organization*. Chicago, University of Chicago Press.

Davey, William J. (1987). "Dispute Settlement in Gatt." *Fordham International Law Journal* 11(1): 51–109.

Davies, Bill (2012). *Resisting the European Court of Justice: West Germany's Confrontation with European Law, 1949-1979*. Cambridge, Cambridge University Press.

Davies, Bill and Morten Rasmussen (2012). "Towards a New History of European Law." *Contemporary European History* 21(3): 305–318.

Davis, Christina (2012). *Why Adjudicate? Enforcing Trade Rules in the WTO*. Princeton, NJ, Princeton University Press.

Davis, Christina and Sarah Blodgett Bermeo (2009). "Who Files? Developing Country Participation in WTO Adjudication." *Journal of Politics* 71: 1033–1049.

Davis, Christina and Sophie Meunier (2011). "Business as Usual? Economic Responses to Political Tensions." *American Journal of Political Science* 55(3): 628–646.

Davis, Christina and Krzysztof Pelc (2013). "Cooperation in Hard Times: Self-Restraint of Trade Protection." Unpublished paper.

Davis, Christina and Yuki Shirato (2007). "Firms, Governments and WTO Adjudication: Japan's Selection of WTO Disputes." *World Politics* 59: 274–313.

De Araujo, Jose Tavares, Carla Maracio, and Karsten Steinfatt (2001). "Antidumping in the Americas." *Journal of World Trade* 35(4): 555–574.

de Vattel, Emerich (1916 [1758]). *The Law of Nations, or, Principles of the law of nature applied to the conduct and affairs of nations and sovereigns*. Washington, Carnegie.

De Witte, Bruno (2011). "The European Union as an International Legal Experiment." In Gráinne de Búrca and Joseph H. H. Weiler (eds), *The Worlds of European Constitutionalism*. Cambridge, Cambridge University Press: 19–46.

Dero, Delphine (2006). *La Reciprocite et le Droit des Communautes et de L'Union Europeennes*. Bruxelles, Bruylant.

Deutsch, Karl W., Sidney A. Burrell, Robert A. Kann, Maurice Lee, Martin Lichterman, Raymond E. Lindgren, Francis L. Loewenheim, and Richard W. Van Wagenen (1957). *Political Community and the North Atlantic Area: International Organization in the Light of Historical Experience*. Princeton, NJ, Princeton University Press.

Devereaux, Charan, Robert Z. Lawrence, and Michael D. Watkins (2006). *Case Studies in US Trade Negotiation: Vol. 2: Resolving Disputes*. Washington, DC, Institute for International Economics.

Downs, George W. and David M. Rocke (1995). *Optimal Imperfection? Domestic Uncertainty and Institutions in International Relations*. Princeton, NJ, Princeton University Press.

Downs, George W., David M. Rocke, and Peter N. Barsoom (1996). "Is the Good News about Compliance Good News about Cooperation?" *International Organization* 1996(3): 379–406.

Due, Ole (1999). "The Danish Ratification of the Maastricht Treaty before the Danish Supreme Court." In Marrianne Dony (ed.) *Mélanges en Hommage Michel Waelbroeck*. Bruxelles, Bruylant: 313–331.

Duguid, Paul (2003). "The making of Methuen: The Commercial Treaty in the English Imagination." *História, Revista da Faculdade de Letras* 3(4): 9–36.

Duttle, Thomas, Katharina Holzinger, Thomas Schäubli, Frank Schimmelfennig, and Thomas Winzen (2013). "The Dynamics of Secondary-Law Differentiation in the European Union." Unpublished paper.

Ecochard, Pierre, Lionel Fontagné, Guillaume Gaulier, and Soledad Zignago (2006). "Intra-Industry Trade and Economic Integration." In Daisuke Hiratsuka (ed.) *East Asia's De Facto Economic Integration*. Basingstoke, Palgrave Macmillan: 32–79.

Eeckhout, Piet (2011). *EU External Relations Law*. Oxford, Oxford University Press.

Elagab, Omer Yousif (1988). *The Legality of Non-forcible Counter-measures in International Law*. Oxford, Clarendon Press.

Emaus, Vegard (2008). "Unilateral Modification and Withdrawal of WTO Concessions and Commitments." MA thesis, *Europa-Institut*, Universitat des Saarlandes.

Esping-Andersen, Gøsta (1990). *The Three Worlds of Welfare Capitalism*. Cambridge, Polity Press.

European Court of Justice (2012). *Annual Report 2011*. Luxembourg, Publications Office of the European Union.

Farrell, Henry (2003). "Constructing the International Foundations of E-Commerce: The EU–US Safe Harbor Arrangement." *International Organization* 57(2): 277–306.

Finger, J. Michael and Julio J. Nogués (2006). *Safeguards and Antidumping in Latin American Trade liberalization: Fighting Fire with Fire*. Washington, DC, World Bank.

Fischer, Ronald D. and Thomas J. Prusa (2003). "WTO Exceptions as Insurance." *Review of International Economics* 11(5): 745–757.

Foster, Neil and Robert Stehrer (2011). "Preferential Trade Agreements and the Structure of International Trade." *Review of World Economics* 147(3): 385–409.

Gaines, Sanford E., Birgitte Elelund Olsen, and Karsten Engsig Sorensen (2012). *Liberalising Trade in the EU and the WTO*. Cambridge, Cambridge University Press.

Garrett, Geoffrey (1992). "International Cooperation and Institutional Choice: The European Community's Internal Market." *International Organization* 46(2): 533–560.

Garrett, Geoffrey (1995). "The Politics of Legal Integration in the European Union." *International Organization* 49(1): 171–181.

Garrett, Geoffrey and Barry Weingast (1993). "Ideas, Interests and Institutions: Constituting the EC's Internal Market." In Robert O. Keohane and J. Goldstein (eds), *Ideas and Foreign Policy: Beliefs, Institutions and Political Change*. Ithaca, NY, Cornell University Press: 173–206.

Garrett, Geoffrey, R., Daniel Kelemen, and Heiner Schulz (1998). "The European Court of Justice, National Governments, and Legal Integration in the European Union." *International Organization* 52(1): 149–176.

Gawande, Kishore and Wendy L. Hansen (1999). *International Organization* 53(1): 117–159.

Gerring, John and Strom C. Thacker (2008). *A Centripetal Theory of Democratic Governance*. Cambridge, New York, Cambridge University Press.

Gilligan, Michael J. (1997a). *Empowering Exporters: Reciprocity, Delegation, and Collective Action in American Trade Policy*. Ann Arbor, University of Michigan Press.

Gilligan, Michael J. (1997b). "Lobbying as a Private Good with Intra-Industry Trade." *International Studies Quarterly* 41(3): 455–474.

Gillingham, John (2003). *European Integration, 1950–2003: Superstate or New Market Economy?* Cambridge, Cambridge University Press.

Glencross, Andrew (2009). *What Makes the EU Viable? European Integration in the Light of the Antebellum US Experience*. Basingstoke, Palgrave Macmillan.

Goldstein, Judith L., Miles Kahler, Robert O. Keohane, and Anne-Marie Slaughter (2001). *Legalization and World Politics*. Cambridge, MA, MIT Press.

Goldstein, Leslie F. (1997). "State Resistance to Authority in Federal Unions: The Early United States (1790–1860) and the European Community (1958–94)." *Studies in American Political Development* 11(1): 149.

Goldstein, Leslie F. (2001). *Constituting Federal Sovereignty: The European Union in Comparative Context*. Baltimore, Md, Johns Hopkins.

Gori, Paolo (1967). *Les Clauses de Sauveguarde des Traites CECA et CEE*. Heule, Belgium, Editions UGA.

Gormley, Laurence W. (1985). *Prohibiting Restrictions on Trade Within the EEC: The Theory and Application of Articles 30–36 of the EEC Treaty*. Amsterdam, North-Holland.

Government of Canada (1993). "North American Agreement on Environmental Co-operation: North American Agreement on Labour Cooperation: Background Information." Ottawa, [Government Printer].

Gradoni, Lorenzo and Attila Tanzi (2008). *"Diritto Comunitario: Una* Lex Specialis *Molto Speciale."* In Lucia Serena Rossi and Giacomo Di Federico (eds), *L'incidenza del Diritto dell'Unione Europea sullo Studio del Diritto Internazionale*. Rome, Editoriale Scientifica: 37–70.

Gray, Julia and Jonathan B. Slapin (2012). "How Effective are Preferential Trade Agreements? Ask the Experts." *Review of International Organization* 7: 309–333.

Grayson, George W. (1995). *The North American Free Trade Agreement: Regional Community and the New World Order*. Lanham, Md, University Press of America.

Green, Edward J. and Robert H. Porter (1984). "Noncooperative Collusion under Imperfect Price Information." *Econometrica* 52(1): 87–100.

Greenaway, David and Robert C. Hine (1991). "Intra-Industry Specialization, Trade Expansion and Adjustment in the European Economic Space." *Journal of Common Market Studies* 29(6): 603–622.

Grimm, Dieter (1997). "The European Court of Justice and National Courts: The German Constitutional Perspective After the *Maastricht Decision*." *Columbia Journal of European Law* 3(2): 229–242.

Grossman, Gene M. and Elhanan Helpman (1994). "Protection for Sale." *American Economic Review* 84(4): 833–850.

Haas, Ernest (1958). *The Uniting of Europe*. Stanford, CA, Stanford University Press.

Haftel, Yoram Z. (2013). "Commerce and Institutions: Trade, Scope, and the Deisgn of Regional Economic Organizations." *Review of International Organization* DOI 10.1007/s11558-012-9162-9.

Hanf, Dominik (2001). "Flexibility Clauses in the Founding Treaties, from Rome to Nice." In Bruno De Witte, Dominik Hanf, and Ellen Vos (eds), *The Many Faces of Differentiation in EU Law*. Antwerp, Intersentia: 3–26.

Hankla, Charles (2006). "Party Strength and International Trade." *Comparative Political Studies* 39(9): 1133–1156.

Hartley, Trevor C. (1999). *Constitutional Problems of the European Union*. Oxford and Portland, OR, Hart.

Hartley, Trevor C. (2007). *The Foundations of European Community Law: An Introduction to the Constitutional and Administrative Law of the European Community*, 6th edn. Oxford, Oxford University Press.

Hartley, Trevor C. (2010). *The Foundations of European Union Law: An Introduction to the Constitutional and Administrative Law of the European Union*, 7th edn. Oxford, Oxford University Press.

Hathaway, Oona A. (2007). "Why Do Countries Commit to Human Rights Treaties?" *Journal of Conflict Resolution* 51(4): 588–621.

Hayes-Renshaw, Fiona, Wim Van Aken, and Helen Wallace (2006). "When and Why the EU Council of Ministers Votes Explicitly." *Journal of Common Market Studies* 44(1): 161–194.

Heisenberg, Dorothee (2005). "The Institution of 'Consensus' in the European Union: Formal versus Informal Decision-making in the Council." *European Journal of Political Research* 44: 65–90.

Heitshusen, Valerie, Garry Young, and David M. Wood (2005). "Electoral Context and MP Constituency Focus in Australia, Canada, Ireland, New Zealand, and the United Kingdom." *American Journal of Political Science* 49(1): 32–45.

Helfer, Laurence and Karen Alter (2008–2009). "The Andean Tribunal of Justice and its Interlocutors: Understanding Preliminary Reference Patterns in the Andean Community." *NYU Journal of International Law and Politics* 42(4): 871–930.

Helfer, Laurence, Karen Alter, and Maria Florencia Guerzovich (2009). "Islands of Effective International Adjudication: Constructing an Intellectual Property Rule of Law in the Andean Community." *American Journal of International Law* 103: 1–47.

Helfer, Laurence and Anne-Marie Slaughter (1997). "Toward a Theory of Effective Supranational Adjudication." *Yale Law Journal* 107(2): 273–391.

Hicks, Raymond and SooYeon Kim (2012). "Reciprocal Trade Agreements in Asia: Credible Commitment to Trade Liberalization or Paper Tigers?" *Journal of East Asian Studies* 12: 1–29.

Hinrichs, Karl and Olli E. Kangas (2003). "When is a Change Big Enough to be a System Shift? Small System-Shifting Changes in German and Finnish Pension Policies." *Social Policy and Administration* 37(6): 573–591.

Hoekman, Bernard (1998). "Free Trade and Deep Integration: Antidumping and Antitrust in Regional Agreements." World Bank Working Paper 1950.

Hoffmann, Leif (2011). "Land of the Free, Home of the (Un)Regulated: A Look at Market-Building and Liberalization in the EU and the US" Ph.D. thesis, University of Oregon.

Hogan, Gerard and Anthony Whelan (1995). *Ireland and the European Union: Constitutional and Statutory Texts and Commentary.* London, Sweet & Maxwell.

Höpner, Martin and Armin Schäfer (2012). "Embeddedness and Regional Integration: Waiting for Polanyi in a Hayekian Setting." *International Organization* 66(3): 429–455.

Horn, Henrik, Petros Mavroidis, and Håkan Nordström (1999). "Is the Use of the WTO Dispute Settlement System Biased?" CEPR Discussion Paper (2340).

Huberman, Michael (2012). *Odd Couple: International Trade and Labor Standards in History.* New Haven, Yale University Press.

Huerta-Goldman, Jorge A. (2010). "Is Retaliation Useful? Observation and Analysis of Mexico's Experience." In Chad P. Bown and Joost Pauwelyn (eds), *The Law,*

Economics and Politics of Retaliation in WTO Dispute Settlement. Cambridge, Cambridge University Press: 281–296.

Hufbauer, Gary Clyde, Jeffrey J. Schott, and Yee Wong (2003). "NAFTA Dispute Settlement Systems." Institute for International Economics Working Paper. Washington, D.C.

Hungerford, Thomas L. (1991). "GATT: A Cooperative Equilibrium in a Noncooperative Trading Regime?" *Journal of International Economics* 31: 357–369.

Iklé, Fred Charles (1961). "After Detection: What?" *Foreign Affairs* 39(2): 208–220.

Inter-American Development Bank (2002). "Andean Report." Buenos Aires, IDB-INTAL. 1.

Inter-American Development Bank (2005). "Andean Report." Buenos Aires, IDB-INTAL. 2.

Inter-American Development Bank (2011). "Mercosur Report." Buenos Aires, IDB-INTAL. 15.

Iversen, Torben and David Soskice (2006). "Electoral Institutions and the Politics of Coalitions: Why Some Democracies Redistribute More than Others?" *American Political Science Review* 100: 165–181.

Jankowski, Richard (1988). "Preference Aggregation in Political Parties and Interest Groups: A Synthesis of Corporatist and Encompassing Organization Theory." *American Journal of Political Science* 32(1): 105–125.

Jensen, Christian B. and Jonathan B. Slapin (2012). "Institutional Hokey-Pokey: The Politics of Multispeed Integration in the European Union." *Journal of European Public Policy* 19(6): 779–795.

Jensen, Theresa (2011). "The Role of Dispute Settlement Mechanisms in the Constitutionalization of Regional Trade Agreements." MA thesis, University of Toronto, Ontario.

Johns, Leslie (forthcoming). "Depth versus Rigidity in the Design of International Trade Agreements." *Journal of Theoretical Politics*.

Kang, Yoo-Duk (2011). "Does East Asian Integration Keep Up the European Pattern? Empirical Evidence from Intra-Industry Trade in Europe and East Asia." *Asian Development Review* 28(2): 133–165.

Kapteyn, Paul, Joan George, and Pieter VerLoren Van Themaat (1973). *Introduction to the Law of the European Communities: After the Accession of the New Member States*. London and Deventer, Sweet & Maxwell, Kluwer.

Kapteyn, Paul, Joan George, and Pieter VerLoren Van Themaat (1989). *Introduction to the Law of the European Communities: After the Coming into Force of the Single European Act*. Deventer, Kluwer Law.

Kapteyn, Paul, Joan George, and Pieter VerLoren van Themaat (1998). *Introduction to the Law of the European Communities: From Maastricht to Amsterdam*. London, Kluwer Law International.

Katzenstein, Peter J. (1985). *Small States in World Markets: Industrial Policy in Europe*. Ithaca, NY, Cornell University Press.

Kelemen, R. Daniel (2011). *Eurolegalism: The Transformation of Law and Regulation in the European Union*. Cambridge, MA, Harvard University Press.

Keohane, Robert O. (1982). "The Demand for International Regimes." *International Organization* 36(2): 325–355.

Keohane, Robert O. (1984). *After Hegemony: Cooperation and Discord in the World Political Economy*. Princeton, NJ, Princeton University Press.

Keohane, Robert O. (2005). "Preface to the 2005 Edition." In *After Hegemony: Cooperation and Discord in the World Political Economy*. Princeton, NJ, Princeton University Press: ix–xx.

Keohane, Robert O., Andrew Moravcsik, and A. M. Slaughter (2000). "Legalized Dispute Resolution: Interstate and Transnational." *International Organization* 54(3): 457–488.

Kilpatrick, Claire (1998). "Community or Communities of Courts in European Integration? Sex Equality Dialogues Between UK Courts and the ECJ." *European Law Journal* 4(2): 121–147.

Knudsen, Ann-Christina L. (2009). *Farmers on Welfare: The Making of Europe's Common Agricultural Policy*. Ithaca, NY, Cornell University Press.

König, Thomas and Dirk Junge (2008). "Veto Player Theory and Consensus Behaviour." In Daniel Naurin and Helen Wallace (eds), *Unveiling the Council of the European Union*. Basingstoke, Palgrave Macmillan: 81–98.

König, Thomas and Sven-Oliver Proksch (2006). "A Procedural Exchange Model of EU Legislative Politics." In Robert Thomson, Frans N. Stokman, Christopher H. Achen, and Thomas König (eds), *The European Union Decides*. Cambridge, Cambridge University Press: 211–238.

Kono, Daniel Y. (2009). "Market Structure, Electoral Institutions, and Trade Policy." *International Studies Quarterly* 53(4): 885–906.

Krasner, Stephen D. (1982). "Structural Causes and Regime Consequences: Regimes as Intervening Variables." *International Organization* 36(2): 185–205.

Krasner, Stephen D. (1999). *Sovereignty: Organized Hypocrisy*. Princeton, NJ, Princeton University Press.

Kravis, Irving B. (1954). "The Trade Agreements Escape Clause." *American Economic Review* 44(3): 319–338.

Kravis, Irving B. (1963). *Domestic Interests and International Obligations: Safeguards in International Trade Organizations*. Philadelphia, University of Philadelphia Press.

Krotz, Ulrich (2009). "Momentum and Impediments: Why Europe Won't Emerge as a Full Political Actor on the World Stage Soon." *Journal of Common Market Studies* 47(3): 555–578.

Krotz, Ulrich and Richard Maher (2011). "International Relations Theory and the Rise of European Foreign and Security Policy." *World Politics* 63(3): 548–579.

Kucik, Jeffrey (2012). "The Domestic Politics of Institutional Design: Producer Preferences Over Trade Agreement Rules." *Economics and Politics* 24(2): 95–118.

Kucik, Jeffrey and Eric Reinhardt (2008). "Does Flexibility Promote Cooperation? An Application to the Global Trade Regime." *International Organization* 62(3): 477–505.

Kuijper, Pieter-Jan (2008). "Does the World Trade Organization Prohibit Retorsions and Reprisals? Legitimate 'Contracting Out' or 'Clinical Isolation' Again?." In Merit E. Janow, Victoria Donaldson, and Alan Yanovich (eds), *The WTO: Governance, Dispute Settlement and Developing Countries*. Huntingdon, NY, Juris: 695–708.

Larsson, Olof and Daniel Naurin (2013). "Legislative Override of Constitutional Courts: The Case of the European Union." EUSA Conference, Baltimore.

Lawrence, Robert Z. (2003). *Crimes and Punishments? Retaliation Under the WTO.* Washington, DC, Institute for International Economics.

Lecourt, Robert (1965). "La Dynamique Judiciaire dans l'Édification de l'Europe." *France Forum* 64 (April–May): 20–22.

Lenhoff, Arthur (1962–1963). "Jurisdictional Relationship Between the Court of the European Communities and the Courts of the Member States." *Buffalo Law Review* 12: 296–326.

Levy, Philip and Thirukodikaval Nilakanta Srinivasan (1996). "Regionalism and the (Dis)advantage of Dispute-Settlement Access." *American Economic Review* 86: 93–98.

Lewis, Jeffrey (2005). "The Janus Face of Brussels: Socialization and Everyday Decision Making in the European Union." *International Organization* 59(4): 937–971.

Lindseth, Peter L. (2010). *Power and Legitimacy: Reconciling Europe and the Nation-State.* Oxford, Oxford University Press.

Lindstädt, René, Jonathan B. Slapin, and Ryan J. Vander Wielen (2012). "Adaptive Behavior in the European Parliament: Learning to Balance Competing Demands." *European Union Politics* 13(4): 465–486.

MacDonald, Chad (2009). "NAFTA Cross-Border Trucking: Mexico Retaliates After Congress Stops Mexican Trucks at the Border." *Vanderbilt Journal of Transnational Law* 42: 1631–1662.

Maduro, Miguel Poiares (1998). *We the Court: The European Court of Justice and the European Economic Constitution: A Critical Reading of Article 30 of the EC Treaty* Oxford, Hart.

Malecki, Michael (2011). "Do ECJ Judges All Speak with the Same Voice? Evidence of Divergent Preferences from the Judgments of Chambers." *Journal of European Public Policy* 19(1): 59–75.

Mancini, G. Frederico (1989). "The Making of a Constitution for Europe." *Common Market Law Review* 26: 595–614.

Marks, Gary W., Fritz W. Scharpf, Philippe C. Schmitter, and Wolfgang Streeck (1996). *Governance in the European Union.* London ; Thousand Oaks, CA, SAGE Publications.

Martin, Lisa L. (1992a). *Coercive Cooperation: Explaining Multilateral Economic Sanctions.* Princeton, NJ, Princeton University Press.

Martin, Lisa L. (1992b). "Interests, Power and Multilateralism." *International Organization* 46(4): 765–792.

Mattli, Walter (1999). *The Logic of Regional Integration: Europe and Beyond.* New York, Cambridge University Press.

Mattli, Walter and Anne-Marie Slaughter (1995). "Law and Politics in the European Union—A Reply to Garrett." *International Organization* 49(1): 183–190.

Mattli, Walter and Anne-Marie Slaughter (1998). "Revisiting the European Court of Justice." *International Organization* 52(1): 177–209.

Mayer, Franz C. (2005). "Europarecht als französisches Verfassungsrecht WHI-Paper 1/05. " Berlin, Walter Hallstein-Institut für Europäisches Verfassungsrecht.

Mayer, Frederick (1998). *Interpreting NAFTA: The Science and Art of Political Analysis.* New York, Columbia University Press.

McCall Smith, James (2000). "The Politics of Dispute Settlement Design: Explaining Legalism in Regional Trade Pacts." *International Organization* 54(1): 137–180.

McGillivray, Fiona and Alaistair Smith (2008). *Punishing the Prince: A Theory of Interstate Relations, Political Institutions and Leader Change*. Princeton, NJ. Princeton University Press.

McNair, Arnold Duncan (1961). *The Law of Treaties*. Oxford, Clarendon Press.

Mearsheimer, John (1994/1995). "The False Promise of International Institutions." *International Security* 19(3): 5–49.

Mill, John Stuart (1993 [1865]). "Considerations on Representative Government." In Geraint Williams (ed.) *Utilitarianism; On Liberty; Considerations on Representative Government; Remarks on Bentham's Philosophy*. London, Dent.

Milner, Helen (1999). "The Political Economy of International Trade." *Annual Review of Political Science* 2: 91–114.

Milward, Alan S. (1984). *The Reconstruction of Western Europe 1945–51*. London, Methuen.

Milward, Alan S., George Brennan, and Federico Romero (1992). *The European Rescue of the Nation-state*. London, Routledge.

Mongelli, Francesco Paolo, Ettore Dorrucci, and Itai Agur (2005). What Does European Institutional Integration Tell Us About Trade Integration? ECB Occasional Paper Series No. 40. Frankfurt: European Central Bank.

Moravcsik, Andrew (1994). Why the European Community Strengthens the State: Domestic Politics and International Cooperation. Harvard University Center for European Studies Working Paper No. 52. Cambridge, MA, Harvard University Press.

Moravcsik, Andrew (1995). "Liberal Intergovernmentalism and Integration: A Rejoinder." *Journal of Common Market Studies* 33(4): 611–628.

Moravcsik, Andrew (1997). "Taking Preferences Seriously: A Liberal Theory of International Politics." *International Organization* 51(4): 513–553.

Moravcsik, Andrew (1998). *The Choice for Europe: Social Purpose and State Power from Messina to Maastricht*. London, UCL Press.

Moravcsik, Andrew (2000). "The Origins of Human Rights Regimes: Democratic Delegation in Postwar Europe." *International Organization* 54(2): 217–252.

Moravcsik, Andrew (2005). "The European Constitutional Compromise and the Neofunctionalist Legacy." *Journal of European Public Policy* 12(2): 349–386.

Morgan, Glyn (2005). *The Idea of a European Superstate: Public Justification and European Integration*. Princeton, NJ and Oxford, Princeton University Press.

Morrow, James (2001). "Institutional Features of the Prisoners of War Treaties." *International Organization* 55(4): 971–991.

Münch, Fritz (1957). *Delimitation du domaine du droit des Communautes Supranationales par Rapport au droit etatique interne*. Actes officiels du Congrès d"études sur la C.E.C.A. Milan, Giuffrè.

Naurin, Daniel and Helen Wallace, eds (2008). *Unveiling the Council of the European Union: Games Governments Play in Brussels*. Basingstoke, Palgrave Macmillan.

Nielson, Daniel L. (2003). "Supplying Trade Reform: Political Institutions and Liberalization in Middle-Income Presidential Democracies." *American Journal of Political Science* 47(3): 470–491.

Nord, Philip (2010). *France's New Deal: From the Thirties to the Postwar Era*. Princeton, NJ, Princeton University Press.

Norwich, John Julius (1995). *Byzantium: The Decline and Fall*. London, Penguin.

Nowak, Jean-Jacques, Sylvain Petit, and Mondher Sahli (2012). "Intra-tourism Trade in Europe." *Tourism Economics* 18(6): 1287–1311.

Nyikos, Stacey (2006). "Strategic Interaction among Courts within the Preliminary Reference Process—Stage 1: National Court Preemptive Options." *European Journal of Political Research* 45(4): 527–550.

Nzelibe, Jide (2008). "The Case Against Reforming the WTO Enforcement Mechanism." *University of Illinois Law Review*: 319–357.

Obermaier, Andreas J. (2008). "The National Judiciary—Sword of European Court of Justice Rulings: The Example of the Kohll/Decker Jurisprudence." *European Law Journal* 14(6): 735–752.

Odell, John (2000). *Negotiating the World Economy*. Ithaca, NY, Cornell University Press.

Olson, Mancur (1965). *The Logic of Collective Action: Public Goods and the Theory of Groups*. Cambridge MA, Harvard University Press; Oxford, Oxford University Press.

Olson, Mancur (1982). *The Rise and Decline of Nations: Economic Growth, Stagflation, and Social Rigidities*. New Haven, Yale University Press.

Oppenheimer, Andrew, ed. (1994). *The Relationship Between European Community Law and National Law: The Cases, Vol. 1*. Cambridge and New York, Cambridge University Press.

Oppenheimer, Andrew, ed. (2003). *The Relationship Between European Community Law and National Law: The Cases, Vol. 2*. Cambridge and New York, Cambridge University Press.

Partsch, Karl Joseph (1981–). "Reprisals." In Rudolf Bernhardt (ed.) *Encyclopedia of Public International Law*. Amsterdam, New York, North-Holland. 4: 200–205.

Pelc, Krzysztof (2009). "Seeking Escape: The Use of Escape Clauses in International Trade Agreements." *International Studies Quarterly* 53: 349–368.

Pelkmans, Jacques (2006). *European Integration: Methods and Economic Analysis*. Harlow, Financial Times Prentice Hall.

Persson, Torsten, Gerard Roland, and Guido Tabellini (2007). "Electoral Rules and Government Spending in Parliamentary Democracies." *Quarterly Journal of Political Science* 2: 155–188.

Pescatore, Pierre (1969). *Droit International et Droit Communautaire, essai de refléxion comparative*. Nancy, Centre Européen Universitaire Nancy.

Pescatore, Pierre (1993). "The GATT Dispute Settlement Mechanism—Its Present Situation and Future Prospects." *Journal of World Trade* 27(1): 5–20.

Peterson, Timothy M. and Cameron G. Thies (2013). "Beyond Ricardo: The Link Between Intra-Industry Trade and Peace." *British Journal of Political Science*: 1–21.

Phelan, Diarmuid Rossa (1997). *Revolt or Revolution: The Constitutional Boundaries of the European Community*. Dublin, Round Hall Sweet & Maxwell.

Phelan, William (2002). "Does the European Union Strengthen the State? Democracy, Executive Power and International Cooperation." Harvard University CES Working Paper Series No. 95. Cambridge, MA, Harvard University Press.

Phelan, William (2008a). "Can Ireland Legislate Contrary to European Community Law?" *European Law Review* 33(4): 530–549.

Phelan, William (2008b). "Why Do EU Member States Offer a "Constitutional" Obedience to EU Obligations? Encompassing Domestic Institutions and Costly International Obligations." IIIS Discussion Paper Series No. 256. Dublin, Trinity College.

Phelan, William (2009). "State Reputation as a Public Good." Institute for International Integration Studies Discussion Paper Series No. 275. Dublin, Trinity College.

Phelan, William (2010). "Political Self-Control and European Constitution: The Assumption of National Political Loyalty to European Obligations as the Solution to the *Lex Posterior* Problem in the National Legal Orders." *European Law Journal* 16(3): 253–272.

Phelan, William (2011a). "Open International Markets Without Exclusion: Encompassing Domestic Political Institutions, International Organization, and Self-Contained Regimes." *International Theory* 3(2): 286–306.

Phelan, William (2011b). "Why Do the EU Member States Accept the Supremacy of European Law? Explaining Supremacy as an Alternative to Bilateral Reciprocity." *Journal of European Public Policy* 18(5): 766–777.

Phelan, William (2012). "What is *Sui Generis* About the European Union? Costly International Cooperation in a Self-Contained Regime." *International Studies Review* 14: 367–385.

Phelan, William (2013a). "Enforcement and Escape in the Andean Community: Why the Andean Community of Nations is Not a Replica of the European Union." Unpublished paper.

Phelan, William. (2013b). "The European Union's Next Nobel Peace Prize." *E-International Relations*, from <http://www.e-ir.info/2013/08/05/the-european-unions-next-nobel-peace-prize/>.

Phelan, William (2013c). "The Limited Practical Relevance of National Constitutional Rights as a Constraint on the National Application of European Law in the Early Decades of European Integration." Unpublished paper.

Phelan, William (2013d). "The Troika: The Interlocking Roles of Commission v Luxembourg and Belgium, Van Gend en Loos, and Costa v Enel in the Creation of the European Legal Order." Institute for International Integration Studies Discussion Paper. Dublin, Trinity College.

Phillipson, Coleman (1915). *International Law and the Great War.* London, T. Fisher Unwin.

Pierson, Paul (1996). "The Path to European Integration: A Historical Institutionalist Analysis." *Comparative Political Studies* 29(2): 123–163.

Poggi, Gianfranco (1978). *The Development of the Modern State: A Sociological Introduction.* Stanford, CA, Stanford University Press.

Pollack, Mark A. (1997). "Delegation, Agency and Agenda Setting in the Europoean Community." *International Organization* 51: 99–134.

Pressman, Jeffrey L. and Aaron Wildavsky (1973). *Implementation.* Berkeley, CA, University of California Press.

Przeworski, Adam and Henry Teune (1970). *The Logic of Comparative Social Inquiry.* Malabar, Krieger.

Puchala, Donald J. (1972). "Of Blind Men, Elephants and International Integration." *Journal of Common Market Studies* 10(3): 267–284.

Rasmussen, Morten (2010). "Constructing and Deconstructing 'Constitutional' European Law: Some Reflections on how to Study the History of European Law." In Henning Koch, Karsten Hagel-Sørensen, Ulrich R. Haltern, and J.H.H. Weiler (eds), *Europe: The New Legal Realism: Essays in Honour of Hjalte Rasmussen*. Copenhagen, Djøf Publishing: 639–660.

Reynolds, Kara M. and Yan Su (2005). "Dumping on Agriculture: Case Studies in Antidumping." Working paper. Department of Economics, American University, Washington, DC.

Rickard, Stephanie J. (2010). "Democratic Differences: Electoral Institutions and Compliance with GATT/WTO Agreements." *European Journal of International Relations* 16(4): 711–729.

Rieger, Elmar (2000). "The Common Agricultural Policy: Politics Against Markets." In Helen Wallace and William Wallace (eds), *Policy-Making in the European Union*. Oxford, Oxford University Press: 179–210.

Risse-Kappen, Thomas (1996). "Exploring the Nature of the Beast: International Relations Theory and Comparative Policy Analysis Meet the European Union." *Journal of Common Market Studies* 34(1): 53–80.

Rodrik, Dani (1998). "Why Do More Open Economies Have Bigger Governments?" *Journal of Political Economy* 106(5): 997–1032.

Rogowski, Ronald (1987). "Trade and the Variety of Democratic Institutions." *International Organization* 41(2): 203–223.

Roitinger, Alexander (2004). "The Institutional Design of Trade Policy Flexibility in the World Trading Order: Analysis and New Direction for Reform." Ph.D. thesis, University of St Gallen.

Rosendorff, B. Peter and Helen V. Milner (2001). "The Optimal Design of International Trade Institutions: Uncertainty and Escape." *International Organization* 55(4): 829–857.

Ruggie, John (1982). "International Regimes, Transactions, and Change: Embedded Liberalism in the Postwar Economic Order." *International Organization* 36(2): 379–425.

Sattler, Thomas and Thomas Bernauer (2011). "Gravitation or Discrimination? Determinants of Litigation in the World Trade Organisation." *European Journal of Political Research* 50(2): 143–167.

Scharpf, Fritz Wilhelm (1988). "The Joint-Decision Trap—Lessons from German Federalism and European-Integration." *Public Administration* 66(3): 239–278.

Scharpf, Fritz Wilhelm (1999). *Governing in Europe: Effective and Democratic?* New York, Oxford University Press.

Scharpf, Fritz Wilhelm (2006). "The Joint Decision-Trap Revisited." *Journal of Common Market Studies* 44(4): 845–864.

Scharpf, Fritz Wilhelm (2009). "The Double Assymetry of European Integration: Or: Why the EU Cannot Be a Social Market Economy." MPIfG Working Paper 09/12. Cologne: Max Planck Institute for the Study of Societies.

Schelling, Thomas C. (1956). "An Essay on Bargaining." *American Economic Review* 46(3): 281–306.

Schermers, Henry G. (1989). "The Suit for Damages as a Means of Pressure on the Member States of the European Community." In Kay Hailbronner, Georg Ress, and Torsten Stein (eds), *Staat und Völkerrechtsordnung: Festschrift für Karl Doehring*. Berlin, Heidelberg, Springer: 883–888.

Schilling, Theodore (1996). "The Autonomy of the European Legal Order." *Harvard International Law Journal* 37(2): 389–409.

Schimmelfennig, Frank (2001). "The Community Trap: Liberal Norms, Rhetorical Action, and the Eastern Enlargement of the European Union." *International Organization* 55(1): 47–80.

Schmitter, Philippe C. (1996). "Some Alternative Futures for the European Polity and Their Implications for European Public Policy." In Yves Meny (ed.), *Adjusting to Europe: The Impact of the European Union on National Institutions and Policies*. London, Routledge.

Schropp, Simon A. B. (2009). *Trade Policy Flexibility and Enforcement in the WTO: A Law and Economics Analysis*. Cambridge, Cambridge University Press.

Secretaría General (2006). "Comunidad Andina: Avances y Perspectivas." SG/di 800.

Shaffer, Gregory (2003). "How to Make the WTO Dispute Settlement System Work for Developing Countries." ICTSD Resource Paper No. 5. Geneva, ICTSD.

Shapiro, Martin (1980). "Comparative Law and Comparative Politics." *Southern Californian Law Review* 53: 537–542.

Sicilianos, Linos-Alexandre (1990). *Les réactions décentralisées à l"illicite: des contre-mesures á la légitime défense*. Paris, Libr. générale de droit et de jurisprudence.

Simma, Bruno (1978). "Termination and Suspension of Treaties: Two Recent Austrian Cases." *German Yearbook of International Law* 21: 74–96.

Simma, Bruno (1981). "Reciprocity." In Rudolf Bernhardt (ed.), *Encyclopedia of Public International Law*, Vol. 4. Amsterdam, New York, North-Holland: 29–33.

Simma, Bruno (1985). "Self-Contained Regimes." *Netherlands Yearbook of International Law* 16: 111–136.

Simma, Bruno (1994a). "Counter-measures and Dispute Settlement: A Plea for a Different Balance." *European Journal of International Law* 5: 102–105.

Simma, Bruno (1994b). "From Bilateralism to Community Interest in International Law." *Recueil des Cours* 250(VI): 217–384.

Simma, Bruno and Dirk Pulkowski (2006). "Of Planets and the Universe: Self-Contained Regimes in International Law." *The European Journal of International Law* 17(3): 483–529.

Simmons, Beth (2010). "Treaty Compliance and Violation." *Annual Review of Political Science* 13: 273–296.

Sjöberg, Ola, Joakim Palme, and Eero Carroll (2010). "Unemployment Insurance," In Francis G. Castles et al. (eds), *The Oxford Handbook of the Welfare State*. Oxford, Oxford University Press: 420–434.

Skidelsky, Robert, (2006). "Hot, Cold and Imperial." *New York Review of Books* 53(12): 50–55.

Slepcevic, Reinhard (2009). "The Judicial Enforcement of EU law Through National Courts: Possibilities and Limits." *Journal of European Public Policy* 16(3): 378–394.

Sorensen, Karsten Engsig (2012). "Non-Discriminatory Restrictions on Trade." In Sanford E. Gaines, Birgitte Elelund Olsen, and Karsten Engsig Sorensen (eds),

Liberalising Trade in the EU and the WTO. Cambridge, Cambridge University Press: 177–202.

Spamann, Holger (2006). "The Myth of 'Rebalancing' Retaliation in WTO Dispute Settlement Practice." *Journal of International Economic Law* 9(1): 31–79.

Staiger, Robert (1995). "International Rules and Institutions for Trade Policy." In Gene M. Grossman and Kenneth Rogoff (eds), *Handbook of International Economics*, Vol. 2. New York, North-Holland.

Stein, Arthur (1982). "Coordination and Collaboration: Regimes in an Anarchic World." *International Organization* 36(2): 299–324.

Stein, Eric (1981). "Lawyers, Judges and the Making of a Transnational Constitution." *American Journal of International Law* 75(1): 1–27.

Steunenberg, Bernard and Torsten J. Selck (2006). "Testing Procedural Models of EU Legislative Decision-making." In Robert Thomson, Frans N. Stokman, Christopher H. Achen, and Thomas König (eds), *The European Union Decides*. Cambridge, Cambridge University Press: 54–85.

Stone Sweet, Alec (1998). "Constitutional Dialogues in the European Community." In A-M. Slaughter, Alec Stone Sweet, and J.H.H. Weiler (eds), *The European Courts and National Courts. Doctrine and Jurisprudence: Legal Change in its Social Context*. Oxford, Hart: 305–330.

Stone Sweet, Alec (2004). *The Judicial Construction of Europe*. Oxford, New York, Oxford University Press.

Stone Sweet, Alec and Thomas L. Brunell (1998a). "Constructing a Supranational Constitution: Dispute Resolution and Governance in the European Community." *American Political Science Review* 92(1): 63–81.

Stone Sweet, Alec and Thomas L. Brunell (1998b). "The European Court and the National Courts: A Statistical Analysis of Preliminary References, 1961–95." *Journal of European Public Policy* 5: 66–97.

Sykes, Alan O. (1990). "Mandatory Retaliation for Breach of Trade Agreements: Some Thoughts on the Strategic Design of Section 301." *Boston University International Law Journal* 8: 301–331.

Sykes, Alan O. (2005). "Public Versus Private Enforcement of International Economic Law: Standing and Remedy." *Journal of Legal Studies* 32(4): 631–666.

Tallberg, Jonas (2000). "Supranational Influence in EU Enforcement: The ECJ and the Principle of State Liability." *Journal of European Public Policy* 7(1): 104–121.

Taylor, Paul (1983). *The Limits of European Integration*. London & Canberra, Croom Helm.

Teh, Robert, Thomas J. Prusa, and Michele Budetta (2007). "Trade Remedy Provisions in Regional Trade Agreements." WTO Staff Working Paper ERSD-2007-03. Geneva, World Trade Organization.

Thibaud, Paul (1991). "L'Europe, essai d'identification." *Esprit* (11): 47–62.

Thomson, Robert (2011). *Resolving Controversy in the European Union: Legislative Decision-making Before and After Enlargement*. Cambridge, Cambridge University Press.

Thomson, Robert, Frans N. Stokman, Christopher H. Achen, and Thomas König, eds (2006). *The European Union Decides: Testing Theories of European Decision-making*. Cambridge, Cambridge University Press.

Tsebelis, George and Geoffrey Garrett (2001). "The Institutional Foundations of Intergovernmentalism and Supranationalism in the European Union." *International Organization* 55(2): 357–390.

Van den Bossche, Peter (2005). *The Law and Policy of the World Trade Organization: Text, Cases and Materials*. Cambridge, Cambridge University Press.

Vauchez, Antoine (2010). "The Making of the European Union's Constitutional Foundations: The Brokering Role of Legal Entrepreneurs and Networks." In Wolfram Kaiser, Brigitte Leucht, and Michael Gehler (eds), *Transnational Networks in Regional Integration: Governing Europe 1945–1983*. Basingstoke, Palgrave Macmillan 108–127.

Vauchez, Antoine (2012). "Keeping the Dream Alive: The European Court of Justice and the Transnational Fabric of Integrationist Jurisprudence." *European Political Science Review* 4(1): 51–71.

Vega-Canovas, Gustavo (1997). "Disciplining Anti-Dumping in North America: Is NAFTA Chapter 19 Serving Its Purpose?" *Arizona Journal of International and Comparative Law* 14: 479–501.

Verdier, Daniel (1998). "Democratic Convergence and Free Trade." *International Studies Quarterly* 42(1): 1–24.

Vinuesa, Raúl Emilio (2005). "Enforcement of Mercosur Arbitration Awards Within the Domestic Legal Orders of Member States." *Texas International Law Journal* 40: 425–442.

Vodopivec, Milan (2004). *Income Support for the Unemployed: Issues and Options*. Washington, DC, World Bank.

von Stein, Jana (2006). "When and Why Do Treaties Work? Commitment and Compliace in International Economic, Human Rights, and Environmental Law." Ph.D. thesis, Los Angeles, UCLA.

Voon, Tania (2010). "Eliminating Trade Remedies from the WTO: Lessons from Regional Trade Agreements." *International and Comparative Law Quarterly* 59: 625–667.

Vroman, Wayne and Vera Brusentsev (2005). *Unemployment Compensation Throughout the World: A Comparative Analysis*. Kalamazoo, Michigan, W.E. Upjohn.

Vroman, Wayne and Vera Brusentsev (2006). "Unemployment and Unemployment Compensation from a Global Perspective." WZB Discussion paper. Berlin, Wissenschaftszentrum Berlin für Sozialforschung.

Vroman, Wayne and Vera Brusentsev (2009). "Unemployment Compensation in a Worldwide Recession." Washington, DC, Urban Institute.

Wallace, William (1983). "Less than a Federation, More than a Regime: The Community as a Political System." In Helen Wallace, William Wallace, and Carole Webb (eds), *Policy-Making in the European Community*. Chichester and New York, John Wiley & Sons: 403–436.

Waltz, Kenneth Neal (1979). *Theory of International Politics*. Boston, MA, McGraw-Hill.

Ward, Alan J. (1994). *The Irish Constitutional Tradition: Responsible Government and Modern Ireland, 1782–1992*. Dublin, Irish Academic Press.

Weiler, Joseph H.H. (1981). "The Community System: The Dual Character of Supranationalism." *Yearbook of European Law* 1: 267–306.

Weiler, Joseph H.H. (1985). "Alternatives to Withdrawal from an International Organization: The Case of the European Economic Community." *Israel Law Review* 20(2–3): 282–298.

Weiler, Joseph H.H. (1991). "The Transformation of Europe." *Yale Law Journal* 100: 2403–2483.

Weiler, Joseph H.H. (1993). "Journey to an Unknown Destination: A Retrospective and Prospective of the European Court of Justice in the Arena of Political Integration." *Journal of Common Market Studies* 31: 417–446.

Weiler, Joseph H.H. (1994). "A Quiet Revolution: The European Court of Justice and its Interlocutors." *Comparative Political Studies* 26(4): 510–534.

Weiler, Joseph H.H. (2000). *The EU, The WTO and the NAFTA: Towards a Common Law of International Trade.* Oxford, Oxford University Press.

Weiler, Joseph H.H. and Ulrich R. Haltern (1996). "The Autonomy of the Community Legal Order—Through the Looking Glass." *Harvard International Law Journal* 37(2): 411–448.

Weldon-Johns, Michelle (2013). "EU Work–Family Policies—Challenging Parental Roles or Reinforcing Gendered Stereotypes?" *European Law Journal* 19(5): 662–681.

Wendt, Alexander (1992). "Anarchy is What States Make of it: The Social Construction of Power Politics." *International Organization* 46(2): 391–425.

Wibbels, Erik (2000). "Federalism and the Politics of Macroeconomic Policy and Performance." *American Journal of Political Science* 44: 687–702.

Wind, Marlene, Dorte Sindbjerg Martinsen, and Gabriel Pons Rotger (2009). "The Uneven Legal Push for Europe: Questioning Variation When National Courts Go to Europe." *European Union Politics* 10(1): 63–88.

Woll, Cornelia (2006). "The Road to External Representation: The European Commission's Activism in International Air Transport." *Journal of European Public Policy* 13(1): 52–69.

Wooton, Ian and Maurizio Zanardi (2002). "Trade and Competition Policy: Anti-Dumping versus Anti-Trust." University of Glasgow Discussion Papers in Economics 02-06. Glasgow, University of Glasgow.

World Trade Organization (2012). *Annual Report.* Geneva, WTO Secretariat.

Yoshinaka, Antoine, Gail McElroy, and Shaun Bowler (2010). "The Appointment of Rapporteurs in the European Parliament." *Legislative Studies Quarterly* XXXV(4): 457–486.

Zimmermann, Claus D. (2011). "Toleration of Temporary Non-compliance: The Systemic Safety Valve of WTO Dispute Settlement Revisited." *Trade, Law and Development* 3(2): 382–406.

Zoller, Elisabeth (1984). *Peacetime Unilateral Remedies: An Analysis of Countermeasures.* Dobbs Ferry, NY, Transnational Publishers.

Zürn, Michael and Christian Joerges (2005). *Law and Governance in Postnational Europe: Compliance Beyond the Nation-State.* Cambridge, Cambridge University Press.

Index

The manufacturer's authorised representative in the EU for product safety is Oxford University Press España S.A. of El Parque Empresarial San Fernando de Henares, Avenida de Castilla, 2 - 28830 Madrid (www.oup.es/en or product.safety@oup.com). OUP España S.A. also acts as importer into Spain of products made by the manufacturer.
Printed and bound by CPI Group (UK) Ltd, Croydon, CR0 4YY
14/09/2026
02216306-0003